RADICAL SEATTLE

RADICAL SEATTLE
THE GENERAL STRIKE OF 1919

Cal Winslow

MONTHLY REVIEW PRESS

New York

Library of Congress Cataloging-in-Publication Data
available from the publisher

ISBN paper: 978-158367-852-7
ISBN cloth: 978-1-58367-853-4

Typeset in Minion Pro and Cheddar Gothic Serif

MONTHLY REVIEW PRESS, NEW YORK
monthlyreview.org

5 4 3 2 1

CONTENTS

INTRODUCTION

"The past is a foreign country, they do things differently there."[1] Our story of revolution in Seattle looks back one hundred years to 1919 and to a very different place indeed. Gone are Seattle's Skid Road and the mean waterfront streets where in times past seamen brawled and the longshoremen struck the great ships. In their place shining towers of glass and steel rule the skyline. Construction cranes are ubiquitous, and developers contrive to belie gray skies and the drizzle that characterizes the not-so-shining climate. There are the poor, of course, and the homeless who shelter in tents beneath the highways that suffocate wide swathes of the city. They worry the authorities, but the developers will have the day. Meanwhile, massive ships from China wait in Elliott Bay to unload, and tour boats head out to Alaska's shrinking glaciers. The Great Wheel amusement ride now towers over Pier 57. Two gigantic arenas dominate the southern end of the waterfront. There are tourists everywhere. The football stadium is the prize of Microsoft cofounder, the late Paul Allen, who obtained public funding for its construction. The best seats in the house can sell for more than $1,000 and the approaches are lined with upscale bistros and bars. Just south of Lake Union, Allen's Vulcan real estate company is transforming the city yet again, this time at the behest of another tech firm, Amazon. Its new headquarters will include a spherical glass house enclosing a miniature rainforest. The "Emerald City," as I write, has the fastest growing population of any major urban area in the United States. The world's two richest men, Jeff Bezos and Bill Gates, reside here. Seattle flourishes; it is an important place. But can we ask what sort of place? A stage set, perhaps, for the new Gilded Age in which corporate wealth and vibrant street life distract the eye from all manner of social contradictions. Seattleites don't mind the rain; in fact, they love the outdoors, rain or shine. Public space, however, is at a premium and access to the city's beaches severely restricted. Tech workers take great pride in Seattle's high rating for livability, yet the cost of housing rises faster than even the Bay Area. The traffic is often unbearable.

In 1919 John D. Rockefeller, titan of the last Gilded Age, was the world's richest man. A man of the East, the West was not foreign to him. He helped underwrite the railroads that would tie Seattle and the Puget Sound country to Wall Street and the financiers of the East Coast, even to those of Europe. The "Interests," that is, the city's youthful industrialists, lured Rockefeller into the Pacific Northwest. This in turn inspired a speculative explosion; the Rockefeller name alone being enough to incite swarms of bankers to follow the rails west in search of wealth, though in timber not gold. Bezos is our twenty-first-century titan, presiding over the trillion-dollar colossus Amazon, its name a byword for low-wage, low-quality work. Three hundred fifty thousand people work for Bezos, more than forty thousand in Seattle alone–just recently beneficiaries of a raise to $15 an hour in one of the world's most expensive cities.

In 1919 timber dominated the economy of western Washington. The vast stands of ancient cedar, western hemlock and Douglas fir would buttress the silver and copper mines of the West, underpin its railroad lines, and build its rapidly expanding cities, above all in California. The midwestern lumberman George Weyerhaeuser would ascend to join Rockefeller and his set in the era's pantheon of wealth. The men in the camps who felled these giant trees toiled twelve hours a day, seven days a week. They ate company food and slept in company shacks. Conditions in the mills were neither easier nor safer than in the woods. It was a world of giant saws, deadly belts, horrific noise, dust, smoke and fire. When the heavy winter rains came, the lumberjacks wrapped up their bindlestiffs and fled to Seattle. There they would remain, sinking into debt, until job sharks and lumbermen herded them back to the woods.

Seattle's first settlers became timber men. The name Skid Road recalls how in the 1850s logs were rolled down the city's steep hills, in the first instance to Henry Yesler's sawmill on the shore. In 1919, the Yesler mill was gone, but not Skid Road. Yesler Way was a backstreet heaving with saloons, brothels, and flophouses. Skid Road became synonymous with places the down-and-out gathered, places that were rough and sometimes radical. The Industrial Workers of the World (IWW) put down its roots in this quarter.

Situated on a strip of land between Puget Sound—an inland sea off the northern Pacific—and the freshwater Lake Washington, Seattle, upon incorporation by the Washington Territorial legislature in 1869, had just more than two thousand inhabitants. This figure would swell to eighty thousand by the turn of the century. The warring railroads brought more than one hundred thousand newcomers into the territory. Two days closer than California to Vladivostok and the Asian markets, Seattle became the main distribution hub for the northern Pacific Rim, usurping San Francisco, its rival to the south. In addition to its command of Washington's forests and the great wheat belt of the Palouse Steppe, Seattle also dominated the trade and fisheries of Alaska, its economy boosted by the influx of prospectors during the Klondike Gold Rush. Then, there were jobs in the distributive and wholesale trades, as well as shipbuilding, attracting migrants fleeing slums, unemployment, and poverty in the East—blacklisted railroad workers, unemployed miners, famished wheat farmers. When the mayor of Butte, the working-class battleground in Montana, visited Seattle in 1919, he recognized large numbers of ex-copper miners work-ing in its shipyards.

Seattle's well-to-do were diverse: merchants, shipbuilders, bank-ers, businessmen of all sorts and their families. The Weyerhaeusers would settle in nearby Tacoma. In Seattle, the rich business-men lived away from Skid Road on the leafy boulevards of First and Capitol Hills, along Magnolia Bluff, overlooking the lake in Madrona and Washington Park. The politicians and their news-papers might feud about what to do with the infamous Skid Road, but Seattle was staunchly progressive, embracing women's suffrage, prohibition, cooperatives, municipal ownership, and growth. The tops of surrounding hills were lopped off or "regraded" for the ben-efit of developers. The neighboring town of Ballard was annexed in 1907 and the harbor municipalized four years later—a blow to the big railway and shipping interests struck on behalf of small manufacturers, minor shipping lines, and farmers anxious to force down rates.[2] The new Port of Seattle developed the best waterfront facilities in the country, including the sort of moving gantry crane still used in container terminals today.

The speed of this development was astonishing. It was uneven development and then some. In 1914, less than a half-century since the first non-indigenous peoples settled there, Seattle had become a modern industrial municipality of 300,000. The Smith Tower, completed that year, climbed thirty-eight stories above Pioneer Square—the tallest building west of the Mississippi River, we learned in school.

The region's indigenous people, the Duwamish and Suquamish, were all but obliterated—murdered, ravaged by disease, and herded from their villages into impoverished reservations. The newcom-ers despised them, finding their way of life incomprehensible, their four thousand years of coexistence with the earth of little or no interest. This was the case throughout the West. Communal societies everywhere fell, lost forever, no matter how stubbornly these people might resist. In an 1853 article titled "Washington Territory–The Future," the *Olympia Columbian* captured the spirit of the settlers: "Of the Indians now in our midst and around us in every direction, and in large numbers, but a miserable remnant will remain, and they, confined within such narrow limits as Government may allot to them in some obscure locality, will ultimately succeed in dragging out to a bitter end their wretched existence."[3] The Nez Perce habitation was east of the mountains in the smoky Blue Range of Washington and northeastern Oregon. Their Chief Joseph would instruct his fighters to shoot only at the officers, lest they exhaust a dwindling supply of ammunition—to no avail. Chased tirelessly by soldiers 1500 miles eastward from their homes in Washington and Oregon, Joseph surrendered in October 1877, both he and his people exhausted in the freezing early winter of Montana. Seattle was named for the Duwamish chief, Sealth, perhaps because he did not resist, at least not with arms. Sealth, however, a survivor, left words defiant in their own way, and they have persisted, powerfully, and are widely recalled:

The earth does not belong to man, man belongs to the earth.
All things are connected like the blood that unites one family.
Man did not weave the web of life, he is merely a strand in it.
Whatever he does to the web, he does to himself.
The earth is sacred and men and animals are but one part of it.
Treat the earth with respect so that it lasts for centuries to come
And is a place of wonder and beauty for our children.

Today, as glaciers on Mount Rainier melt and the Sound's salmon perish, these words seem prescient, even prophetic. They speak of another relationship with the earth, of another way of life. They inspire people desperately in search of one. In school we learned little of this. Rather, we learned the story of the poor Whitmans, Marcus and Narcissa, killed in 1853 near Walla Walla. The Indians are said to have believed these missionaries were responsible for spreading deadly measles among their people. We did not learn that.

The irony is that scarcely had this blood dried when new

settlers came to Puget Sound bringing communal dreams of their own, compacting all of history—hunter-gatherers to "scientific" socialists—into mere decades. In the 1880s and 1890s, anarchists, utopian socialists, idealists and free-thinkers founded "colonies—Home, Equality, Freeland, Burley. These were the outposts of what the Brotherhood of the Cooperative Commonwealth believed would become the first socialist state, an alternative in the here and now to everything they hated about the industrial capitalism of the East. Harry Ault, editor of the Seattle Central Labor Council's *Union Record*, spent his teenage years in Equality Colony, Skagit County, in a family of disenchanted Populists. The railroad man and socialist icon Eugene Debs, imprisoned in 1895 in the aftermath of the defeat of the Pullman Strike, became an advocate of colonization and the secretary of the Commonwealth. But not for long. He soon abandoned this position in favor of a more conventional socialism and became a founder of the Social Democratic Party, later the Socialist Party of America. The colonies would not endure, but the idea of Washington as a workingman's paradise persisted. Debs would maintain his view that Washington would be the first socialist state. Many went to Washington with this in mind.

In truth, however, in the 1910s Seattle's working-class communities were far from idyllic; the city's industries were certainly not democratic. Ballard, "south of Yesler," and the Rainier Valley were neighborhoods blighted by poor housing, threadbare amenities, and lack of access to the Sound, the green forests, and the great mountain ranges beyond—all that the city cherished, and still does. Shipyard life was brutal, with long days and longer weeks. Still, the experience of the cooperators and communards of Puget Sound and the high hopes of Debs kept the dream of a better world alive. It whetted appetites and stretched the imagination.

Seattle workers overwhelmingly supported the principle of industrial unions—the organization of workers by industry, not skill or craft. They looked for leadership to James Duncan, chair of the Seattle Central Labor Council (CLC) and a critic of the

Industrial Workers of the World. He rejected its challenge to the American Federation of Labor (AFL) from the left. Still, he acknowledged the Wobblies as "pacesetters" and admired their commitment to working-class solidarity. Seattle's Socialist Party members were also proponents of industrial unionism. They were a thorn in the side of the Party's national officials, who supported Samuel Gompers, the conservative president of the craft-based AFL. The IWW had its base camp in Seattle and published its western newspaper, the *Industrial Worker,* there. In this setting, "two-card" workers—belonging simultaneously to an AFL affiliate and the IWW—were commonplace. They held the "AFL card for the job, and the IWW card for the principle." In this environment, trade unionism, social democracy, and industrial unionism intermingled.

Sadly, the anti-Chinese movements of the 1880s remained a stain on class solidarity in the Northwest. Seventeen thousand Chinese workers had worked to bring the Northern Pacific Railroad to the coast. Some five thousand remained in western Washington, though anti-Asian riots in Tacoma in 1885 and Seattle in 1886 violently reduced their numbers. In the new century, Japanese immigrants replaced Chinese as Seattle's largest minority. The relatively few black workers in Seattle, just one percent of the population, took what work they could, including as strikebreakers in the longshoremen's strike of 1916.

The IWW opposed Chinese exclusion, and Seattle's socialist movement included a strong current of anti-racism. Still, as late as 1917, the *Seattle Daily Call* reported striking butchers demanding a "white" cook. Alice Lord, talented organizer of the city's women workers, above all its waitresses, was a committed exclusionist. Seattle's most popular street speaker, however, the socialist firebrand Kate Sadler, was a scathing critic of Asian exclusion, above all when practiced by the unions. She was not alone. Anna Louise Strong, an advocate of child welfare, had been to Japan where she documented the plight of Japanese women workers. The *Union Record* insisted on the need "to break down racial barriers in the

West." When Harry Ault, editor of the *Record*, testified for the
Seattle unions at a congressional hearing on Japanese immigration
held in Tacoma, he opposed exclusion and the Japanese Land Act.
The historian Katsutoshi Kurokawa wrote that Ault and Duncan
had "little patience with racial prejudice."[4]

Seattle's workers rose in these years. It was a decade of intense,
bitter conflict in the Pacific Northwest, by then widely known for
strikes and radicalism. This ascent was far from steady. Seattle's
working class grew in fits and starts, building through fierce struggles, often interrupted.[5] These conflicts, incessant in the timber
camps and sawmills, bloody on the waterfront, outrageous in
Everett, were commonplace in the movement and made Seattle a
union town—a city where workers could imagine themselves running industry. Seattle's working people, women and men, in unions
or not, its families and communities, became class conscious in
these years. This development cannot be understood as an isolated
event. The General Strike of 1919 makes no sense if extracted from
history, or from its environment; no sense if understood as simply
an episode, limited to a week or perhaps a month. "Studying a
single event," the late historian Herbert Gutman argued, "cannot
answer the basic questions, not even the general strike. . . . We need
the background, of the discontent of working people in the Pacific
Northwest as well as of the Seattle social and economic structure.
. . . Only then [can we understand why] in that era a general strike
occurred only in Seattle and indigenous radicalism hung on so
tenaciously."[6]

Seen this way, the General Strike represented the highest point
in a longer process of socialist and working-class organization.
In a range of workplace struggles and political battles, working
people built an infrastructure for radical politics. Seattle's workers
became a class and were conscious of this. They became political
actors in their own right. This book, then, is not just a description
of the heady days of February 1919; it is also an attempt to recover
the decade-long making of the collective capable of launching one
of America's most gripping strikes.

IN WHAT FOLLOWS, IT WILL NOT BE DIFFICULT to detect the influence of my mentor, Edward Thompson, author of the magnificent *Making of the English Working Class,* a masterpiece still in uninterrupted print after more than fifty years. I make no apologies for this. I was lucky enough to experience, first from a distance, then firsthand, the shock waves this work sent through the polite smoking rooms of universities in the sixties, permanently changing the academic landscape of that epoch. *The Making* was about class and class consciousness, as well as how debilitating and disarming the ideology of classlessness—"we're all middle class"—was then, and still is. In place of "great men" and Whig historiography, the work offered history from below and unashamedly celebratory, partisan accounts in "the long tenacious revolutionary tradition of the British commoner."[7] Here, I am especially reminded of Thompson's much-quoted preface and stated mission: rescuing his subjects from "the enormous condescension of posterity."[8] Seattle's workers built one of the great movements in our history, their achievement rarely matched. However, not just mainstream scholars but also leftist writers customarily belittle the movement and above all the General Strike itself. Time and again, one sees these workers described as "naïve" and "self-destructive" and of their great strike as a "blunder" or "disaster"—at best, more generously, as casualties of history, not its makers.[9]

I think that this disparagement is deeply mistaken. Few felt this way at the time, certainly not Anna Louise Strong and her comrades at the *Union Record,* not those in the Labor Temple, nor those in socialist and IWW circles. At a minimum, the strike answered the IWW's Bill Haywood's question, "Is the general strike an effective weapon for the working class?" with a resounding *yes.*[10] On the far side of the continent, the *New York Call* pronounced the Seattle strike "a forecast of the fall of the Capitalist system."[11]

The truth is that the Seattle General Strike terrified Seattle's authorities, sending shivers through the nation's bourgeoisie—in February and in the days and months that followed. The city's mayor, Ole Hanson, may have been a fool. It's not clear how many

people really believed his bluster, his claim to have all but sin-
gle-handedly defeated "Bolshevism" in Seattle. But certainly the
authorities encouraged him. The Seattle papers' invention of the
revolution and its utter demise was not simply wrong. They wanted
the strike—revolutionary or not, real or imagined—dead, buried
and forgotten, and did their best to see that it was. So did the Wilson
government, and so did the American Federation of Labor. They
feared the workers' movement, above all its rank and file, its immigrants, its rebellious women, its blacks and Mexicans, and its general
strikes to come (as one did in Winnipeg). In those years, the workers' challenge to industrial capitalism was unparalleled. Thus, in
Seattle, workers confronted a "red scare" before *the* Red Scare, and a
campaign to discredit the strike and its organizations, to belittle its
leaders, and to erase the event entirely from history.

Finally, a note on the strike's aftermath. The retreat of radicalism
in Seattle and the Northwest was neither immediate nor total. It
began with the shattering of the IWW, the splintering and demise
of the Socialist Party, and the employers' counterrevolution—the
anti-union "American Plan." In Seattle itself, the Emergency Fleet
Corporation cancelled orders for new vessels, forcing thousands
of shipyard workers into unemployment just as demobilization
was at its peak. It was deindustrialization with a sharp political
edge. The Waterfront Employers' Association fought to reintro-
duce the open shop. The depression of 1920–1921 came early to
Seattle and lasted longer than in other places. But working-class
radicalism didn't die. The General Strike and IWW militancy lived
on, if underground, in the vivid recollections of old Wobblies and
in the battles of young socialists in the 1930s. This legacy laid the
foundation for Washington's Cooperative Commonwealth movement, which, allied with the Democrats, brought a progressive
alliance to power in Olympia and elected the communist Hugh
DeLacy to Congress in 1944. In governing circles, the strike
wasn't forgotten. In 1936 FDR's postmaster general, James Farley,
would ironically raise a glass to "the forty-seven states and the
Soviet of Washington."

Working-class radicalism lived on in our house in Holly Park, a public housing project in Seattle's south end. With Yesler Terrace, Holly Park was integrated, the first such public projects in the country. My parents were children in the Great Depression. My father spent his teenage years fleeing landlords and bill collectors in the tow of a jobless father. He attended Garfield High School. On graduating, he joined the Army Air Corps. My mother went to Franklin, then became a wartime telephone operator. Her worst moment was when, as a child in 1942, her Japanese classmates failed to appear one morning. Internment meant empty chairs, friends gone forever. My father returned home to work as an Alaskan fisherman and sheet metal worker, then as a union organizer. Both were activists in the Democrats' solid South End, where party loyalists, supporters of the Washington Commonwealth Federation and Communists collaborated in a much-revived labor movement and broad left.

As a child, I learned that one never crosses a picket line. I was quite at home in the Labor Temple. I knew what Teamster goons were. My father once returned home badly beaten by some of "Dave Beck's boys." I knew all the words to the songs on the *Talking Union* recording.[12] More to the point, I learned about the IWW—Wobblies—and the General Strike then, vividly, about Centralia. It wasn't a pilgrimage, we were just visiting friends in Centralia. My father wanted to see "Hangman's Bridge," and I went along for the ride. The lynching of the Wobbly Wesley Everest was a singularly gruesome lesson for a child of seven.

I am not sure how many children there were like me. There must have been many. McCarthyism, however, hit hard in Seattle and Washington State. Its local manifestation, the Canwell Committee, headed by the right-wing legislator Albert Canwell of Spokane, wreaked havoc on the left. It targeted Communists, but also the Commonwealth Federation, the longshoremen's union, the University of Washington, and more. On July 19, 1948, the Camwell Committee convened five days of hearings at the university in a vicious witchhunt. In the end, six tenured faculty members received sanctions from the university and three lost their jobs; the university's reputation, rightly, was sullied.

My father continued to work in the union and my mother coordinated the statewide fight against right-to-work legislation. We detested the Weyerhaeusers. As environmentalists before the movement got going, we held them responsible for the devastation inflicted on our forests—so evident in trips to the mountains or drives to the ocean beaches. But politics receded, except in national elections. We supported Stevenson. My mom kept the faith or regained it. As a single parent in the sixties, she opposed the Vietnam War, joined up with feminists at work, and supported her rebellious kids.

My school friends were all working class, the children of bakers, barbers, pipe fitters, carpenters, and railroad clerks—but they seem to have known nothing of the great strikes of the past. I'm still not certain why. They were not mentioned in our textbooks. What little we learned of history focused on the Oregon Trail, the so-called Indian Wars, the First World War, then the new war with communism. Much, to say the least, was lost.

The thoughtful editors at *New Left Review* were right to suggest, when I published a version of chapter 6 of this book in their journal, that here archaeology and considerable excavation was called for. The Seattle story had indeed been buried, lost in United States memory. I started college at Antioch in the early sixties when it was perhaps the most radical college in the country. One spring, I lived in Corey Hall (Corey was a pseudonym of Louis Fraina, a founder of US communism, though at the time this was known to only a few of us). The young radicals at Antioch, like the new movements nationally, knew little of the socialist tradition. Antioch's curriculum was rather traditional, despite its radical reputation. In the history department, for example, we studied the muckrakers and reforms of the 1910s. They certainly were not unrelated to the workers' movements. We might discover this but only if we searched. We studied the French Revolution, but there also, to capture its relevance, we had to read between the lines,

which we could do and did. So, we became radicals outside the classroom. The activists at Antioch were educated by and in the South's civil rights movement, then the antiwar movement. It was not the Lawrence Strike that moved us, nor the Everett massacre, but rather Greensboro, North Carolina; Birmingham and Selma, Alabama; and Philadelphia, Mississippi. But this came with a cost.

It was not until the emergence of Students for a Democratic Society (SDS) that the history of labor returned to the fore. However, this reappearance, often rather crude, arrived in what had become a bitterly contested terrain. If a victory, it was Pyrrhic. In the summer of 1969, SDS imploded, and the US student movement collapsed.

In response, disheartened but not defeated, I joined the doctoral program at Warwick University in England, there to study with Thompson. I wanted to learn history from below, especially working-class history from below. I wanted a way to understand US working-class history, in a period when it seemed incorrigibly conservative. US labor history was taken seriously at Warwick. Thompson, that year, was joined by IWW historian Melvyn Dubofsky, as a visiting professor. The Warwick experience was interesting not only because of the professors, however. We, the students of Thompson, were nearly all activists, socialists as well, belonging to a generation marked by upward mobility bu often with working-class origins. This was an identity for whic we were prized at Warwick. It was a highly unusual experienc for a student from the United States, to be recognized as worl ing class not as an identity denied but as a positive identity. Th reawakened my own history. There, at Warwick's Center for t Study of Social History, working-class history was elevated, a deep excavations were undertaken with zeal. As a result, it v the rare student indeed with no knowledge of Big Bill Haywc or Elizabeth Gurley Flynn. Today, happily, the same can be : of this country's labor studies centers, including the thriving : grams at the University of Washington.

During the Second World War, Seattle was transformed int(

City." The Boeing bombers—the B-17s, B-29s and B-47s, as well as the B-52s of *Dr. Strangelove* fame—which rained destruction from the skies on Japan and Occupied Europe and then on Korea, were constructed in a sprawling plant backing on to the Duwamish River and another in Renton, together employing as many as forty-five thousand people. When government orders began to dry up in the mid-1950s, the company invested heavily in passenger jet airliners to escape what executives nervously referred as to "the peace problem."[13] The success of the 707 and 737 made Seattle all but a company town. The sudden termination of the postwar boom in 1971 therefore came as a shock. Boeing slashed its production workforce from 85,000 to 20,000 and unemployment climbed to 14 percent, the highest rate in the country.

A three-decade tech boom, however, beginning in the mid-1980s with Microsoft's expansion in the suburb of Redmond, fifteen miles to the northeast, has erased the decline of 1971 too from memory. Amazon presently employs thousands in the city—spread across three dozen sites—and occupies more office space than the next forty largest companies combined. It has used this leverage to block a municipal employment tax intended to raise funds for affordable housing. The company congratulates itself for investing in its hometown, yet five-sixths of the $668 million poured into infrastructure improvements around its South Lake Union campus has come from the public purse—such is the fine print in today's "gospel of wealth."[14] There are now gated suburbs in the foothills of the Cascade Mountains, once the habitat of the IWW loggers. The Port of Seattle still thrives, but the old labor gangs upon which the waterfront's solidarity was constructed have been replaced by crane operators and truck drivers, far fewer in number, though still occupying strategic positions in global commodity chains.

Does anything of 1919 endure? Is there an inheritance? In the time since then there have been moments containing glimpses of this older history, as well as potentially offering something new. Eight decades after the General Strike, a rare alliance of blue-collar

workers, environmentalists, and other alter-globalization activists—the "Teamsters and Turtles"—disrupted the World Trade Organization conference in Seattle, temporarily overwhelming the police and cutting off the convention center from the rest of the city. Steelworkers marched on the waterfront. Defying curfews, orders to evacuate, and the imposition of a fifty-block "no protest zone" in the downtown district—edicts that the Seattle and King County police, Washington National Guard and US military enforced with tear gas, rubber bullets, concussion grenades, and baton blows—the protesters forced the WTO to adjourn in confusion, cancelling Clinton's gala address.[15] Yes, there is an inheritance well worth celebrating this centenary year, a year begun with the massive strike of Los Angeles teachers. The workers of 1919 were brazen and courageous, and then some. They were defiant even in the face of the cruelest measures taken against them, mass incarceration, deportation, and murder. If their rule over Seattle lasted only five days, they were five days that mattered, five days well worth remembering.

—MENDOCINO, CALIFORNIA

1. THE UNION'S INSPIRATION

On February 6, 1919, Seattle's workers, all of them, struck. In doing so they literally took control of the city. They struck in support of shipyard workers, some thirty-five thousand, then in conflict with the city's shipyard owners and the federal government's US Shipping Board.

Seattle's Central Labor Council (CLC), representing 110 unions, all affiliated with the American Federation of Labor (AFL) and all craft unions, called the strike. They brought the city to a halt—a strange silence settled on the normally bustling streets, and on the waterfront where "nothing moved but the tide."[1] The CLC's *Union Record* reported sixty-five thousand union members on strike. It was a general strike, the first of its kind in the United States. Perhaps as many as one hundred thousand working people participated.

The city's authorities were rendered powerless—there was indeed no power that could challenge the workers. There were, of course, soldiers in the city and many more at nearby Camp Lewis, not to mention thousands of newly enlisted armed deputies, but to unleash these on a peaceful city? The regular police were reduced to onlookers; the generals hesitated.

Rank-and-file workers, union by union, elected the strike leadership, a strike committee. The strike committee elected an executive committee. Meeting virtually nonstop, they ensured the health, welfare, and safety of the city. Garbage was collected, the hospitals were supplied, babies got milk, and the people were fed, including some thirty thousand a day at the strikers' kitchens.

The streets were safe, rarely safer, patrolled by an unarmed labor guard of workers. It was reported that crime abated. Nevertheless, the rich, those who could not or would not escape to Portland or California, armed themselves. The *Seattle Star* asked, "Under which flag?"–the red, white, and blue or the red. The mayor, Ole Hanson, knowing well that this was not the case, claimed the latter and warned that–a revolution was underway. The AFL piled on, denouncing the strikers and sending emissaries by the hundreds.

The General Strike, however, was not a revolution. It was in support of the city's shipyard workers. Still, never had there been anything quite like it, not in the United States. Moreover, these strikers left their jobs amid the great strike wave of the First World War years and an international crisis that in fact was in some places revolutionary—a crisis evolving in the shadow of revolution in Russia. It was no wonder, then, that revolution was in the air—terrifying some, inspiring others. Then, too, no one knew for certain just how far this strike might go. The strike was simple and straightforward for many, a powerful statement of solidarity and nothing more. But others did indeed want more: all-out victory for the shipyard workers, for example. Some wanted much more, but surely no one could know, not on that cold February morning, not with any certainty, just what lay ahead.

THE STRIKE EXPOSED A WIDENING CRISIS then confronting the working-class movement, in which Seattle would play a central role. At stake were not just shipyard issues but the nature of the labor movement as it existed. Its very form was challenged, as well as its values, actions, tactics, and goals, both long term and short. The fundamental issue was craft unionism versus industrial unions. Millions of workers seemed ready to abandon craft unions in favor of industrial unionism: unions organized by industry, not craft or job. Industrial unionism meant that the power of workers was in the workplace, not at the ballot box or in political action. It also reckoned that workers' power would be expressed in the strike, including, for some, the general strike. This was the program of the IWW, the One Big Union (OBU) movement, in well-established organizations such as the United Mine Workers of America (UMWA) and the Western Federation of Miners (WFM), and even among dissidents within the Socialist Party, which was founded as the embodiment of parliamentary democracy. This was anathema to the AFL's leadership. Organized in 1886, the AFL insisted it alone could be the representative of American workers. Yet-the rift had opened between even its most loyal affiliates; industrial unionism had become a current within the AFL itself.

Nowhere, perhaps, was this as true as in Seattle. Seattle's trade unionists were in craft unions, some 120 of them, organized by the job and divided by lines of jurisdiction. The history of Seattle labor in those years was the struggle to change this. And surely to the dismay of the officers of the AFL's national unions, it was in many ways successful. Its workers sought common contracts, common strikes, common conditions, and common politics. They insisted that the power of the strongest workers be available for the weakest. Thus, the sympathy strike, or at least the threat of it. In these years, the CLC routinely used this threat in bargaining. The national officers of the AFL supported craft unions with strict jurisdictional divides. They opposed sympathy strikes, denounced any discussion of the general strike, and considered IWW members to be dual unionists. Seattle, then, was different. In Seattle, the AFL's red line of demarcation faded, obscuring the divides between Seattle's AFL, its socialist leaders, the IWW, and an array of independent radicals and organizations. Strikes and sympathy strikes underpinned union power; inevitably, this included the general strike, putting its power, if only implicitly, on the table.

In 1919, the movement to free Thomas Mooney came to a head. Mooney along with Fred Billings were San Francisco trade unionists framed in the aftermath of the deadly 1916 Preparedness Day bombing, and were serving life sentences. It was an international movement but in few places was it as inspired as in Seattle. "It lies within your power to get him [Mooney] out of there, but to do so you must exercise a power that you do not realize you possess," roared Kate Sadler, speaking at a street meeting of thousands.[2] The "power" she referred to was the general strike. Sadler was Seattle's best-known Socialist, the workers' Joan of Arc. She led some forty Seattle delegates to Chicago in January to attend a national labor convention addressing the Mooney issue. There, before one thousand delegates, Sadler would defy the conference leadership, appealing with her delegation for a May Day general strike to free Mooney.[3] To no avail. The "reds" were defeated. There would be no general strike, and Mooney and Billings would remain imprisoned.

Whether the worker on the street in Seattle was indeed aware of the power alluded to by Sadler remains somewhat unclear, yet the returning delegates found the shipyard workers on strike and a movement that was itching for a fight. Seattle's unions represented the city's tens of thousands of workers, supported a daily, union-owned newspaper, the *Union Record*, and a score of cooperative enterprises: markets, butchers, barbers, and a laundry. Seattle was a closed-shop town, unique among American cities. On street corners, soap box orators abounded, as did socialist newsstands and newspapers. Sadler was far from the only incendiary. The Socialist Party, left-wing and working class, was entrenched in a workers' movement that widely supported the idea of workers' power. "I believe that 95% of us agree that the workers should control industry," said Harry Ault, the editor of the *Union Record*.[4]

Seattle was also the regional center of the IWW. The Wobblies championed industrial unionism. It was for them foundational, the indispensable element in their outlook. Though always a minority, the Wobblies would everywhere shape the discussion of industrial unionism, in theory and practice, and of the general strike as well. Speaking in New York in 1911, Bill Haywood, the future IWW leader, then still a Socialist Party member, insisted that the question was "whether or not the general strike is an effective weapon for the working class."[5] He paid tribute to the Paris Commune, referred to the theorists of the movement, and apologized for not being a "better theorist" himself. Then Haywood turned his attention to Colorado, where he had been a miner, and the bitter experience at Cripple Creek. The workers there had not been "thoroughly organized." That is, they were not organized in an industrial union and without industrial unionism, he said, the general strike was not possible: "I want to urge [this] upon the working class: to become so organized on the economic field that they can take hold of and hold the industries in which they are employed." Political power, he argued, came through industrial organization. "The industrial organization is capable not only of the general strike, but prevents the capitalists from disfranchising the worker, it gives the vote to women. It re-enfranchises the black man and places the ballot in the hands of every boy and girl employed in a shop, makes them eligible to take part in the general strike, makes them eligible to legislate for themselves where they are most interested in changing conditions, namely in the place where they work."[6]

Haywood and the IWW claimed the general strike as their own while denying any association with the strictly defined syndicalist tradition. Neither were they anarchists, let alone romantically attracted to fantasies of violence and martyrdom—though certainly they had their martyrs. Solidarity was their mantra, folded arms their power. The general strike was about workers' power in the here and now, in the future as well, but beginning today. Haywood projected three types of general strike—a general strike in industry, a general strike in a community, and a national general strike—contending that each remained untried.

Still, in theory, the IWW insisted that the general strike was its ultimate weapon. The general strike was the instrument with which "the capitalist system will be overthrown." Rarely more precise than this, the Wobblies believed that when the day came "control of industry would pass from the capitalists to the masses and the capitalists will vanish from the face of the earth." The workers would then possess the machinery of production and distribution, enabling them to create "a new society without poverty, police, jails, armies, churches . . . blessed with freedom and abundance."[7] Haywood's fixation, however, remained on the practical and immediate utility of the general strike to class struggle. He routinely referred to the question "[Is] the general strike an effective weapon for the working class?"—in the immediate sense, in the class struggle. In fact, simply the threat of a general strike terrified the authorities. In the 1910s, such threats were not unusual. They came mostly from the IWW, being issued, however, not as calls to storm the gates. On the contrary, they were responses to practical crises: how to win a strike or how to defend the organization. These strikes failed to materialize. Neither the threat to strike to keep the United States out of the war, nor the threats to strike to free Mooney and other political prisoners would be put to the test. The closest the IWW came to leading a general strike was during the 1917 timber strike in the Northwest. There some fifty thousand loggers and millhands struck for the eight-hour day and won. The full impact of this was considerable, certainly in Seattle and the Pacific Northwest.

Seattle's trade unionists lived through this strike and many more. They understood that the general strike—a potential weapon but not necessarily the ultimate one—was in their arsenal. The literature they read tells us this. They were aware of the Chartists and the Commune, the Belgian strikes, and the 1905 Russian strike. Six times between 1900 and 1918 the CLC voted in favor of a general strike—each time in disputes with the employers. Each time settlements rendered the threat immaterial. The hysteria of the authorities aside, the CLC and the IWW understood strikes in terms of immediate, short-term reforms: the general strike in the woods began with demands for clean bedding, showers, and decent food in the logging camps, then the eight-hour day. This was the path to power, in both the short and long term; the new society would be built piecemeal in struggles in the shell of the old. The CLC's view was much the same as the IWW's, though the long term was longer. Was, then, the general strike an effective weapon? In the forests? Yes, it seemed. In Seattle? A strike going beyond a work stoppage, beyond a single industry, had never been tried in a city. Not until 1919. No one knew.

NOVEMBER 11, 1918. THE WAR WAS FINISHED. There were wild celebrations everywhere, in France, Britain, and the United States, spontaneous demonstrations of relief and happiness. Millions took to the streets of Paris and New York. In London, "a primitive jamboree" ensued, with crowds roaring, cheering, drinking, copulating in the shadows. In Brest, in Brittany, where the American soldiers first disembarked, the city was "wild with joy," factory sirens howling, the ships' whistles screaming in the harbor. The American soldiers still there were hugged and kissed. On November 7, the *Seattle Star* had pronounced, "War Is Over!" At once, people took to the streets. In the morning, the mayor was awakened to find the streets already filled, his planned proclamation of a "holiday" irrelevant. Makeshift bands appeared, people banging garbage can lids, lunch buckets, car horns blasting. Then came the sailors, ordered out to make the celebration official and properly patriotic. Then the shipyard owners closed the yards, foremen shepherded the men into the streets, swelling already huge crowds. The entire length of Second Avenue became gridlocked.

"The war to end all wars," the patriotic papers repeated without a blush. Ten million lost in the slaughter on the Western Front, 36 million casualties. In Central and Eastern Europe, there were millions more dead, vast swathes of devastation, and the heart of the continent in ruins. New armies emerged, this time of scavengers and homeless, creatures without hope. The *Seattle Star* featured a half-page, triumphant Jesus, captioned "Peace on Earth." Then came the mindless boastings of victory and babble about "sacred unions," "homes for heroes," and "democracy at full tilt."

The workers of Seattle had never really supported the war, unless, of course, one reduces it to "supporting the troops," the mantra in all wars. The *Union Record*'s response to the war's end was rather more subdued. News from the front competed with accounts of "revolution" in Germany and the shortcomings of the wage awards promised to the shipyard workers.[8] Still, workers celebrated, especially if it meant an end to long hours, short pay, and conscription, on the one hand, or charges of "sedition" and "criminal syndicalism," the red squads, raids, prison sentencess on the other. The death toll was high: of the nearly five million Americans who served in the First World War, 116,000 were killed. The Battle of Meuse Argonne alone took the lives of 26,000.

The "peace," however, was short-lived. The same day the *Seattle Star* cried out, "War Is Over!" it reported that sailors in Kiel, the home of the Kaiser's high seas fleet, had seized the ships. "The crew of the dreadnoughts *Kaiser and Schleswig* mutinied and waved red flags yesterday morning. They arrested their officers, 20 of whom were shot. . . . The sailors threaten to blow up the ships if they are attacked."[9] Soldiers in the town's garrison had joined them, and the city was effectively governed by a council of sailors, soldiers, and workmen. Thousands more were soon marching with red flags, and the revolt was spreading. There was street fighting in Hamburg, mutinies spreading. "Several garrisons in Holstein have deserted and are reported marching on Kiel, waving red flags."[10] The revolution in the West, it seemed, had begun.

In the winter of 1918, much of Seattle—the schools and most public places—was closed, as a result of Spanish influenza. Fifteen hundred were dead already; it was unclear if the epidemic had ended. Still, the first loggers were drifting back. They joined others—wandering, homeless men on the city's mean streets, waiting for work to resume. This was ordinary in Seattle's winter. Now, however, newcomers appeared, some still in uniform, wanting work. The *Union Record* reported that peace abroad was bringing hunger at home. A union representative from the Metal Trades

Council told reporters that he had been approached "by 15 sol-diers in just one night, all for bed and board."[11]

The paper foresaw unemployment and "bread lines coming." "It looks as if that move for the six-hour day or even the four-hour day, in order to pass the jobs around, may be needed in a hurry, right here in Seattle."[12] The Machinists of Hope Lodge responded by ruling that "no member shall under any circumstances be allowed to work more than eight hours during a current work day, or more than 44 hours in a working week." They proposed "a shortening of the work day policy as palliative to unemployment, for civilians and discharged service men alike, as a result of the large number of men suddenly thrown on the labor market." The Lodge also adopted "a clause for their new working agreements providing that when conditions arise in any plant whereby men are to be laid off, that instead of reducing the force, the hours be reduced to six hours per day, five days a week." The Lodge also instructed mem-bers that "they must accept employment only through the union offices so that the disgraceful features of the 'job hunting' to which American working men have been submitted may be eliminated as far as possible."[13]

The shipyards, the core of Seattle's economy, nevertheless still seemed to prosper. The *Star's* lead headline read, "American Shipbuilding Will Continue, Declares Schwab."[14] Charles Schwab, the head of Bethlehem Steel, who had been charged but not con-victed of war profiteering, was viciously anti-union. President Wilson appointed him Director General of the Emergency Fleet Corporation, its board given wartime control of all shipbuilding in the United States. Seattle's shipyard workers had chafed under his wartime regime, and the high cost of living became *the* issue. Thus, the killing in Europe, most of it, had not been finished a month before the Metal Trades Council, representing the shipyard unions, took a strike vote. Members overwhelmingly rejected the pay "awards" (salary adjustments) of both the shipyard owners and the wartime Emergency Shipping Board. Their demands were for wage increases and for raising the pay of the least skilled to reduce inequality in the yards. They were not alone; across the country workers believed they had sacrificed for the cause of war, but that the "high cost of living" had been an unfair burden. The demand everywhere was for wage increases. Real enough in itself, the demand was also an indication of deeper frustrations and dissatisfactions. The strike wave of the war years—an epidemic of strikes—was both national and international, inspired in part by syndicalism, the new workplace radicalism. Seattle was at once a strike center and a radical center, a stronghold of working-class socialism with a vision of a better world. Mocking Wilson and the local "interests," Seattle's workers called for self-determination and democracy at home.

The *Union Record* thrived in this setting. Seattle's workers, informed by the paper, made the rebellions abroad their rebellions: London's dockers, laborers in Buenos Aires, the "Golden Triangle" of revolt in Italy—Turin, Milan, Genoa—where the young Antonio Gramsci urged the creation of workers' councils. It brought news from the Red Clyde in Scotland and its shop stewards' movement. John Maclean and Willie Gallagher became well-known figures: Maclean the revolutionary socialist and Gallagher the worker who "never had a salary, never had expenses paid by the movement . . . the skilled brass finisher who has always worked at his trade when he wasn't in jail."[15] Then came the Soviets in Budapest, insurrection in Bavaria, and the German revolution. On December 27, 1919, an article from Berlin opened: "Wives and sweethearts of the mutinous sailors have seized rifles and joined in defense of the royal palace against the loyal guard."[16] The ordeals of Karl Liebknecht and Rosa Luxemburg would be featured on the *Union Record*'s front pages as, alas, were their deaths.[17] It ran news from Johannesburg and Mexico and Winnipeg. Closer to home, it warned readers, "Southerners Plan Terror Against Negro."[18]

In the United States, rebellion emerged in crises on several fronts, including the strike wave. It began early in the decade, accelerated in the war years, then reached its peak in 1919. In 1917, more than six million workdays were lost to strikes. The metal workers led the first strikes, then the shipbuilders (separate from metal workers), coal miners, copper miners, textile and timber workers followed. Sixty-seven of the strikes in 1917 involved more than ten thousand workers per strike; one-sixth of lost workdays were due to strikes led by the IWW. The latter included strikes in the forests of the Pacific Northwest, in the Butte, Montana, and Arizona copper mines, in the Mesabi Range and on Philadelphia's docks.

The year 1919 was the high point in the decade, beginning with the victory of the Amalgamated Clothing Workers-winning the 44-hour week plus wage increases. In New York, impatient marine workers waited for "the findings of the War Labor Board," comfortable that "at a day's notice they can tie up the whole vast traffic of New York Harbor."[19] In January 17,000 struck, the first of four harbor strikes that year; the longest, by longshoremen, shut down the harbor for six weeks in the fall. The Lawrence Textile workers walked out in January and held out until victory in May. The Cleveland Cloak Makers struck. Cincinnati clothing workers, teachers, library workers, office workers, telephone workers, and the Boston police also struck. In one of the largest strikes ever, 350,000 steelworkers shut down basic steel, unleashing an unprecedented reign of terror in retaliation. In Pittsburgh, the Interchurch World Movement discovered that Slavic steel workers were radicals. In West Virginia, coal miners were "insurrectionary"; their 1919 strike carried on into the next decade, culminating in an armed assault on Blair Mountain.

In the streets, there were food riots in New York City; in Cleveland the May Day rally turned into a day-long battle with police and vigilantes; looters took advantage of the police strike in Boston.[20] The Mooney movement, aimed at freeing jailed San Francisco labor leaders, estimated that as many as one million workers participated that summer in strikes and demonstrations demanding their release.

The summer of 1919 also remains a time of national shame,

of gruesome episodes in the oppression of black people. Alas, far from glorious, the "Red" in the "Red Summer" refers to blood, black blood, not revolution. At year's end, authorities could identify at least forty localities as sites of "race riots." More like pogroms, they were outbursts of mob violence in which whites, alleging offenses, attacked black individuals, black neighborhoods, especially returning black soldiers, and black workers. In that summer, some forty-three African-American men were reported to have been lynched—hanged, shot, some burned alive. The violence accompanied and impelled the Great Migration of hundreds of thousands of southern blacks—500,000 to the North, more to southern and border cities. Most sought to take advantage of wartime labor shortages and to escape the misery of the Jim Crow and sharecropping South.

Chicago was a major destination for blacks migrating north. It was a vast concentration of industry and commerce, the nation's second-largest city, with a population approaching three million. The black population on the city's crowded South Side had doubled in the war years, challenging racial boundaries and workplace segregation. On a hot summer Sunday, Eugene Williams, a black teenager, swimming in Lake Michigan, was alleged to have crossed into whites-only waters; he was attacked by rock-throwing whites and drowned. Fighting followed, spreading into the South Side neighborhoods. Individual blacks were attacked, sometimes whites. White mobs roamed through black neighborhoods, torching houses, businesses, and churches. By the time, belatedly, the Illinois Militia arrived, twenty-three blacks and fifteen whites had been killed, while five hundred people, the majority black, had been wounded, and one thousand black families were left homeless. Wilson, the Bureau of Investigation, and the Red Squads were alarmed, but not by white violence. Wilson himself believed that returning black soldiers were "conveying Bolshevism." Whites, overwhelmingly, were appalled by demands for racial equality, union rights, and self-defense, linking these to the general unrest.[21]

Wilson and his advisers were, in their way, quite correct. This was also the time of Harlem's "New Negro" and of a resurgence of "fierce race consciousness" and internationalism.[22] Black workers, with courage and pride, were opening a new chapter in their history by fighting back—in Omaha, Washington, and Chicago. Soap-box socialists Chandler Owen and A. Philip Randolph joined W. E. B. Du Bois in believing that "we are cowards and jackasses if now that the war is over, we do not marshal every ounce of our brain and brawn to fight a sterner, longer, more unbending battle against the forces of hell in our own land. '*We return. We return from fighting. We return fighting.*'"[23] Owen and Randolph opposed the war and supported the Russian Revolution, urging blacks to organize themselves. They produced the *Messenger* and collaborated with Max and Crystal Eastman at the *Liberator* and with other Greenwich Village radicals. Their goal was to raise class consciousness among black workers by connecting the cause of black freedom to class struggle. Military intelligence considered the *Messenger* "the most dangerous of all the Negro publications."[24] James Weldon Johnson was a New York writer, a figure in the Harlem Renaissance and a leader of the NAACP. He reported that it was the most widely read of all the radical publications in New York. In the summer of 1919, the *Messenger* claimed 33,000 Negro workers and a few thousand whites as readers and urged them to join the IWW, "a revolutionary organization that draws no race, creed, color or sex line."[25]

SEATTLE'S REBELS, LEFT, RIGHT, AND CENTER, had little use for the East, seeing the cities there as venal, slum-ridden sites of child labor, wretched working conditions, and ecological disaster. James Duncan, the CLC secretary and the architect of industrial unionism in Seattle, expressed sympathy for the workers of the East but believed they were backward, and their unions relics. He suspected it might take years for them to catch up. The West was the future.

Kate Sadler, no "Easterner," flourished in this West. She was born in poverty in Scotland, where she "learned socialism at her father's knee." In the United States, she came first to Philadelphia, where she worked as a domestic. There she met Sam Sadler, the longshoremen's future leader, and in 1909 they moved west, settling in Seattle. In the decade that followed, Sadler worked tirelessly to build the Socialist Party. Harvey O'Connor, the historian of Seattle's rebels, considered her "a peerless socialist orator," on the level with Kate Richards O'Hare and Elizabeth Gurley Flynn.[26] Sadler was Seattle's representative to the Socialist Party's National Committee, but she rarely returned east; her commitment was to the workers of Seattle and its hinterland. Here, she supported workers whenever called, as long as someone could pay expenses. Sadler was as well known in the mining camps and mill towns as in the Puget Sound cities. She was also the featured guest at Colville's 1916 socialist "encampment," a weekend educational event in the tiny mining and timber town in Washington's far northeast corner. "Kate Sadler," they announced, welcoming her, "is one of the great socialist women of the nation.... She is known throughout the length and breadth of Washington as a fearless champion of the working class. A veritable reincarnation of Joan of Arc, Kate Sadler's splendidly fiery eloquence inspires hope, kindles courage, arouses enthusiasm among the workers wherever she is heard." Organizers promoted her as "full to overflowing with what Debs so aptly calls 'the fine spirit of revolt.' We especially invite the women and the young people to hear her. You will never regret it."[27] A 1917 report from Everett recounts her giving an "inspiring lecture," speaking on the "War Crisis" to a large, outdoor crowd: "In spite of the fact that the weather was cold, the crowd stayed with the meeting until it was adjourned."[28] Other accounts find her in Sumas on the Canadian border, in Liberty, a mining camp in the Cascades, and in Pierce County's coal camps. At Butte's metal mine workers' June picnic in 1919, "the event of the day [was] an address by Kate Sadler of Seattle, labor's gifted woman orator, who [talked about] world happenings and their relation to the working class."[29] O'Connor wrote that "when workers called for help, in strikes, jailings, free speech struggles, Kate came. Kate the fearless one. . . . The police, of course, knew her, [but] always hesitated to drag her off the soapbox, for the workers formed an iron ring, daring them to touch *our* Kate."[30]

Seattle was different, many thought better, a belief not uncommon in the West at the time, but in Seattle the difference was connected to its workers and their movements. Seattle's white settlers brought with them the ideas of the times—Manifest Destiny, US exceptionalism, the "White Man's Burden," and Empire—though, as elsewhere, these ideas were contested. Seattle sits in the far northwestern corner of the nation, barricaded to the east by the Cascade Range beneath its magnificent yet ominous volcanic peaks, sheltered from the sea on the west by the Olympic range. Seattle in 1919 was, to be sure, a western city, sitting on the far edge of the continent, the end of the line, the sea the "last" frontier. It was surrounded by the vast rural West, with all the accompanying myth, but it was not home to cowboys, nor prospectors—if people came looking for gold, it was in Alaska.

Seattle early became an industrial city, but not a mill town—a city in the West, but not of it. Two thousand miles from Chicago; rail connection was completed in 1893, but trains were slow, the stops many. By ship, travel was even slower; San Francisco, 900 miles away, was reached only by sea. Travelers in the Puget Sound Basin seem to have preferred travel by sea; a "mosquito" fleet of steamers plied the Sound. Obstacles, to be sure—yet as elsewhere in the West obstacles had to be overcome, the aggressive capitalism of the new century, aggressive, dominant, thrived on such obstacles. The railroads opened the "wide open spaces" and would continue to do so; free land was promised on the final frontier, but ranchers and farmers all too often became collateral damage. The object was not a new "garden," but rather access to and exploitation of the West's wealth: the silver and gold of California, the copper of Arizona and Montana, coal in Colorado, the immeasurable forest land of the Pacific Northwest. The robber barons like James J. Hill, the "Empire Builder" and president of the Great Northern Railroad, were agents of an empire conceived in the

East, financed by eastern, often European bankers, and savored in the East. Globalism was already a fact, isolation was spatial at best. Whatever westerners may have wanted, they got capitalism; its imperatives and its booms and busts in the East shaped their lives, however far they might have been from New York City and Washington, DC.

The East meant the big banks, Wall Street, capitalism and capitalist catastrophes. The Depression of 1893 was the worst ever at that time: five hundred banks closed and thousands of businesses failed. Railroads, including the Northern Pacific, Union Pacific, Atchison, Topeka and Santa Fe, slipped into bankruptcy. Thousands of farmers lost their land. The cities teemed with the jobless, as the unemployment rate rose to 20 percent (and even higher in the great cities). There were protests and strikes. Jacob Coxey led a march of jobless (Coxey's Army) from Ohio on Washington, DC, demanding the government create work. Copycat marches, often composed of railroad workers, set off from Seattle and Tacoma; with Washington, DC, far in the distance, they attacked railroad centers and yards. The Populist Party soared in 1892, then crashed in disillusionment with the defeat of William Jennings Bryan in 1896. Federal soldiers routed the workers in the Pullman Strike, the great railroad strike of 1894; more workers became unemployed and the blacklist ubiquitous.

Debs, the railroad worker who led the great strike, was jailed in federal prison at Woodstock, just west of Chicago. There he took the time to read. Victor Berger, the Milwaukee socialist, is said to have introduced him to the writings of Karl Marx, giving him a copy of *Capital* which he found dull, preferring the German socialist Karl Kautsky. Of his many visitors, Kier Hardy, the Scottish socialist and founder of the Labour Party, seems to have most impressed him. "Debs did not learn much in jail," his biographer Ray Ginger wrote. "He could only learn by actively taking part in the battles of the outside world. When that form of activity was denied him, his entire method of educating himself came to pieces, and it was useless to give him books."[31]

Voters in Washington State supported Bryan for president; more important, they elected the Populist John Rogers as governor. The Populists campaigned for free schoolbooks, state aid to education, women's suffrage, and direct election of US senators, all of which enhanced the idea of the state as a haven in a hostile nation, a colony in "working man's country." Thus, new settlers arrived—blacklisted railroad workers, redundant coal miners, wheat farmers in despair—fleeing bankruptcy and eviction. Some were the followers of the new utopianism of the era, inspired by Laurence Gronlund's *The Cooperative Commonwealth* (1884) and Edward Bellamy's *Looking Backward* (1888). Others had read Robert Owen, the Welsh textile manufacturer and founder of utopian socialism, or followed William Morris, the English designer and revolutionary socialist, author of *News from Nowhere*. The Brotherhood of the Cooperative Commonwealth promoted establishing settlements in Washington, as did Debs, though he soon rejected this idea. The Brotherhood inspired half a dozen "colonies" in Puget Sound Country, all socialist to some degree: the Puget Sound Cooperative Colony on the Straits of Juan de Fuca, Equality in the Skagit Valley, Burley on the Kitsap Peninsula, Glennis near Eatonville, Freeland on Whidbey Island, and Home, an anarchist settlement, on the Longbranch Peninsula.[32]

Social relations in the colonies varied, as did the meaning of socialism. However, they were not merely back-to-the land settlements; however isolated, the colonists remained engaged. The first institutions everywhere, shelter aside, were the post office, the print shop, and the newspaper office. At Burley, they published *The Cooperator*; at Equality, *Industrial Freedom* and the *Young Socialist*; at Port Angeles, the *New Light*; at Home, the *Agitator* and *Discontent*; at Freeland, the *Whidbey Islander*. All the colonists championed equality, democracy, and socialism. All colonists were to work, though again how this was managed varied. None were to be poor. And there would be no government, no police, no church.[33]

The utopians have received a bad press, from the left as much as anywhere. The truth is they suffered quarrels and disagreements, their visions often seem fantasies, and they didn't last forever. Yet they are not without interest, certainly not in the history of the Seattle General Strike and its participants, who were often themselves disparaged as utopian. The colonists of Puget Sound rejected with their feet the notion that "there is no alternative" and did so in real time. They had the courage to question society and its most basic values, to imagine alternatives to the wretchedness of the present. And they were not mere spectators. They attempted to merge the world of the dream with the world of reality.[34]

This history never really died, nor did the idea that the Northwest was special ever entirely disappear, though the central idea of winning the country's workers to ideal communities was pressed in vain. They, with Debs, turned instead to socialism and socialist organizations, by that time well established both as an international movement and as a current in the farms and factories of Washington. Seattle's socialism is said to have been born in 1900 with Dr. Herman Titus as its founder.[35] A graduate of the University of Wisconsin and a Baptist preacher for several years, Titus settled in Seattle where he became a Skid Road social worker. There he read *Capital*, was persuaded, then founded his own paper, the *Socialist*. His wife, Hattie, managed a small hotel, a hangout for radicals. In 1906, Titus and Hattie joined the young Alfred Wagenknecht and Hulet Wells to lead the first of the West's free-speech fights. They took to soapboxes on the city's busiest street corners, holding forth on socialism and the issues of the day. They drew large crowds, disrupting commerce and traffic, repeatedly facing arrest. Titus himself was jailed six times. Imprisoned, they refused to work on the chain gangs, agitated the other prisoners, and exposed the foul prison conditions, forcing the Health Department to close the jail down. Juries refused to convict them.

Seattle socialists, as elsewhere, struggled; they stumbled into blind alleys and suffered foolish fractures and discord. Nevertheless, they grew in these years, both in numbers and in their presence in the working-class movement. By 1910, Seattle had become one of the Socialist Party's strongholds—Debs would win a million votes in the 1912 presidential elections. Still, Seattle remained special, even singular. Kate Sadler was not just a unique individual. Importantly, she brought to light the spirit of the Seattle workers' movement as it rose. This movement—militant, egalitarian, and deeply humane—did not emerge spontaneously. Rather, it was the creation of years of sustained work and sacrifice, often at great personal cost, by an exceptional group of socialists and trade unionists—Sadler perhaps foremost among them. She did not make this movement, of course. She was just one in this collective of gifted organizers and orators. Movements of thousands are the creations not of individuals but of communities. Rather she was the product of her relationship with the workers' movement. Indeed, we never hear of Sadler except in relation to workers— their meetings, their strikes, the struggles in their lives. She had the rare qualities of a true mass leader, the ability to address the workers' most pressing needs without losing sight of theory, in this case her vision of the socialist society to come. Her life was rooted in working-class struggle; this experience shaped her outlook, as it did the workers', and ultimately, that of their class.

The making of Seattle's working class, then, involved the relationships and the experience of workers themselves—with one another, with the authorities, with the employers and their press, and with the police. These were historical relationships in a process. The story of the great General Strike of 1919 and why it occurred in Seattle and nowhere else can only be understood with this in mind. The challenge is to expand our field of vision in time, stretching it both backwards and into the future, and geographically not contract it. We have to consider the roots of the strike, to follow the development of a movement, to see this historical moment in context. And this is well worth doing, all the more so as it happened one hundred years ago, far from the strategic centers, isolated from revolutionary strongholds, on the very edge, hidden in the shadow of rain forests, in the gray morning light of the Sound. Much of the Seattle story is forgotten. However regrettable, this is understandable. What is not understandable is that when people refer to the history of the General Strike, it is often as something insignificant or peripheral, simply a blip on the graph of lost causes—or worse, condescendingly corrected to make it fit into more acceptable narratives.

2. TWO CITIES

Seattle was both a boomtown and a radical center in the war years. The economic panic of 1907 was past, as was the recession of 1913–14. The city was by 1914 structurally complete. The city center was in place. To accomplish this, the tops of hills were literally chopped off, regraded for the benefit of the developers, with millions of tons of earth sluiced into Elliott Bay.

The construction of the ship canal that would connect Puget Sound with Lake Washington was underway. The Smith Tower was the tallest building west of the Mississippi River. Seattle's well-to-do inhabited leafy boulevards. They boasted a flourishing cultural life and founded a fine university. City planners foresaw an economic base that was diverse and with a large middle class. The politicians and their newspapers might feud about what to do with the infamous Skid Road and its flophouses, saloons, cheap booze, and brothels, but Seattle remained staunchly progressive. It supported women's suffrage, prohibition of alcohol (sales and manufacturing, but not consumption), cooperatives, municipal ownership, and growth. Its population had surpassed 300,000 when the war broke out.

Above all, Seattle had its port. More, its new municipal piers, equipped with gantry cranes (huge, moving cranes, a type still used on container terminals today) that were among the finest in the nation. And Seattle was two days closer to Vladivostok and the Asian markets than San Francisco. It was the "gateway to Alaska." Terminal space was abundant, wharfage and warehouse rates were cheap. In 1914, the Panama Canal opened, ensuring the city its place in world trade. By the war's end, Seattle would surpass San Francisco as the West Coast's leading port. Unlike other Puget Sound cities, it was not a mill town except for the shingle mills of Ballard, an adjacent small city annexed in 1907. Shipbuilding, always subject to economic booms and busts, exploded during the war. "Where only yesterday lay miles of empty tidelands," wrote the young radical Joseph Pass, "today monster yards are laboring day and night, giving birth to vessels of steel and wood."[1] Its yards would deliver more ships to the nation's fleets than any other single port. In 1917, Seattle had 1,300 manufacturing plants employing fifty thousand workers. Of these, thirty thousand were shipyard workers. In Tacoma, thirty miles south, there were fifteen thousand more.

Seattle, then, was an industrial city. Its unions were clean, not run by gangsters. It did not have a dominant political machine or bootleggers of any importance. Still, the city could be a tough place. "The Metal Trades, which dominated the Seattle labor movement and the Central Labor Council, were composed of a rough lot of men . . . torrid oaths and profanity prevailed" wrote a contemporary historian. "Men came out covered in soot and red paint, exhausted from wielding thundering riveting guns. Every day or so some unlucky shipyard worker would be carried out in the dead wagon." Its trades, then, were no less dangerous than elsewhere.

Seattle became a center for these loggers in winter, when rains made work in the woods impossible. The state's loggers, "hardworking, hard fighting, hard drinking," fled the woods to Skid Road. Their boots and bindlestiffs made them unwelcome almost every place else. In some years there were as many as ten thousand. There they might stay until poverty forced them back into the woods, often in debt, at the mercy of the job sharks and lumber men.

Seattle was founded in 1860. It was just one of several outposts on the Sound. The Territorial Assembly incorporated Seattle in 1865, unincorporated it in 1867, and then reincorporated it in 1869. The city survived the early booms and busts of the timber industry. Shamefully, it participated in the ethnic cleansing. After the anti-Chinese riots of 1885–86, the Chinese population, driven from both Seattle and Tacoma, was reduced to less than 4 percent of the population. In 1889, the Great Fire razed the central business district. The nationwide depression of 1893 was devastating in Seattle, leading to a run on the banks, foreclosures, and plummeting land values. Some residents simply fled, taking with them whatever they could. Seattle's city treasurer, Adolph Krug, escaped to Canada, taking with him $225,000 in public funds. The president of the Buckley State Bank of Tacoma left with $30,000.

By chance, gold was discovered in the Yukon Territories in 1896. Next year, the arrival of the SS *Portland* from Alaska, carrying sixty-eight miners and "one ton of gold," transformed Seattle. It was estimated that as many as 100,000 men (plus a few women) passed through Seattle on their way to Alaska and the Klondike. Only a fraction of this number would become actual prospectors. Far fewer became rich. However, in Seattle, every business prospered, and real estate values soared. "Anyone who owned or could lease a ship, no matter how old, no matter how unseaworthy, could find passengers. One captain hitched up a series of rafts, loaded two hundred passengers and a herd of cattle."[2] The merchants outfitted would-be mining men, then refitted them. The banks financed whatever they could, offering cash to those who returned gold. Salmon canners fed the hordes, beginning the deadly onslaught on the species.

Seattle in those years was recast. An essentially Wild West frontier town became the progressive regional center of the 1910s. This occurred remarkably fast, but not evenly. Seattle would never become a boss-driven urban catastrophe of the kind revealed by the work of the turn-of-the-century muckrakers, including Lincoln Steffens's pathbreaking account *The Shame of the Cities*.[3]

Shipbuilding and associated industries thrived, but none did better than the saloons and brothels on Skid Road. With thousands of single men pouring into the city, men with money to spend and time to kill, prostitution thrived. There were more saloons in the business district than there were restaurants or dry-goods stores. The city's Hillside Improvement Company would, at one point, purchase several acres for a "model red-light district"; it would include a 500-room brothel, the biggest in the world. Seattle, at least in Skid Road and its environs, became an "open town" where easy money abounded.[4] Certainly, then, there was enough to be ashamed of. Seattle's political battles in the decade were framed by Skid Road and what to do about it. In these struggles, the working-class movement, although most often siding with the progressives, found itself increasingly isolated.

Ironically, it was the infusion of gold-rush wealth that under-wrote this transformation and shaped economic development. It created the basis for a diversified economy. Seattle would not become a single-industry, company town (not until the 1950s anyway). James E. Casey founded United Parcel Service in 1907. William Boeing founded his corporation in 1910. The new wealth also shaped the city's class system. It gave Seattle's professional classes independence from the timber employers, railroad men and their like, the masters of the frontier economy. It also under-lay the politics of municipal reform and enterprise, efficiency in government and management, and moral virtue. These were all in line with the national progressive movement. Then, too, it created the structures of a class system that had more in common with the industrial centers of the East than the company towns of the frontier West. Its population, diverse in occupation, skill, gender and national origin, was overwhelmingly comprised of industrial wage workers.

Seattle's progressive middle class pursued a "beautiful city," free from the vice and corruption of the East. It supported plan-ning, municipal ownership, provision for health, education, and the future. The feminists of the movement, the middle class "club women," suffragists, social workers, and others worked to improve the conditions of the city's poorest, children, single mothers, the elderly. They supported prohibition and sought relief for women workers, campaigning with labor for the eight-hour day for women. The civic planners' public projects won working-class support. The labor movement opposed private ownership of utilities and public facilities, including the port, associating the direct rule of the wealthy, the "Interests" as they were called, with corruption. Socialists too, including the remnants of nineteenth-century Populists, supported the programs of the reformers. However, they also held fast to a vision of another world. Overall, organized labor's policy in city politics was one of picking and choosing. It supported women's suffrage and measures making the city more democratic but was against prohibition—the latter increasingly an important issue for the middle classes.

In Seattle, legislation supporting "direct democracy," including the initiative, the referendum, and recall, and opposition to the ward system, helped clear the path for social reform. It reinforced the movement for clean government. This latter was essential if women, whose votes would threaten the vice economy, were to obtain the vote. Its antithesis, in the wings, was the wide-open city run by saloonkeepers and gangsters, which was the scourge of reformers everywhere.[5] These reforms in place, the state legislature in 1909 put a referendum on the ballot amending the state constitution by granting votes for women. It passed in every county, two to one. The victory of the women reinvigorated the anti-saloon movement, a cause that vexed Seattle's progressive politics in the run-up to war. The labor movement was divided. James Duncan, the long-time leader of Seattle's Central Labor Council, was a teetotaler, but there was the issue of personal liberty and "the working man's right to whiskey," as Chicago lawyer Clarence Darrow once argued in a Seattle lecture. Booze, some argued, was a long-standing masculine prerogative; it was also relief from the exhaustion of a day's toil. There was the worry that enforcement would be punitive and class-biased (which turned out to be the case).

On November 3, 1914, Washington's voters approved a measure prohibiting the manufacture and sale (although not the consumption) of liquor statewide. Washington women had gained the right to vote in 1910, and their votes contributed to passing the initiative. City people in Seattle, Tacoma, and Spokane opposed prohibition, whereas small-town and rural people were in favor. The prohibitionists drew upon what were believed to be long-standing middle-class American values—values rooted in a rural, Protestant, and Anglo-Saxon countryside. "Where else shall we look," asked an editorial in a prohibitionist paper, "but to the farmer to counteract the venality and corruption of the slums of our cities' populations, that seem to be so rapidly increasing by the aggregation of alien voters, anarchist and saloon influences?"[6] Still, reasonable people supported the case against the saloon. Drunks and the liquor traffic were undoubtedly causes of "alcohol-related crime, delinquency, poverty, prostitution, disease and political corruption."[7] There were fanatics in the field, none perhaps so inflamed as the Reverend Mark Matthews, the Presbyterian minister who led the city's fundamentalists in the crusade against the saloon. "The liquor traffic is the most fiendish, corrupt and hell-soaked institution that ever crawled out of the slime of the eternal pit," he claimed. "It is the open sore of this land."[8] Matthews's congregation, ten thousand strong, was among the largest in the country. With his followers, Matthews raided red-light district establishments, exposed politicians, and offered a preview of the "citizen's arrest."[9]

In the 1910 elections, the lawyer Hiram Gill was elected mayor. Gill campaigned promising a "wide-open town." He was supported by Alden Blethen, the flag-waving owner of the *Seattle Times*. Gill believed "in letting people alone"; if a "man wanted to go to hell . . . [he] was unwilling to set up roadblocks."[10] Gill made his fortune representing brothel keepers and saloon owners; as a city councilman he opposed municipal ownership, taxes for city projects, and labor unions. Blethen agreed, believing that the saloons and brothels were essential in maintaining the Alaska and maritime

trade. Downtown bankers and property owners profited, securing income both legally and illegally. Gill promised that the saloon
and brothel district would be contained. He fulfilled this promise, according to a *McClure's* magazine's reporter, by giving the
"vice concessioners" an "almost legal status." Gill wanted a sheriff who knew how to run such an area and found one in Charles
Wappenstein who imposed a semi-official shakedown: his police
kept close watch on the city's estimated five hundred prostitutes,
with Wappenstein to be paid $10 a month by each. *McClure's*, then
the flagship of the muckraking press, reported, "The city seemed
to have been transformed almost magically into one great gam-
bling hell.... No American city has ever seen anything comparable
with it."[11] Gill did not keep his promise to confine saloons to the
restricted area. The city's streets, the cafes, even the better hotels,
were still crowded with prostitutes. The old conditions were as
prevalent as before, and it was chiefly new arrivals who populated
the restricted area.

This provoked the city's middle classes and reformers, who
circulated a recall petition. As a result, an election was held in
February 1919 in which Gill lost. Women, having obtained the vote
three months earlier, no doubt contributed heavily to his defeat,
with an estimated 20,000 of 23.000 registered women voting. The
recall itself was a result of the recent reforms. Gill was the first US
mayor to be subjected to one. An angry Blethen defended both
Gill and his sheriff, Wappenstein, the latter having provided him
with a free personal bodyguard. Blethen survived the episode, but
Wappenstein was sent to the state penitentiary at Walla Walla.

Despite the opposition of Gill and the industrialists, the reformers succeeded in creating a municipal port, founded in September
1911. They followed up with projects at Harbor Island, the construction of the Fisherman's Terminal, and the completion of
the Ship Canal, a waterway that would eventually connect Lake
Washington with the Sound. The Klondike wealth underwrote
these municipal projects. But these would be the progressives'
last great achievements, the high point of public works in Seattle.

Private construction flourished too, but not, of course, according to an overall plan.[12]

"Wrestling order out of chaos is the order of the municipal day," claimed the reformers. They circulated calls for a comprehensive plan, one that envisioned a "City Sensible" or "City Beautiful."[13] In September 1911, Virgil Bogue, nationally known as a successful city planner and a friend of F. L. Olmsted, the landscape architect, was selected to develop a "Plan for Seattle." Bogue revived the Olmsted Plan for Seattle Parks of 1903, though emphasizing efficiency over beauty more than Olmsted had.[14] He proposed a massive new civic center—"more European than New York, beaux-arts" in design—to be built on the soon-to-be-completed Denny regrade. In addition, he envisioned an adjacent railroad station, a system of wide, freewheeling roads radiating out from the city's center, a rail link to Kirkland (via a tunnel through Lake Washington), a subway system, and thousands of acres of city parks, including all of Mercer Island, the 4,000-acre island in Lake Washington. All three Seattle dailies and the wealthy opposed the project. The labor movement supported the plan, though not, it seemed, with enthusiasm. It offered little for the growing working-class neighborhoods of the Rainier Valley or for industrial enclaves like Ballard. Alas, it was defeated, clearing the way for the future "Freeway Bridge," the bifurcation of the city by I-5, and Seattle's traffic nightmares of today.

Gill's best-known opponent and eventual successor was George Cotterill, a surveyor and civil engineer born in England and working in Seattle as an engineer. Blethen attacked him as a foreigner. A nominally nonpartisan candidate for mayor, he was effectively a Democrat. Cotterill supported public ownership of utilities and public control of the port. His heart, however, was in the prohibitionist movement, a movement becoming more conservative over time. His parents had been members of the United Kingdom Temperance Alliance. As a child, he attended the Band of Hope, a school for temperance education.

The Potlatch Riot of 1913 all but ended his political career. The

Potlatch Days Festival, an annual Seattle event, was named for Northwest Coast Indian gift-giving feasts, which were banned in Canada and "discouraged" in Washington, DC. It culminated that July in a riot. The origins of the episode lay in ugly reports by Blethen in the *Seattle Times* that a woman soapboxer on Washington Street near Occidental Avenue, when heckled by soldiers, had "insulted their uniforms." This provoked fistfights; the soldiers regrouped and reinforced, then attacked. Soldiers and sailors, supported by a large mob, looted and burned the IWW and Socialist Party offices. It was a dark preview of things to come. Cotterill responded by shutting saloons, closing the *Seattle Times,* and banning street speakers. Judge John Humphries, Blethen's good friend, blocked these orders, but Cotterill followed up with a campaign to clean up Skid Road; thousands were arrested, alarming all sides. Cotterill supported police raids on hotels and cafes without warrants. He vetoed efforts to spell out police powers. Critics pointed to 17,078 arrests made without warrants in 1912 (5,699 of these dismissed in court) as well as to attacks on free speech and assembly. Police could dictate when, where, and what meetings could be held. They also seized printing presses and papers, and arbitrarily closed businesses. Gill, returned as mayor in 1916. Now "reformed," he shocked "respectable" people by sympathizing with the workers massacred in Everett.

The Municipal League, the voice of progressive reform in Seattle, had been organized in 1910, primarily in opposition to the downtown elites. The unions joined the League in supporting electoral reform and municipal ownership of the docks, the electric company, streetcars, public markets, and laundries, even if these demands fell short of the unions' core goals of workers' control, social ownership of production, international solidarity, and, of course, opposition to war. Collaboration between liberals and labor only went so far, however. The state's socialists contested city elections from the left; in the 1912 elections, Hulet Wells, an editor of the weekly *Socialist Voice*, ran on a platform of jobs for the unemployed. Wells, the son of Canadian farmers, crossed the border frequently as a youth, working as a farmhand. He spent two years with his father in the Klondike, then worked as an itinerant laborer, a logger, and a shingle weaver before entering the University of Washington in 1905 to study law. His mission: "I do not pretend to represent anyone but the working man and have been a working man all my life and understand their problems." His vision included improving the shacks that crowded Ballard's shingle mills; the tiny, cheap working-class homes of the South End rarely appeared as problems for the city's reformers. Neither did poor services, overcrowded schools, or severe limitations in the viewshed. Slums, went the well-worn banality, were eastern.

Then the renewal of industrial conflict further undermined labor's relationship with liberalism. The Municipal League supported the open shop, as did the employers' new management schemes, their efficiency experts, and scientific managers. In Seattle, this was personified by Carlton Parker, a University of Washington professor, author of *The Casual Laborer and Other Essays*, and his sponsor, Henry Suzzallo, the university's president. Parker investigated migrant camps and casual laborers in California. This led employers to worry that he was pro-IWW, yet this was far from the case. In his brief tenure at the university, Parker collaborated with the reactionary New York leadership of the national longshoreman's union (the International Longshoreman's Association, ILA) and J. Edgar Hoover, then head of the Bureau of Investigation, in their efforts to rid Seattle's docks of the IWW and maintain the open shop on the waterfront. Suzzallo, equally anti-IWW, became a leading proponent of the war as well as a fierce critic of the General Strike. This was progressivism in crisis.

The IWW, champions of "anarchists and aliens" that they were, excoriated the Skid Roads of the West, yet these were their urban terrain, their point of contact with the bums and the hobos, the homeless migrants. In the Northwest, the loggers fled from the forests in the rainiest season. This meant men had no alternative but Skid Road, its saloons, its flophouses, its job sharks, and cops on the take. The Wobblies were appalled by the raw exploitation of men and women in these places. They disapproved, if not in the lurid language of *McClure's* or with the moral sanctimony of the ministers, then in the lexicon of class war and industrial socialism and with a sympathy and solidarity not found elsewhere. Cotterill's "cleanups" targeted not just saloon owners but also the bums and hobos, the people celebrated by the IWW. The action, then, moved increasingly from City Hall and the pulpits into the streets. The street speakers on their soapboxes were the people's voice, their connection with the movement, and their "universities of the streets." Another hotspot was the Great Hall at the Labor Temple, the place where Seattle labor gathered, including socialists and IWW "two-card men"—workers simultaneously members of the IWW and the AFL—to debate and set policy under the watchful eyes of the rank and file, packed into rowdy and highly politicized galleries.

Seattle was "divided into two hostile camps," wrote Anna Louise Strong: "Good business men of the city and the women of the upper strata, 'our best people,'" on the one side, and "the invading host, the lowest of the low, about whom nothing too bad could be said, destroyers of everything good, jailbirds and criminals," on the other.[15] Class lines were hardening. The Everett events would embitter working-class people; the prospects of the timber strike heartened them. On the city's streets, the fight for the closed shop escalated, and class consciousness was surging. People had to choose sides.

Strong, with a PhD from the University of Chicago, came to Seattle well-grounded in the progressive movements of the times. She had been close to Roger Baldwin, future founder of the American Civil Liberties Union (ACLU), and had worked with and remained friends with Florence Kelley, the child welfare advocate and a future founder of the National Association for the Advancement of Colored People (NAACP). Strong too became an advocate of child welfare. She organized an exhibit on the topic— an outgrowth of child labor legislation—focusing on hygiene, recreation, and education. She toured with the exhibition in the

United States and abroad, bringing it to Seattle in May 1914, where it was seen by forty thousand people.

Her father was Rev. Sidney Strong, the best-known progressive minister in Seattle, pro-labor and a founder of the Municipal League. His estrangement began with supporting the strikers in the forests. He became a central figure in the middle-class antiwar movement, and hosted an anti-conscription conference. The meeting was broken up by police, with their attempt to arrest Kate Sadler provoking a "near riot."[16] This led to Reverend Strong's expulsion from the League and the demand that he be jailed and removed from the Seattle Ministerial Federation. It was claimed that he had once compared IWW members to the early Christians. The League, once the bastion of reformers, now found itself defending the war at home. The League also expelled Robert Bridges, the elected chair of the Port Commission. Bridges became a Seattle Port Commissioner when the Commission was formed in 1911. He was a leading fighter for municipal ownership of the port. Bridges, however, had always been far from a typical League member. In Scotland, he had been a coal miner. Bridges tried farming in the United States, then union organizing in the Black Diamond coal mines of southern King County. He was progressive but pro-labor. His opposition to the scheme to privatize the port's Harbor Island brought the enmity of the "Interests." Bridges opposed the military buildup by not allowing Port of Seattle employees to march in the "Preparedness Day" parade.

"I WENT DOWN TO THE [IWW] HALL," Strong wrote, then a fledgling reporter, "I went because I wanted to know the truth." There, she found herself embarrassed. "It is down in the part of town where respectable women seldom go—except to hurry through to the railroad station . . . a district where poverty has robbed even vice of its concealments."[17] The hall was up a narrow staircase, above a movie theater. She was met there by "a kindly, motherly-looking woman" who introduced her to the others present.[18] She wondered why they had not opted for a better location, suspecting that this place was chosen "because they want to reach these unskilled workers, these wandering men who come into town from the harvest, who sleep in fifteen cent 'flops' and eat in cheap joints, and wear calks in their shoes that would hurt the floors of a decent place."[19] She learned they had no choice: alternative quarters were unavailable, the "good business men" elsewhere being unwilling to rent to them. Strong met IWW leaders: Red Doran, the organizer, Herbert Mahler who "handled the finances," and James Thompson, the leader of the loggers. Thompson told her, "We are going to have a revolution . . . the labor process [will] take on the cooperative form, and the tools of production become social . . . social ownership. . . . [The] things that are used collectively should be owned collectively . . . this is the irresistible force to the people of the twentieth century." She met workers, all migrants, and most young. One was an eighteen-year-old from a North Dakota farm who followed the harvest west, did haying in Montana, returned to Minneapolis, where he spent nine days in the hospital with tonsillitis, then went to Spokane and Wenatchee for apple picking, finally going to Seattle, where he would work on the waterfront occasionally, waiting for summer.[20] Another named Savery was a logger. He was "slow of speech and understanding, but sure and unhurried in every movement," wrote Strong. Savery was a Russian who had come to Montreal when he was two. His people died when he was seven, and he went to work for a French farmer. Savery left the farm at age twelve; he had done mostly common labor. Since he "grew up big enough to handle logs [he worked] in the woods." He joined the IWW, "to better my conditions."[21]

Strong reckoned there were three and a half million such men in the country, not counting seven million more unskilled laborers who drifted in and out of casual work, including tens of thousands in the Pacific Northwest. She quoted a US Department of Labor report claiming that "over a tenth of the people in the United States are in the ranks of unskilled labor, frequently changing jobs." These were men, she believed, "who would never have a home of their own, men who follow the harvest or work in the mines or the woods, men who live from day to day, almost hour to hour, men who sleep in the fifteen-cent flops and to whom a woman, and children, and a room or two for a family, is, and will always remain, a bitter, impossible dream."[22]

In these years Seattle's labor movement shifted steadily leftward; the experience of the past decade had been one of recurrent recession, unemployment, lost wages, and the struggle to recover. At the end of 1913, unemployment had reached 30,000 statewide. Seattle's jobless were joined by the refugees of seasonal employment: agriculture, logging, fishing, and canning. The city converted a former hospital into the "Liberty Hotel," a haven for the unemployed. Women, however, were not allowed. Even Seattle's settled workers often survived through seasonal work on the waterfront, in the shipyards and canneries, and in related occupations. The economy would recover, however, and the recuperation continued throughout the war years. The world's longest dock was completed on Elliot Bay at Smith Cove and a 1,500-foot wharf was under construction. Salmon canning flourished, as did flour exporting and the Alaska trade. Then, the war brought large-scale manufacturing, primarily shipbuilding, which in turn stimulated foundries, boiler-making, metalworking, transport and services, sales, restaurants, and personal services. The demand for timber and timber products increased, even as steel ships replaced wooden ones. The chronic housing shortage eased, as home construction boomed.

The year 1912 marked the beginning of the great strike wave. The ratio of strike participants to the total labor force grew higher than it had ever been before.[23] Skilled workers struck to make up for what had been lost in the Depression years. Unskilled workers fought in a vain attempt just to catch up. Workers everywhere struck for higher wages, in the face of a steadily rising cost of living. The IWW participated in these strikes, always as a minority but never as isolated as its critics claimed. Its litany of appeals—for the downtrodden, direct action, trade union democracy, working-class solidarity, and big changes in the world—were widely heard, very much part of the scene. In the long summer of 1917, the number of strikes in the United States outran those of earlier years. Solidarity became the workers' watchword, and in working-class neighborhoods life could become unbearable for scabs. Large funeral processions for slain workers became commonplace, and entire families joined in workplace struggles.[24] Seattle was no exception to this nationwide surge in workers' struggles.[25] When the US Commission on Industrial Relations met in the city for five days of hearings, John R. Commons, Wisconsin's labor specialist, observed that in Seattle there was "more bitter feeling between employers and employees than in any other city in the United States."[26] As the power of the labor movement increased, workers focused on fighting for the closed shop—abhorrent to employers large and small. In Seattle, the CLC sought to make the closed shop universal. The advantage of the closed shop was that unions did not have to continually recruit new employees to maintain their presence. Most employers resisted any form of organized labor, and they especially opposed the closed shop. They revived the open shop campaigns of the first years of the century, often with the addition of a jingoistic "Americanism" and supporters such as Presbyterian minister Mark Matthews. They sought to outlaw the closed shop, as well as boycotts and sympathy strikes. In this effort, countrywide employers' organizations like the National Association of Manufacturers (NAM) were joined by regional employers' associations and local Chambers of Commerce. On the West Coast, the shipping interests fought hard to keep trade unions off the docks, while the lumber businessmen worked to keep unions out of the mills.

The long, bitter Teamsters' strike of June 1913 to March 1914 began as a dispute with the Globe Transfer Company, but it quickly became citywide and combative. The drivers of Teamsters' Local 174 struck for wages. The employers resisted, and the conflict significantly disrupted the city's business. The union drivers discouraged the strikebreakers that the employers had engaged, who more often than not voluntarily returned to the barns. There was picket-line violence, however, and the violence escalated when the King County Sheriff began deputizing professional strikebreakers from nearby towns. The company-friendly Judge Humphreys was asked for an injunction limiting picketing, and he delivered. With the strike at an impasse, the Washington Employers Association took direct control of negotiations and imposed the open shop. Four thousand gathered at the Dreamland Rink to protest but to no avail. The police began arresting picketers, and the strike collapsed.

This outcome was a clear but costly victory for the Employers Association. One by one, the owners eventually settled with the union, and the arrested strikers were acquitted. These years saw the emergence of class consciousness, even among the skilled and better paid workers, who undoubtedly felt their job security and living standards were threatened by the open shop campaign.[27] Union growth and the accompanying threats to the employers' prerogatives exacerbated the growing ambivalence of the middle-class progressives. They supported reform in general, but when the Municipal League reported in its organ News on the longshoremen's strike and lockout of 1916, it showed its hand. The report claimed that blame for the violence and wharf fires could be attributed equally to both sides. Yet it asked only that longshoremen cease such activity, making no such request of the Waterfront Employers Association.[28]

There followed strikes of miners, waitresses, streetcar drivers, shipyard workers, laundry workers, and longshoremen. These were all contested, but backed by the CLC, they were mostly won. At the same time, a feminist women workers' movement emerged within the larger Seattle working-class movement. Organized in 1911, the Seattle Women's Union Card and Label League (SWUCLL) grew through the war years, assuming an increasingly important role in the labor movement. According to historian Maurine Greenwald, the SWUCLL's work was multifaceted: members promoted or challenged labor movement policies, encouraged consumers to purchase only union-label goods, discussed writings, attended lectures by well-known women activists, worked with middle-class club women, and responded to changing economic conditions. Label League activists came to identify themselves as "houseworkers" and women workers in the home, who wanted to liberate women from confinement to the household.[29] Greenwald also writes that the SWUCLL "had a membership of five hundred women, including most of the working-class female activists in the city."[30] It supported the strike at and subsequent boycott of Seattle's then largest department store, the Bon Marché, leading to the recognition of the Retail Clerks Union.[31] The SWUCLL often took the initiative in labor's political campaigns, organizing in favor of the initiative and the referendum. It led the 1914 campaign for a universal eight-hour day and was a driving force in organizing parades and demonstrations, recruiting Mother Jones to lead the Workers' Memorial Day March of May 30, 1914.[32]

3. THE TIMBER BEAST

Seattle was an island in a still immeasurable sea of timber. The Pacific coastal forests were estimated to contain nearly two-thirds of the timber in the country, and the Washington State forests accounted for the largest part of these. Washington had the greatest concentration of softwood trees in the world.[1]

Forests blanketed the lower slopes of the Cascades, the southern and western sides of the Olympic Mountains and the uplands in the southwestern corner of the state. On the coast itself moss-laden cedars anchored the earth's last-standing temperate rain forests. The region's prevailing northwesterly winds swept in from the Pacific to meet first the coastal ranges, then the Cascades. Together they wrung rain from moisture-laden air down upon a unique region. This is the wettest area of the country, and the great conifer forests thrived in it. The climate's year-round precipitation, including during the summer's warm months, coastal fog, and cloudy skies favored the conifers. Their ability to withstand late-summer drought and occasional winter freezes gave them an advantage over deciduous trees.

Western Washington's forests were, and are still, dominated by Douglas firs. Commercially they are the most valuable. These massive trees could reach a height of 380 feet and a girth of sixteen feet. They were just one of a dozen giant conifers in the lush, ancient forests of Sitka spruce, western hemlock, western red cedar, and yews that might contain thousand-year-old trees. Thirteen species surpassed heights of two hundred feet. Cool summers, the dense canopy of the forest, and limited undergrowth created gardens of ferns and flowers. There was an abundance of wildlife—deer, Roosevelt elk, black bear, wolves, plus countless smaller creatures and dozens of species of birds. This ecosystem was sustained in part by the massive salmon runs. Salmon fed the animals, fertilized the land, and was the lifeblood of the indigenous peoples.

The people—Makah, Suquamish, Puyallup—coexisted with the forest. They did not live in it; it was too dense to encourage everyday travel. Instead they lived in permanent villages along the shore, often where rivers met the Sound or the sea. They carved cedar logs into canoes and totem poles. They split cedar for the planks of their longhouses. Women pounded cedar bark into rope, mats, baskets, and garments. These people led rich lives; there were few places where life was as easy, encouraging extensive arts and crafts, and allowing for ceremonies and celebrations. The rivers teemed with fish, and the tidelands were a cornucopia of sustenance. The people did, however, collect berries and herbs in the forests. They hunted there and sometimes sought solitude for reflection and prayer. There might be clearings, but it was limited. They were not farmers.

When the white settlers came there to farm, they encountered obstacles. Clearing, the first necessity, was a challenge. The great trees had to be felled, which was difficult enough and left behind massive stumps, nearly impossible to remove. The soil itself was thin; what there was was sandy, gravelly, and acidic. Cultivators made instead for the Willamette Valley in Oregon or sought out river bottoms, though these were relatively few, and the limited flatland in the region often lay beneath steep mountain slopes in narrow valleys always subject to seasonal flooding.

In the 1880s, the new railroads brought many thousands to the

Washington Territory, but the majority were not seeking farms. Rather they sought work, finding it for better or worse in the burgeoning extractive industries. They became miners, fieldhands, and above all, loggers—the men who would strip first the shores of the Sound, then the river valleys, and finally the foothills of the great mountain ranges—the Cascades and the Olympics—of their ancient forests. The West was transformed by settlers: the farmers and the pre-proletariats. They were, however, just the hired hands of others, the eastern, often European financiers who orchestrated the invasion of telegraph lines and railroads, tools of choice in the scramble for the riches of the West. They tied this new economy to an expanding global market, thereby linking it also to crises, competition, and global booms and busts, and making it dependent on the government.

Timber was at the center of this economy, but it was years before the railroads became the prime shippers of timber. Rough timber first left on coastal schooners, often those leaving from Seattle's deepwater, sheltered Elliott Bay. The railroads revolutionized transportation. They also cleared a path for speculators, land agents, bankers—men seeking wealth, by fair means or foul. They came from the banks and offices in New York, Boston, and St. Paul, and included the point men for the greatest "Interests" of the era: the railroad men, James J. Hill and Edward Harriman; the banker J. P. Morgan; the world's richest man, John D. Rockefeller; and the lumber baron George Weyerhaeuser. In 1900, two out of three workers in Washington State toiled in its woods, in the lands of the Lumber Trust. The Trust, according to IWW organizer James Rowan, was "the ruling power, [which controls] not only the industry, but the local, and sometimes the State machinery of government, with its powerful and corrupt influences." It was "industrial feudalism . . . in its worst form."[2]

The Seattle settler Henry Yesler built the city's first lumber mill in 1853. It was steam-powered and sat just above Elliott Bay, cementing Seattle's relationship to its waterfront. But the transformation of a local, near subsistence economy based on milling into a massive industry was driven not by the early settlers. Rather, it was the work of that new class of men, the robber barons, individuals of great wealth, ambitious in extreme, and utterly ruthless when they needed to be. Rockefeller personally underwrote the industry that would transform these forests forever, turning this last frontier into an industrial colony. These men sensed their chances instantly, and each in his way rushed to seize the resources and the key positions of the industrial society being hastily assembled. They established themselves as "lords of 'empires' in iron, railroads and oil, to be held naturally for private gain, and once held, defended them to the last breath of financial life against all comers."[3]

The party of Lincoln initiated the massive transfer of power to the new captains of industry in an emerging large-scale capitalism. By the 1850s timber was already an essential component in the development of large-scale industry. Timber too had its "conquistadores," every bit as avaricious as California's. By the end of the century, half a dozen men owned the Northwest's forests. "Great central lumber companies like the Weyerhaeusers," wrote the historian Frederick Jackson Turner, "moved to the Pacific Northwest, where they secured imperial forests." Power in the West came with land, and Congress stage-managed the allotting of this land, the people's land. It got rid of the land as fast as it could. In 1862, the Homestead Act made available millions of acres and signaled the distribution of the public domain, which was then held by the federal government, amounting to fully half the present area of the United States. The nation's natural treasures were sacrificed to unparalleled exploitation, most notably by the railroads and the mining interests but also by the lumber barons. Timber was wanted in the mines, along the railroads, and in the new towns.

Congress sold the land, granted it, donated it, acquiesced to trespass, and then watched as it was stolen. The land was privatized on a massive scale. The wealthy were always favored, and the auctions invariably enriched the well-to-do. "Intrigue, fraud, bribery, corruption, legal chicanery, violence and murder were

freely used by these 'respectable' and 'patriotic' gentlemen,'" wrote
Rowan.[4] The lumber barons looted the government land and
Indian reservations of their timber.[5] There were the settlers, of
course, the farmers and ranchers who fueled the myth of the winning of the West. Some succeeded, many did not. The government
would never develop a systematic way to evaluate claims under
the Homestead Acts. The land offices relied on witnesses to show
that a claimant had lived on the land for the required time and had
made the required improvements. In practice, however, witnesses
were often bribed, and collusion with land agents and speculators
was virtually universal, with the pursuit of private gain prevailing.
Mythology aside, speculation and monopolization were the norm,
while the benefits mainly went to enriching the railroads.

In 1898, Congress set aside "Forest Reserves," 150 million acres
as National Forests, yet much of this too would fall into the hands
of the lumbermen, the government selling to the highest bidders.
It was estimated that Weyerhaeuser and other timber companies
in the Pacific Northwest had acquired control of about four million
acres of this prime timber. In 1914 the US Board of Corporations
reported that "whereas three-quarters of the standing timber was
publicly owned in 1870, now four-fifths were privately owned, primarily in the Pacific Northwest and California." The government's
forest "guards," that is, its Forest Service, would become the lumbermen's handmaidens.

Anna Louise Strong became one of Seattle's most powerful
voices opposing the lumber barons and the financiers who stood
behind them, calling them the "great titans, railway kings and
lumber barons [who] seized the public's wealth."[6] Strong was a
mountaineer. She traveled from Seattle to the high glaciers of Mt.
Rainier and was witness to the clearcuts, burned-over river valleys,
and fishless streams that lay along the path. The IWW historian
Walker Smith shared her concerns, writing, "The forest lands of
the nation are being denuded," and the result, he predicted, would
be floods and droughts.[7] "Where a logging company operates,"
Smith wrote, the rule is that "it takes all the timber on the tract"

then the brush and refuse is burned, leaving lunar landscapes and the horror of naturalists. Such destruction was not of concern, however, to Theodore Roosevelt, who claimed to be a naturalist, nor to Gifford Pinchot, his chief of the US Forest Service, himself a lumber tycoon's heir. Both were crude utilitarians, through and through, something never lost on preservationists and aesthetes, who detected collusion with the lumbermen. Roosevelt survives in myth. Pinchot is memorialized in the Gifford Pinchot National Forest in southwest Washington. Yet Pinchot is also remembered for saying, "Wilderness is waste."

The volume of timber taken from these forests and the sheer destructiveness of the loggers' onslaught is astonishing. Why this seemingly unquenchable appetite? One reason was that in a new nation bursting at its seams the forests of the East, from Maine through the Great Lakes, were exhausted. No sense of sustainability seems to have existed, no thought given to renewal. The timber barons, like locusts moving westward, left behind ruined lands and a legacy of waste and devastation by fire. In 1900, there were 80 million acres of charred and decimated stump lands east of the Mississippi and a long history of logging. In 1871, the Peshtigo Fire killed 1,500 people and burned 1.28 million acres in northeastern Wisconsin. Ten years later, the eastern Michigan "thumb" was burned in a fire claiming 160 lives. Then, in 1885, nearly all of the Wisconsin Valley was swept by fire.

Vast areas of the Great Lakes region—some 50 million acres stretching from Lake Huron in the east to the Red River in the west in Minnesota—had been laid bare through the clearcutting techniques of the highly mechanized and efficient lumber industry. Efficient perhaps, wasteful certainly. Saws that made wide kerfs (slits left by saws), the cutting of trees to leave high stumps, and felling for roads and tracks all took their toll. Only the best trees would be taken; the rest were left to rot or burn. Sometimes the burning was intentional, sometimes a result of hot, dry summers. Fire was the curse of the forests; fire that fed on the slash, the mass of debris that piled feet-deep on the forest floor after the timber was taken out. Flames probably consumed about as much timber every year as reached the mill.[8] Summertime smoke could suffocate western Washington. "The smoke from these fires," wrote an English tourist in 1883, "for weeks and for months troubles the air and obscures the landscape."[9]

The exploitation of land and people followed the "Interests" west. They reproduced the East's squalor in the pristine Puget Sound coves and inlets and in the literally hundreds of logging camps. These were built along the shore, in the low hills of the southwest of the state, and sometimes in the high valleys that sat beneath Washington's great line of volcanos—St. Helens, Adams, Rainier, Glacier, and Baker. This volcanic arc separated western Washington from the hot, dry "short log" pineland of the East. Everywhere the mills became sites of heavy industry, belching smoke and fire, while the great saws screamed. Then, too, came instant slums, the shacks and bunkhouses of the workers. A study conducted during the First World War found that half the logging camps in the Northwest lacked adequate bunks or showers and a third were without toilet facilities. It was a "sad travesty," reported Rexford Tugwell, the economist who would later join Franklin Roosevelt's "Brains Trust" after a tour of the region.[10]

Two Maine lumbermen, William Talbot and Andrew Pope, came to San Francisco in the aftermath of the Gold Rush seeking fortune in the western woods, before migrating north to Washington where they built a mill at Port Ludlow on the Olympic Peninsula. Soon there were mills at Seabec, Madison, Blakely, and Port Gamble (with its imitation New England village). These were all on the Sound, accessible to the new West Coast lumber schooners, ships designed with shallow drafts to cross coastal bars and navigate the tiny ports where these mills were found. The first mill towns were temporary habitations; these outposts lasted only as long as the trees did.

Seattle too had its mills, including the shingle mills of Ballard. But this would change. As the result of the development of its harbor, trade with Asia, the Alaska Gold Rush, and the opening of the Panama Canal, Seattle's economy diversified. The mill towns, however, remained fiefdoms. The Wobblies called them "company towns." Rowan wrote, in a description that might seem more like that of a West Virginia coal mine camp, "The entire life of the community resolved around the saw mill. The workers in the saw mills live in company-owned houses or boarded at the company boarding house. They trade at the company store; when they are sick, they go to the company hospital or are treated by the company doctor. When they are dead, they are buried in the company cemetery, and their souls are saved by the company preacher."[11] The larger towns—Tacoma, Aberdeen, Hoquiam, Chehalis, and Centralia—offered more "freedom," but it was freedom in a savage environment occupied by guards, vigilantes ,and small-town gangsters. "Everett on Port Gardner Bay took pride in the designation 'City of Smokestacks,'" wrote the Wobbly Walker Smith, and it was from these mill towns and forests that "the lumber industry dominated the whole life of the Northwest."[12] James Hill brought his railroad first to Everett, where he promised that he and John D. Rockefeller would make the town into the Boston of the Pacific Coast. However, the Cascades produced little gold, and in 1893 the Great Northern passed Everett by to terminate in Seattle.

Frederick Weyerhaeuser was born in Germany; he came to Rock Island, Illinois, where he found work in a sawmill. In 1857 he bought the mill, then began building a confederation of logging and milling operations in the Mississippi Valley. In 1872, he organized the Mississippi River Boom and Logging Company, handling all the logs milled on the Mississippi. He became the most powerful lumberman in the country even before he moved west. In 1891, Weyerhaeuser settled in St. Paul, Minnesota, next door to his future partner, James J. Hill. The two decided that their futures were in the Pacific Northwest. Weyerhaeuser founded the Sound Lumber Company in 1899. Then, in 1900, he negotiated one of the largest land transactions in American history: 900,000 acres of timber from the Northern Pacific Railroad's land grants at six dollars an acre, "a price estimated then as about

ten cents a thousand feet for the wood."[13] That was the beginning; Weyerhaeuser then organized the Weyerhaeuser Timber
Company and proceeded to build the new company's first mill:
Mill B in Everett. Then the largest in the world, it produced an
amazing 70 million board feet in 1912.

The Weyerhaeuser Company was initially based in Tacoma,
then in the suburb of Federal Way, now part of Seattle. The company is one of the largest owners of timberland in the world. It is
an international conglomerate; its holdings include seven million
acres of land in the United States, much of it in Washington where
the "primeval" forests it once logged have been reduced to tree
farms, the trees a "crop" on a thirty-year rotation. Weyerhaeuser
manager George S. Long apparently coined the term "tree farm"
in 1908 while proclaiming that "timber is a crop."[14] Weyerhaeuser
also retains logging rights to 35 million acres of land in Canada.
Now diversified, it leaves behind old mills and deforestation—in
addition to deadly contaminants including heavy metals, polycy-
clic aromatic hydrocarbons (PAHs), PCBs, phenols and dioxins.

From the start, booms and busts plagued the timber industry.
The Northern Pacific's arrival in Tacoma in 1893 did not deliver
on its promises. The Midwestern markets were still too many miles
away. Nevertheless, the railroads brought population growth, the
development of new towns, and the expansion of cities. In 1906, the
San Francisco earthquake and fire temporarily increased demand
for timber, and 1912 to 1913 were "good" years but short-lived.
The life span of the smallest timber firms was brief; few weathered
the hard times. The larger companies grew at the expense of struggling rivals, and the result was an industry dominated by a handful
of giant corporations, with Weyerhaeuser, "The Trust," at the top
of the heap.

THERE WERE TENS OF THOUSANDS of loggers and mill workers in the Pacific Northwest on the eve of war, the large majority
working in the forests of western Washington. They worked ten-
hour days, often more, in logging camps and mills. IWW writers

insisted that in addition to working loggers "there were thousands of their fellow workers vainly seeking work," successful only when "those employed happened to lose their jobs." Hence unemployment plagued the industry, in good times and bad. Their overlords, the lumbermen, "were as ruthless and competitive" as any New York City garment manufacturer. They created their own sweatshops in dreary and brutal camps, isolated from the towns, that in any case offered little more than saloons and brothels. In the woods, labor was the chief production cost; competition pressed wages downward and working conditions with them.[15]

The timber industry initially relied on human muscle power, the ax, and the hand-held saw. There was, however, a slow and steady development of new technologies, including steel cables and the Dolbeer steam donkey, invented by a California lumberman, which greatly increased productivity but was disastrous for the forests. Cable hauling meant extreme clearcutting; it broke young trees and tore up seedlings, leading to logging "deserts." The method of "high-lead" yarding, developed somewhat later, lifted the logs rather than dragging them. However, the giant logs, now airborne, brought new dangers. Then the railroads came—short lines through rugged terrain connecting the difficult-to-reach interior to the mills. The promise of technology was always double-edged. For the forest, new techniques spelled new horrors. The loggers' task was to take down every tree within reach. The slash was burned. The flames consumed limbs, bark, other trees, undergrowth, birds and animals, the ferns and flowers, everything that could not escape. Entire ecosystems were destroyed, leaving ridges charred and streams unrecognizable.

Workers in groups felled the trees. It might take a week for a team of six to bring down one very large tree. The use of black powder and dynamite was commonplace. The impact of the fall could make a tree shatter, so a blanket of brush and branches was woven to soften the fall. The thick bark also protected the fallen tree. Once a tree was down, the workers cut the huge logs into sections which were hauled to the mills one section at a time, first by oxen, then by steam engines or rail and much later by tractors and trucks.

Conditions were dangerous in the hills and equally brutal in the mills. There men and boys worked on and among giant saws, with their deafening noise and in air that seemed more sawdust than nitrogen and oxygen. Asthma was as common as missing limbs. In camp or mill, the specter of terrifying accidents and gruesome injuries haunted the workers, and death by saws, cables, falling trees made logging and lumber work five times more lethal than in any other sector of Washington industry.[16] Workers were forced to sign agreements absolving their employers of responsibility; the injured were reported to be victims of accidents or their own misstep. When the lumbermen made agreements with the closest hospitals, they deducted costs from the loggers' paychecks.[17]

Much is made of IWW propaganda ridiculing, above all in song, the employers and their supporters: the long-haired preachers, the Salvation Army, the railway and mining bosses, the police, and the jailers. In fact, they were merely responding in kind. The mill owners made no effort to disguise their contempt for the loggers: "timber beasts" to be driven like "cattle." They called Swedes "stupid," and Southern and Eastern European workers were referred to as "blacks" at a time when the outrages of Jim Crow were no secret, not even in this far frontier. Half the workforce was foreign-born. Some mill owners in Bellingham hired Japanese workers, others imported "Hindus." One tragic consequence was the Bellingham Riot of 1907, when mobs of "exclusionist" whites attacked East Indian immigrants., while others attacked the Japanese. The intention was to drive them both from the mills and the towns.[18]

The first IWW strike in the Northwest was in Portland in 1906 for wage increases and the nine-hour day. The employers retaliated everywhere. Every mill had its detective or team of them; guards were armed with automatic weapons and dogs. The mill at Cosmopolis on Grays Harbor was surrounded by chain-link fence; the workers called it the "Western Penitentiary." The employers in response swore that "they all want rooms with a bath, and Waldorf-Astoria fare."[19] And, "when people threaten what you have, crush them, any way you can." Nevertheless, wrote George Emmerson, for the Grays Harbor lumberman, there were dangers. "The industry," wrote George Emmerson, "was very close to a volcano."[20]

In a highly volatile industry, the employers organized to combat price slumps and overproduction and to control the labor market. The West Coast Lumber Manufacturers' Association became one of the most powerful of these organizations. They insisted that the timber workers were unskilled, and, as such, were entitled to as little as possible in return for their work. Above all they resisted contracts, fixed wage rates, seniority rights, and any form of job security. Preferring men they viewed as "bums" and "hobos," they shamelessly sought out the youngest workers and transients, men who could be hired cheaply and dismissed without cause. The logger W. L. Morgan reported, "I worked in the Northwest lumber camps and am able to tell you about them from personal experience. Ten hours a day, which was our working day, is far too long for men who are employed at . . . labor which taxed the endurance of the most powerful of men. Besides [that] we walked to and from the job on our own time which stretched the working day to ten or twelve hours. When we got back to camp at night, we were so played out that we had no strength for recreation or study but were overcome with a desire for sleep. We existed like horses or mules. The work on the job was not only hard but dangerous and we were continually speeded up to the limit of our endurance. For giving our entire strength, our entire lives, as you might say, we were paid a bare subsistence."[21]

Who were the "timber beasts"? They were essentially homeless men, widely despised by the region's middle class, subject to discrimination when the heaviest rains of winter forced them out of the woods, their worldly belongings in a bindle. Why were they called "beasts"? James Thompson, the IWW's lumber industry organizer, explained to the Industrial Commission in Washington, DC, that these workers were thought to live in the forests like "animals." He testified, however, that they were just working men, mostly young people who "worked hard" but received wages below the "Dead Line." That, he explained, meant wages for a worker "below the line necessary to keep him alive." The loggers, Thompson argued, "are being murdered on the installment plan . . . they breathe bad air in the camps, that ruins their lungs. They eat bad food, that ruins their stomachs. The foul conditions shorten their lives and make their short lives miserable."[22]

The physical hardships associated with the lumber industry, including isolation deep within the rain forests, made working conditions an even more miserable burden than low wages. The work was seasonal and layoffs common; the completion of one job might mean termination and the search for work elsewhere. When the winter rains brought an end to work in the woods, the state's loggers fled to the city, not welcome elsewhere. In some years there might be thousands on Seattle's streets.[23]

4. HOLD THE FORT

The volcano exploded in 1916. It was set off by a simple strike in Everett. The "City of Smokestacks" was then a stronghold of Washington's timber workers, the "only union town in the State," according to industry spokesmen.[1] That year, the city's shingle weavers struck to protest a wage cut.

Everett was home to thirty-five thousand people. The chief employers were the lumber and shingle mills, but also shippers and salmon canners. The former employed more than five thousand men. These included the shingle weavers, who predominated, as well as the workers at the new Weyerhaeuser sawmill and a host of smaller mills. The employers, with the banks that underwrote them, dominated the local industry and, with it, the city. James Hill's Great Northern Railroad had supplied Everett's first workers: thousands of migrants, farmers, and millworkers from the Midwest and New England, plus men, women and children from farther afield—Canada, England, Germany, and Scandinavia.[2]

In 1915, Everett was still recovering from long lean years. It was always a hard and depressed place. Everett was an open town, with so few payrolls that the saloons were often overwhelmed by destitute men seeking shelter. Each month hundreds of the unemployed lodged themselves in the city jail for the sake of simple food and shelter. In 1909, there were 1,143 mills in the state. Of these, 389 remained in 1915, with the loss rarely resulting from combinations and mergers.[3] The industrial work year was just 129 days.[4] These figures are cruel reminders of the precariousness of life in the industrial West where the approach of winter "brought a rush of grim incongruities: new streets where men stood in line to wait for the indignity of free bread; railroad cars swarming with hobos who rode new rails to the idle factories of new cities."[5]

It was the war in Europe that brought increased demand, first for ammunition boxes and caskets, later ships, then planes. The return of "good times" for workers meant back to the mills. Innovation spurred productivity, and for shingle weavers new technologies meant thinner cuts and a faster pace. 1n 1916 there were dozens of shingle mills in Everett, more than in any city in the world. Everett's mills were among the most modern, notably the million-dollar Clough-Hartley Mill, employing 165 men, capable of turning out a million shingles in a ten-hour shift. Together, they shipped out six million cedar shingles a day, dominating the market.

The International Shingle Weavers Union was formed in 1901, the result of a successful strike. Of the unions in the timber industries, the Shingle Weavers' was consistently the most radical and militant. So, in 1916, Everett was a center of industrial turmoil in the state. In the conflict between shingle weavers and their employers there had been disputes, including strikes in the very first mills, going back to the era of the Knights of Labor, the workers' movement of the late nineteenth century.

Located some thirty-five miles north of Seattle, where the Snohomish River meets Port Gardner's Bay on Possession Sound, Everett had elites who were quite proud of the city's origins. Above all, they honored Rockefeller, who had invested early in Everett, and his hirelings. City streets were named accordingly, though this was controversial. The IWW historian Walker Smith recalled that some of these were in fact "slave-built streets—unemployed workers, even though they were plentifully supplied with money, were arrested and without the alternative of a fine were set to work clearing, grading, planking and, later on, paving the streets."[6]

Smith was an organizer and editor, as well as a leading member of the Wobblies. He managed to survive a decade in the trenches of class war in the Northwest. He was born in Washington, DC, in a family with nine children that migrated west, eventually settling in Colorado, where Smith learned about the Western Federation of Miners (WFM), the radical industrial union of the hard rock miners. In 1910, Smith settled in Spokane, becoming editor of the IWW's western paper, the *Industrial Worker*. He moved to Seattle in 1913, where he became the Wobblies' leading journalist, known for his widely read history of the Everett Massacre.[7]

Smith would make Everett a household word and for good reasons. The Everett Massacre belongs with the bloodiest labor battles in the West—Coeur d'Alene, Cripple Creek, Bisbee, and Ludlow. More than that, it played an important role in shaping working-class consciousness in the Northwest and certainly in Seattle. Max Eastman, describing the 1914 massacre in Ludlow, Colorado, said "it was no pleasure to tell."[8] There the National Guard attacked a camp of striking miners and their families, killing at least twenty-five, many of them women and children.[9] Much the same could be said of Everett, where defenseless protesting workingmen would be murdered in broad daylight. It would shake the working people of Seattle, themselves no strangers to violence, as nothing had done before. Writing in *The Masses,* Eastman worried that "if the public does not learn the lesson of Ludlow" there would be more such episodes to come. Come they did to Gardner Bay. And the killing there, like that at Ludlow, was "no local brawl." It was not merely local, and it was not "Western." "You cannot dismiss the bleeding with that old bogus about the wild and woolly west." Rather, Eastman insisted, it was about America—a "little America," and, Walker Smith concurred, the cost workers paid for "the right to organize within the confines of the Lumber Kingdom."[10]

The Shingle Workers Union had survived the Panic of 1907

and the recession of 1913–1915. In 1911, it could count some two thousand members, the majority of whom, according to Smith, supported the IWW, though the union itself was affiliated with the AFL.[11] In early 1916, encouraged by thousands of unemployed seeking work, the employers slashed wages statewide, with a view to provoking the workers. Led by the West Coast Lumbermen's open-shop association, the employers targeted Everett for a fight. They saw this timber town as an ideal site to inaugurate their open-shop campaign. They were highly confident, believing they had effectively beaten the Wobblies elsewhere in Washington State. They also seemed to have gained the upper hand in the recent West Coast strike of longshoremen and the strike of Gardner Bay tugboat operators. The employers thought themselves well prepared, equipped with "a system of repression including a massive reference file on workers, hundreds of experienced detectives and an array of guards and vigilantes in waiting."[12] One would boast that "manufacturers and merchants are better organized today than ever they were."[13]

Sunset Magazine, no friend of the worker, described the shingle weavers' work as "not a trade; it is a battle."[14] Its description of the labor process is worth quoting at length:

> For ten hours a day the sawyer faces two-teethed steel discs whirling around two hundred times a minute. To the one on the left he feeds heavy blocks of cedar, reaching over with his left hand to remove the rough shingles it rips off. He does not, he cannot, stop to see what his left hand is doing. His eyes are too busy examining the shingles for knot holes to be cut out by the second saw whirling in front of him. The saw on his left sets the pace. If the singing blade rips fifty rough shingles off the block every minute, the sawyer must reach over to its teeth fifty times in sixty seconds; if the automatic carriage feeds the odorous wood sixty times into the hungry teeth, sixty times he must reach over, turn the shingle, trim its edge on the gleaming saw in front of him, cut out the narrow strip containing the

knot hole with two quick movements of his right hand and toss
the completed board down the chute to the packers, meanwhile
keeping eyes and ears open for the sound that asks him to feed
a new block into the untiring teeth. Hour after hour the steel
sings its crescendo note as it bites into the wood, the sawdust
cloud thickens, the wet sponge under the sawyer's nose, fills
with fine particles. If "cedar asthma," the shingle weaver's occu-
pational disease, does not get him, the steel will. Sooner or later
he reaches over a little too far, the whirling blades tosses drops
a deep red into the air, and a finger, a hand, or part of an arm
comes sliding down the slick chute.[15]

   In a similar vein, Smith wrote that it was simple to identify a
shingle worker. They were "set apart from the rest of the workers
by their mutilated hands and the dead grey pallor of their cheeks."[16]
It was "a merciless bloody vocation."[17]
   In early 1916, the employers posted notices of wage reductions
in the Everett mills. The weavers promptly struck, and violence
followed, with guns and clubs in the hands of vigilantes, sheriff's
deputies, and the police.[18] The strike was quickly broken, yet the
employers promised—in a "gentleman's agreement"—that wages
would be restored once prices began to rise again. These "gentlemen," of course, were none other than the elders of Everett's
Commercial Club, the inheritors of Rockefeller's pioneers who
"first set foot in the virgin forests of Snohomish County" and ever
since had "crushed . . . the spirit of democracy . . . by greed and
cupidity."[19] The promise was not kept, and on May Day 1916 the
shingle weavers struck again, demanding the increased wages.
The employers responded with a united front led by the employers' associations and the lumbermen. Their goal was to smash the
union and establish the open shop in the city. Again, they hired
gunmen and deputizing businessmen. The waterfront swarmed
with armed guards; everywhere there were guns, barbed wire,
bunkhouses, and searchlights.
   The workers resisted through May and June, despite vicious

opposition. "The ranks of the pickets were constantly being thinned by false arrest and imprisonment on every charge and no charge, until in August there were but eighteen men on the picket line."[20] On one occasion, police searched the pickets for weapons and, finding none, forced the strikers to march across "the narrow trestle bridge that extended across an arm of the bay." When the pickets were well out on the bridge, some seventy imported thugs, directed and urged on by their employer, Neil Jamison, poured in from either side. "They left no means of escape save that of making a thirty-foot leap into the deep waters of the bay, and with brass knuckles and blackjacks made an attack on the defenseless weavers. The pickets were unmercifully beaten."[21] That night the pickets returned with hundreds of supporters, only to be driven from the waterfront by police. Several strikers were shot and wounded. The mill owners appeared well on the way to securing victory for the open shop in Everett.

THE NATIONAL OFFICE OF THE IWW in Chicago dispatched organizer James Rowan, "a fiery young Irishman," to Everett with a mandate "to check things out."[22] He arrived on July 31, 1916. There is no reason to think the authorities knew who he was, though he was immediately arrested while speaking. They later released and rearrested Rowan—while speaking again—then threatened him with thirty days in jail, if he chose not to leave the city. Rowan left, though with Sheriff Donald McRae's warning that the Wobblies would not be allowed to involve themselves in the city's conflicts. Rowan's real assignment was to help the IWW in Seattle prepare for the timber strike planned for the following year. Nevertheless, the intensity of the conflict in Everett demanded attention. The shingle weavers were by all accounts defeated, but there remained hundreds of workers, many of them IWW members, on strike in the city.

Back in Seattle, Rowan's report fueled an anger already building. The IWW had established itself in the Northwest with the Spokane free speech fight half a decade earlier. In eastern Washington,

Spokane was the center of the "Inland Empire" comprising eastern Oregon and Washington, on the one hand, and western
Montana and Idaho, on the other: a vast space of forest, wheat
fields, mines, and mountain valley orchards. Like Seattle, a magnet
for the migrant worker a winter haven following the harvest. It
was a place for workers needing a break, and in Spokane, as in
Seattle, they found rest in flophouses and saloons. Spokane was
also home to the hated employment agencies and their "sharks,"
the men who contracted workers for another season in the woods,
in the fields, or on the railroad lines. In the winter of 1908–1909,
there were more than thirty documented employment agencies in
Spokane "doing a thriving business in human flesh and blood."[23]
The sharks not only collected a fee for the job but also colluded
with the bosses in the field to ensure a high turnover. All this
boiled over in January when a crowd of several thousand unemployed men attacked an agency office with rocks and chunks of
ice. A full-blown riot was avoided only by the intervention of the
Wobblies. IWW spokesman James H. Walsh led the men away to
the oganization's hall, where he assured them that a riot was just
what the police and the Pinkertons wanted.

The IWW was already engaged in a "Don't Buy Jobs" campaign, and the Spokane authorities, apparently not seeing what
was coming, responded with an ordinance prohibiting the holding of public meetings on any of the streets, sidewalks or alleys
within the fire district.[24] They routinely arrested IWW speakers,
who were sometimes beaten and often "deported"—taken to the
county line and told never to return. This pattern of repression
continued into the spring of 1909, with fines increased, restrictions multiplying, and prison terms prolonged. More than once
the jails were filled well beyond capacity, with ten to twelve men
crammed into tiny cells, unable to sit or lie down, fed a diet of
bread and water. Unbowed, the prisoners responded by refusing
work on the rock piles, as well as with song, "The Red Flag" or "The
Marseillaise." In November, the authorities escalated the repression
once more. James P. Thompson, then the IWW's lead organizer in

the Northwest, mounted a soapbox and began to speak, only to have the police pull him down, arrest him, and take him to jail. This time, however, many more arrests followed, and by the end of the day 150 men and three women had been detained. At the same time, there was a raid on the IWW hall and the offices of the IWW's *Industrial Worker* were closed. The authorities pledged to eradicate "violence and conspiracy" in the city.[25] The *Industrial Worker* survived only by escaping to Seattle, where William Z. Foster, then an IWW member, briefly served as editor.[26]

The violence in Spokane was entirely one-sided, meted out by the police, company guards, and vigilantes. The IWW insisted on passive resistance. The *Industrial Worker* warned its readers, "It must be understood that any person, at any time, who would try to incite disorder or 'rioting' is an enemy of the IWW. Nothing of this kind will be tolerated at this time."[27] It was a policy that would be severely tested, again and again.

In the face of relentless repression, the IWW held on, even though "between November and March, 334 of the 400 men in prison for 110 days were treated in the emergency hospital a total of 1,600 times. Many left prison with permanent scars and missing teeth. The more fortunate walked away with weakened constitutions."[28] Still, the IWW persisted, and the conflict continued into 1910, with hundreds more arrested, beaten, and tortured. In response, Wobblies descended on Spokane from throughout the West, some from as far as Chicago.

Elizabeth Gurley Flynn was the best-known of these. She was nineteen when she arrived in Spokane, just released from jail in Missoula, Montana. Flynn would achieve international fame at the mills in Lawrence, Massachusetts, where she championed the battles of immigrant strikers, mostly women, thereby becoming the IWW's "Rebel Girl." She was born into poverty in the Bronx, the child of Irish Americans. Her father was a Fenian, and their flat was a refuge for Irish freedom fighters such as James Larkin and James Connolly. She learned about the IWW from Connolly and joined it at age sixteen as a "junior."

The authorities in Spokane considered Flynn the most dangerous of the IWW "agitators." She was arrested on arrival and charged
with criminal conspiracy. However, a sympathetic jury acquitted
her. The prosecutor, livid, savaged the jury foreman, "What in hell
do you mean by acquitting the most guilty and convicting the man
far less guilty." To this the foreman responded, "She ain't a criminal, Fred, and you know it. If you think this jury or any jury is goin'
to send that pretty Irish girl to jail merely for being big-hearted
and idealistic, to mix with those whores and crooks down at the
pen you've got another guess comin'." [29]

Flynn was jailed anyway, after chaining herself to a streetlamp.
She was "placed in a cell with two other women, poor miserable
specimens of the victims of society." One woman was held on the
charge that her husband put her in a "disorderly house" (brothel).
The other was serving ninety days for robbing a man in Spokane.
"Never before had I come in contact with women of that type, and
they were interesting." Also, she recalled, "One is always safer with
others than alone. One of the worst features of being locked up is
a terrible feeling of insecurity, of being at the mercy of men you
do not trust a moment." The women, however, "did everything in
their power to make me comfortable. One gave me the spread and
pillow cover from her own bed when she saw my disgust at the
dirty grey blankets."[30]

In the end, with the Wobblies threatening to bring thousands
more to Spokane, the overwhelmed authorities relented. The
IWW won its major demands: the right to assemble, speak on
the street, hire halls for meetings, and sell the *Industrial Worker*
on the street. A dozen employment agencies were shut down.
There were many such battles to come: in Aberdeen, Wenatchee,
Kansas City, Denver, Minot, Fresno, and San Diego. Most were
won, though defeat in San Diego meant a setback for the movement there. Instead of mass arrests, the San Diego authorities
responded with murderous repression and deportations. Still,
the IWW fought on for "free speech," even after that defeat.
Seattle was a special case; instead of a single free speech fight,

there was a sort of rolling guerrilla war along the streets south of Yesler, on again, off again.

Roger Baldwin, a founder of the American Civil Liberties Union (ACLU), would later explain that the IWW "wrote a chapter in the history of American liberties like that of the struggle of the Quakers for freedom to meet and worship, of the militant suffragettes to carry their propaganda to the seats of government, and of the Abolitionists to be heard." This rebellious component of the working class represented in the IWW "blazed the trail in those ten years of fighting for free speech which the entire American working class must in some fashion follow."[31] Baldwin assured that in no case did the IWW resort to violence, but the "violence used against them was colossal." He estimated that ten Wobblies were killed and two thousand jailed in the free speech fights.[32]

However, behind the IWW's fight for free speech lay the more important goal of building the union, and this was a struggle. The years since the battles in Spokane were difficult, and not just in the Northwest's woods. The strike at Lawrence had been a great victory, but heroic stands in Patterson and Akron met with defeat. Internal and external criticism of the IWW grew louder. This contributed to the IWW's decision to move westward and concentrate its resources on organizing the wheat fields of the Great Plains, the hard-rock miners of the Rockies, and lumberjacks of the Pacific Northwest. Success came first on the Plains, where the Wobblies founded the Agricultural Workers Organization (AWO Local 400) in April 1915 in Kansas City. It was led by Walter Nef, a trusted comrade of Bill Haywood's, who was a veteran of the Spokane fight, with a history of organizing on both coasts as well as in the Wheat Belt. Nef had worked as a longshoreman, miner, and construction worker. The AWO aimed to organize all farmworkers. Soapboxing was set aside in favor of building membership and collecting dues. By the end of the year, there were AWO branches in Omaha, Sioux City, and Kansas City, as well as an outpost in California. Plans were made to organize corn harvesters and loggers. By the end of August

1916, the AWO claimed twelve thousand members and "job control" in farm districts where wage rates and hours were enforced by the union. By the time of the 1916 harvest, the AWO had twenty thousand members. The organization became a model, and its income helped to underwrite others. Reviewing the year 1916, Haywood reported growth "in all branches of industry": agricultural workers, metal mine workers, iron miners, railroad workers, and marine transport workers.[33] In Seattle and Spokane, timber workers, once again, were set to battle the Lumber Trust. The July 4 conference in Seattle, attended by five hundred delegates, represented nearly that many logging camps in the district. In Smith's words: "Enthusiasm ran high!"[34]

There were IWW members in Everett in 1916, on the docks and in the mills. Yet with a small office its presence was minimal, and those Wobblies involved in the city's disputes were there "as individuals," Smith would insist. "It is true that among the longshoremen who helped the shingle weavers on the picket line in July there were a number of members of the IWW," wrote the *Industrial Worker*'s Everett correspondent C. E. Payne, "but they went as members of the Longshoremen's Union, and not as IWWs."[35] Smith recalls that "striking longshoremen from Seattle aided the shingle weavers on their picket line . . . and individual members of the IWW, holding duplicate cards in the AFL, stood shoulder to shoulder with the strikers, but officially the IWW had no part in any of the strikes."[36] Nevertheless, the IWW "was drawn into the fray," and "encouragement given the shingle weavers." Inevitably, the Wobblies "became a menace to the mill owners, and the police were ordered to prevent any more street meetings."[37]

The free speech fights had been central to gaining attention for the IWW, for building its reputation, as well as for recruitment—in few places more so than in the woods of the Northwest. Perhaps less noted, the fights also helped make the IWW a force throughout the working class, surely in the forests, but on the docks too, and in large shops and small. Wobblies worked alongside ironworkers, dishwashers, coal miners, tailors, machinists, and railroad workers, among others. The organization was growing, as was its mantra: industrial unionism.

The question in 1916 was whether the IWW would turn Everett into a Spokane. That is, would it turn an already bitterly divided town into a battlefield, invade its streets with soapbox agitators and fill its jails with revolutionary workers? Certainly, the bosses of Everett, led by the Commercial Club, and their collaborators in the state's employers' associations, anticipated this. And they were determined to not let it happen. They looked back to San Diego and its lessons. Everett's sheriff, Donald McRae, would be their point man. In turn, he would set out to recruit a small army of vigilantes. He deputized businessmen, veterans, unemployed workers, strikebreakers, and criminals and armed them.

The IWW was reluctant to call Everett a free speech fight, though it had many such characteristics. This may seem simply a semantic issue, but it reveals the degree to which the IWW— so often a master of tactics and with an array of veterans on its benches—had no idea what it was getting into. They foresaw nothing on the scale of Spokane. On the one hand, the shingle weavers remained defiant and militant, still "reporting a good crowd on the picket line, including women. . . . The women have the men beat two to one doing picket duty. They succeed in getting the men out as fast as the scab herders bring them in."[38] On the other hand, the Commercial Club's goons had by no means retreated; a new tactic was firing into the homes of the best-known pickets. None of this, sad to say, was so unusual. The IWW seems to have gone to Everett mostly on principle, envisioning its presence there as symbolic, a rehearsal for the battle in the woods to come. However, its foundational principle was "solidarity" and the embattled workers of Everett deserved support. The IWW calculated that if the shingle weavers lost, it would be in part the result of their own tactics, including their affiliation with the AFL, which had offered very little support. So the IWW expected at a minimum to pick up some of the pieces. There were scattered shingle weavers' pickets still active, and the strikes of the longshoremen and the tugboat men continued. As the fighting escalated, Haywood, taking stock of the situation, exhorted the workers: "It is a fight on the part of the bosses for the open shop and the destruction of all unionism on the Pacific Coast," a struggle of "the working class against a reign of terror and the iron heel of the master class on their necks, through the destruction of the IWW and all other organizations of the workers."[39]

In August, the IWW announced a street corner meeting featuring James Thompson. Sheriff McRae, learning of the event, responded that the "man won't be allowed to speak in Everett."[40] To make his position clear, McRae ordered an assembly of men near the IWW office to be "rounded up." They were seized, roughly questioned, searched, and all of those without families or properties in Everett were forcibly deported. That night, ten more were removed from the shingle weavers' picket line and taken to the county line.[41]

"Treatment of this kind became general," wrote Smith.[42] It led the secretary of the Building Trades Council, Jake Michel, to declare, "Men just off the job with their paychecks in their pocket have been unceremoniously thrown out of town just because they are working men."[43] On the morning of August 4, Thompson arrived with a small group of supporters, including Rowan. Among the women in the group was the IWW veteran Edith Frenette, a popular speaker on Seattle's Skid Road, who had been arrested in the Missoula and Spokane free speech movements. First, Thompson ascended the soapbox and spoke on the recent hearings of the Industrial Relations Commission in Washington, DC. Before he finished, the police interrupted Thompson and ordered him to report to the chief of police. Rowan took his place, only to be dragged from the stand and taken away by the same police. Then Frenette spoke—in turn she was arrested along with Lorna Mahler. The listeners, a large crowd by this time, frequently intervened with song, as so often, "Red Flag" and the "Marseillaise." Lettelsia Fye, a self-described housewife, took the stand to read from the Declaration of Independence. Her arrest led Michel to protest, and he too was taken away by police. And so it went. Thompson was informed that he would not be allowed to speak, but that he was free to leave Everett. He refused and was jailed along with the others, though none were charged or ever tried. All this took place in the presence of an angry crowd. The prisoners were deported by boat and train the next morning. Undaunted, the IWW promised to give Everett "a drastic dose of direct action."[44] The authorities dug in, angry but also afraid with "the middle classes increasingly feeling under siege, terrorized."[45]

This dynamic continued, off and on, throughout August and September. There were arrests and beatings, with "the strikers' ranks constantly thinned by the jailing of the picketers."[46] The Wobblies' response was to promise to bring hundreds more into the conflict. The vigilantes grew ever more vicious, but the IWW remained confident that it would prevail. To the alarm of the Commercial Club and its allies, the public was sympathetic to the IWW. Several times angry crowds, sometimes five hundred strong, followed arrested speakers to the jails. In September, two hundred people gathered at the Labor Temple, where they "censured the sheriff as an inhuman tool of the masters of Everett," calling for a gathering of all the city's residents. In the event, more than one-third of the city's population responded. A massive protest was held in the City Park, with over ten thousand in attendance.[47] "The sentiment was with the IWW and the actions of the police force and other illegal gunmen and hoodlums were scathingly condemned."[48]

The culmination of the Everett struggle came late that month. Here is Elizabeth Gurley Flynn's account, as reported in the *Industrial Worker*, a story she repeated to shocked listeners in dozens of Northwest mill towns, logging camps, and union halls in the months to come, and at a massive meeting of thousands at Seattle's Dreamland Rink:

> On the morning of October 30: About thirty men left Seattle for Everett by steamer, with the intention of peaceably trying out their right to hold a street meeting in the town. At the dock, they

were met by a large party of gunmen, armed with loaded saps [a leather weapon weighted with lead] and guns and with scarves around their necks which they drew up, masking their faces.

The men were loaded into waiting machines [cars] and driven out to Beverley Park, a wild patch of woodland on the outskirts of town. Here they were received by another gang of Commercial Club helots in full sapping trim. The men were released one by one and forced to run the gauntlet down between the long ranks of gangsters, all of them bloodthirsty and many drunk on bootleg whisky. A perfect hail of blows fell on the bodies and heads of this handful of defenseless workers; and the air was full of vile abuse of labor and threats against unionism, together with some hurrahs for the sacred "Open Shop." Some of the men were also dragged so roughly across cattle guards on the car-tracks that the guards were found, the next day, to be clotted with blood.[49]

Flynn omits that the men had been stripped, and that farmers, some at great distances, were wakened that night by their screams. Many had been battered by each side and "kicked full booted into gut and testicles."[50] She concludes, nevertheless, that "the wonder of Beverly Park is that the Wobblies lived at all."[51] The party struggled back, some walking as a far as twenty-five miles, to Seattle, where many were taken to the City Hospital to be treated for internal injuries, broken shoulders and arms, broken teeth, scalp wounds, lacerations, and bruises. Despite the beatings having taken place in Beverly Park, the IWW referred to the event as the "Everett Massacre."

The Everett *Tribune* ran a banner headline, "IWW Entitled to No Sympathy,"[52] while rumors spread that "thousands" of "leering maniacs" were on their way "to burn their homes" to the ground, to "loot" and "rape" in an invasion of the "barbaric Huns."[53] Who would these people be, this "leering, jeering army of vagrants and bums"? Here again Flynn's words give us the best description of the IWW's bases. They are, she wrote in the *Industrial Worker*, "the migratory worker, the element that while necessary is ferociously exploited in this Western country. They are the men who fell the timber, they make the rivers navigable, they are the ones who build the mighty bridges and traverse the mountains with the railways. They are the ones who help harvest the food supply of the world. Upon their backs rest the pillars of our industrial world."

Flynn continued, "They are driven from pillar to post, as the seasons must come and go, they must also come and go. They are homeless, no family ties, no opportunities for anything other than labor, yet they are young and strong, they want good homes, good food, and good clothing. They want the good things in life as much as any other member of the human race and they are organizing in the IWW to get them."[54]

THE IWW IMMEDIATELY RESOLVED to settle the situation in Everett, because common decency demanded it and because they saw it as a pivotal battle. Under the headline, "IWW Must Answer the Terrorism of Everett," the editors wrote: "The IWW must answer these outrages or admit that they cannot function on the Pacific Coast or elsewhere as an organization representing the fighting part of the working class. . . . The conditions demand an answer immediately and decisively. They demand not talk, but action; unmistakably and unanswerable."[55]

The Wobblies understood their enemies to be implacable. They pointed to the "assembled army of thugs, with guns and saps." The authorities, they perceived, were "outspoken in their statement that they are going to destroy the IWW and every other organization of the workers." The Wobblies concluded, "In this struggle there are no laws they have to respect, not even those of humanity . . . Their silence is a clearer statement than any word that workers cannot expect any rights, even altho guaranteed by the Constitution, except such as they have the power to enforce."[56]

Seattle sent out the call for two thousand volunteers. By the next morning, there were five hundred assembled. They decided to travel by boat, the inter-urban train offering insufficient space.

Traveling by boat also meant a chance to avoid the vigilantes' tactic of stopping northbound trains and evicting anyone suspicious in their eyes. Two passenger steamships in Puget Sound's fleet, the *Verona* and the *Calista*, were chartered and packed with men and boys, harvest workers, lumber workers, hard-rock miners and lumber workers, few foreign-born, nearly all young.[57] "Mere boys" wrote Smith, "youthful enthusiasm shining on their beard-less faces. Scattered among them were a few men of middle years, and here and there a grey beard stood out in bold relief—but the majority of them were mere boys, youthful soldiers in the Social Revolution, fine and clean and loyal material called together by the compelling idea of a New Society."[58] Perhaps 250 boarded the *Verona*; another thirty-eight would follow on the *Calista*.

Smith described the atmosphere on board: "Laughter and jest were on the lips of the men who crowded the *Verona*, and songs of one big union rang out over the sparkling waters of Puget Sound. Loyal soldiers were these in the great class war, enlightened workers who were willing to give their all in the battle for bread, happiness and liberty."[59] This latter was rhetorical yet prescient. Everything indicates that they did not expect violence. Smith wrote that "not for a moment did they think that the Everett Klu-Klux-Klan [*sic*] would dare resort to violent and criminal tactics in the broad day-light of that beautiful sunny day and in plain view of a host of conscientious Everett citizens."[60]

In Everett, meanwhile, the Commercial Club made its prepara-tions: new deputies were sworn in and arms distributed. A drunken Sheriff McRae brazenly appeared at the IWW hall to threaten the staff there: "I won't have a lot of sons of bitches hanging around this place like in Seattle. I'll bet you a hundred dollars you bastards won't hold that meeting tomorrow."[61]

When the *Verona* entered Port Gardner Bay, its passengers were singing the English transport workers' song:

> *We meet today in freedom's cause,*
> *And raise our voices high;*

We'll join our hands in union strong,
To battle or to die.

Hold the fort for we are coming,
Union men be strong,
Side by side we battle onward,
Victory will come! [62]

The dock was silent as the *Verona* approached, though a cheer rose from the hillside beyond, where thousands of Everett workers and their families assembled to welcome the Wobblies.[63] Those on board did not know that another "army" was on site, nor suspect what was in store for them. Certainly no one expected a warm welcome from the authorities. Neither did they foresee murder.

A makeshift army had headed for the waterfront, following back roads and alleys. "It included mill owners, executives, sons who happened to be home from college, foremen, thugs, dentists, physicians, lawyers, merchants," writes Clark, who observes that it was sustained "at least in part by the courage of bootleg whisky, or by mob inertia, or by the assurance that it must save Everett from the satanic hosts."[64]

The Wobblies crowded the ship's bow, anxious to disembark, but instead saw Sheriff McRae, hand on his gun, shouting, "Who is your leader?" The IWW response, famously, "We are all leaders." McRae: "You can't land here!" The IWW: "The hell we can't," and down went the gangplank, followed by a surge of men.[65] McRae raised his gun, a signal it seemed. The first shot was fired, apparently by deputy W. A. Bridges, then a volley that drove the men back onto the boat. Hugo Gerlot was the first killed. "A youthful free speech enthusiast," Gerlot had climbed the ship's flagpole to greet the expected supporters on the docks; he was shot through the head, legs, and hip, and crashed onto the crowded deck.

There followed a barrage, sending the ship's passengers in desperate search of safety. The passengers first surged starboard, only to have the ship become unbalanced and list dangerously.

Several men were pitched into the sea, having lost their footing "on the blood-stained decks. . . . There, struggling frantically in the water—by no possible chance active combatants—a storm of rifle bullets churning little whirlpools around their heads, one by one they were made the victims of the lumber trusts' greed."[66] The assailants attacked from both sides of the ship, from the end of the city dock and from the dock to the south. "The bay was reddened with their blood. Of all who went overboard, James Hadley alone regained the deck, the rest disappearing beneath the silent waters to be dragged by the undertow out to an unknown and nameless ocean grave."[67]

The Wobblies were in a deadly crossfire, yet there would be victims on the docks as well. McRae had made no preparations for the assault. He had not anticipated the lines of fire, perhaps expecting an IWW retreat. Fall back they did, but not before dozens more were shot and five on board killed. Chaos ensued. A wounded passenger, Oscar Carlson, would report from his Seattle hospital bed: "I tell you as it comes to me now, it seems one shot came from the dock. Then three or four from the other side, then all sides at once."[68] One deputy, also wounded, sought safety in the crowd of bystanders where he shouted hysterically, "They're crazy in there, firing in all directions."[69] The ship's captain had taken refuge in a locked cabin. Wobblies forced a terrified engineer to restart the engines and steer the *Verona* erratically away from the site of the catastrophe, the battered survivors warning the *Calista* to turn back. Deputies and vigilantes continued to shoot until the ship was well out of range. Then they searched the water for bodies, shooting at anything that moved. In all, the attack lasted little more than ten minutes.

There were 31 wounded. They were offered at best crude first-aid, though this may have saved many. Three of the wounded were simply unsuspecting passengers. The IWW carried the dead into a cabin: Hugo Gerlot, John Looney, Gustav Johnson, and Abraham Rabinowitz. Felix Baron would die in a Seattle hospital. They would subsequently claim that at least half a dozen more had been lost, unidentified and never recovered from the harbor. The victims were young men mostly, Gerlot, twenty at best, thirteen were under twenty-five, four under twenty-one, two just eighteen.

On the dock, two deputies lay dead: C. O. Curtis, a mill manager, and Jefferson Beard, a deputy who had been among the thugs at Beverly Park. Sheriff McRae himself was wounded, as were some twenty others, all middle-aged men. They were carried to the Port Commission's cars, to be taken to the hospital, though they were first confronted by crowds of angry workers who cursed and threatened the killers. A terrified McRae begged officers to call out the naval militia. Edwin Marsh, president of the State Federation of Labor, phoned the governor, fearing the prospect of "thousands of working people of Everett . . . enraged toward members of the Commercial Club who participated in the gun battle."[70] Edith Frenette, Lorna Mahler, and Joyce Peters were in the crowd, having come by car to Everett to prepare for the never-to-happen street meeting. When they returned to Seattle, only to be arrested there, the Everett authorities charged that Frenette had threatened McRae with a gun and attempted to throw red pepper into his eyes as he retreated from the docks, and again as he lay crippled. Frenette was released on $2,500 bail. This exorbitant sum reflected, apparently, her unreliability in the eyes of the authorities.[71] The Seattle *Union Record*, reporting on her hearing in December, suggested that "this appear[ed] to be one of the crudest frame-ups which the hysterical authorities have produced as yet."[72]

Police ambulances waited as the *Verona* returned to Seattle's Coleman dock. They took the wounded to the city hospital where Portland doctor Marie Equi was among those who attended them. The others were transported to the city jail. Those on board the *Calista*, which followed, were dispatched to the county jail. Seventy-four men, identified by undercover Pinkertons on board the *Verona*, were charged with murder of the deputies. The men on the *Calista* were charged with "unlawful assembly."

Seattle received the news from Everett at first with shock, then bitter recognition of the terrifying events so near home. The city's dailies followed the lead of the employers' organizations and the Everett papers, but it was an uphill battle. By contrast, Seattle's progressives—among them Robert Bridges, the chairman of the Port Commission—joined what quickly became a movement in support of the workers, as did politicians and clergy. Mayor Hiram Gill responded: "The men who met the IWWs at the dock were a bunch of cowards. They outnumbered the IWWs five to one, and in spite of this they stood there on the dock and fired into the boat, IWWs, innocent passengers, and all." He suggested that "if indeed shots had come from the ship, they were in self-defense," and argued, "If I were one of the party of 40 IWWs who was almost beaten to death by 300 citizens of Everett [at the Beverly Park outrage] without being able to defend myself, I probably would have armed myself if I intended to visit Everett ever again."[73]

The IWW itself reacted with a sequence of horror, grief, and anger—then all three at once—which they expressed on the *Industrial Worker*'s front pages. There they published (more than once) photographs of the dead men, so all the world might see the extent of the massacre in gruesome detail.[74] The newspaper proclaimed: "Louder, clearer, more insistent than any words are the call of the dead bodies of our murdered fellow workers."[75] The victims' death masks became emblems of a campaign to exonerate the prisoners, then symbolic reminders that these deaths should never be forgotten. Gus Johnson had been buried by relatives, and Rabinowitz's body was shipped back to his family in New York. Funerals for Baran, Gerlof, and Looney took place on Saturday, November 18.

Fifteen hundred marched behind the hearses, with automobiles of mourners and pallbearers following. Then came "the long line of marching men, four abreast, swinging in regular time and wearing red flowers and ribbons to a man."[76] The men were buried in Mount Pleasant Cemetery on Queen Anne Hill, "upon the crest of a mighty hill, from the eminence of which one can survey the city of Seattle laid out below in all its complex ramifications and overbrooded by a great pall of smoke."[77] There they joined the IWW martyr Joe Hill. (His ashes had been divided into small packets and sent to fellow workers around the world, except in Utah, where Hill "did not wish to be caught dead.") The Seattle Wobblies' "tramp poet," Charles Ashleigh, called on those assembled to never give up the fight. With his fine English accent, this mild-mannered London-born man said: "Today, we pay tribute to the dead. Tomorrow we turn, with spirit unquenchable, to give battle to the foe!"[78]

EVERETT, NOVEMBER FIFTH
by Charles Ashleigh

Song on his lips, he came;
Song on his lips he went;
This be the token we bear of him;
Soldier of Discontent!

Out of the dark they came; out of the night
Of poverty and injury and woe,
With flaming hope, their vision thrilled to light,
Song on their lips, and every heart aglow;

They came, that none should trample on Labor's right
To speak and voice her centuries of pain.
Bare hands against the master's armored might!—
A dream to match the tolls of sordid gain!

And then the dark went red; and the grey sea
Was written crimsonly with ebbing life.
The barricade spewed shots and mockery
And curses, and the drunken lust of strife.

Yet, the mad chorus from that devil's host —
Yea, all the tumult of that butcher throng,—
Compound of bullets, booze and coward boast,
Could not outshriek one dying worker's song!

Song on his lips, he came;
Song on his lips he went;
This be the token we bear of him;
Soldier of Discontent!

Everett had come to Seattle, and the Seattle labor movement supported the cause. However unexceptional this might seem, solidarity was one of their important achievements and not at all foreordained. Certainly not when the IWW and the AFL were involved. One lesson learned from the victory of the women textile workers' strike in Lawrence, or so it seemed, was that "for the strikers . . . the Federation was a force almost as dangerous . . . as the employers themselves."[79]

Nevertheless, the day following the funerals the CLC convened a meeting five thousand strong, the "greatest meeting ever held at Dreamland Rink." The purpose of the assembly was to demand that "the lawlessness of Everett be investigated, and the real criminals punished." The CLC had already established a committee on Everett. Its members included Duncan, the secretary of the CLC, Harry Ault, the editor of the CLC's *Union Record*, and C. W. Boyle of the Boilermakers' Union. The committee provided funding for the defense of the prisoners and bail for the men arrested on the steamship *Calista*. It convinced the Seattle lawyer George Vanderveer to assist in the case of the *Verona* defendants.

Jointly organized by the CLC and the IWW, the Dreamland meeting was chaired by Seattle judge Richard Rinsor. Speakers included Jake Michel, secretary of the Everett Building Trades (AFL), who told the audience, "I have come here to tell all I know, and I don't care if they stop me on my way back to Everett and hang me to the nearest telegraph pole . . . I'm going to tell it . . . [in Everett] not a man in overalls is safe."[80] He was followed by the Reverend Sidney Strong, whose statement that the "best thing that could be done would be to open the jail doors and let the men go" was met by thunderous applause.[81]

Hulet Wells, state chairman of the Socialist Party and president of the CLC, spoke for the Council: "We of the American Federation of Labor and our friends in the Industrial Workers of the World do not always agree on methods and tactics. But we of the AFL never forget that these men are our brothers of the working class and are with us in the great class struggle."[82] The Socialists joined the CLC in arguing that the IWW had become involved in Everett while assisting the AFL shingle weavers' strike. Charles Ashleigh repeated this in the February edition of *The Masses*: the issue had been solidarity with the strikes of longshoremen and shingle weavers, he wrote, affirming that "the strikers had . . . 'Fellow Workers' in Seattle, members of the IWW, who believe that a strike of any workers in any industry is the concern of every other worker."[83] In Spokane, the Socialist Party sponsored another big meeting.[84] The spirit was infectious.

In January, there was a "monster" meeting at the Dreamland Rink, this time with six thousand in attendance. It began with "Hold the Fort," now the anthem of the Seattle labor movement, regularly sung at all such gatherings. Sam Sadler, the president of Seattle's International Longshoreman's Association (ILA-AFL), a leading socialist, viewed by his comrades as "one of the most trustworthy and vigorous revolutionary propagandists on the Pacific Coast," was the first speaker: "Too long has labor turned the other cheek . . . The martyrdoms in Everett are but a goad to us. These workers did not die in vain; those who are in jail are but our representatives in the class war."[85] The *Industrial Worker* recognized how these other organizations had supported the Wobblies: "The AF of L Unions of Seattle have responded splendidly to the occasion and have shown great energy and interest in the struggle for free speech in Everett and the tragedy that preceded it. The *Union Record*, organ of the Central Labor Council, has devoted most of its space for the last two issues to the matter and has been a publicity organ of the greatest value." J. A. Macdonald, editor of the *Industrial Worker*, argued that Everett was just one front in an international conflict, pointing to Britain "where workers have broken the fetish of Parliament and forced the release of twelve men from jail."[86] The final featured speaker at Dreamland Rink was Elizabeth Gurley Flynn, who was greeted with a roar of appreciation. Surely, this was an unprecedented display of trade union unity and working-class solidarity.

The Wobblies were now making the Everett victims their *cause célèbre*, working to raise money and awareness. James Thompson toured the East. In New York, he spoke to a big gathering at the Manhattan Lyceum.[87] Yet few had the feeling and power of Flynn. She recalled how a recent speaking tour had brought her in contact with "Jews, Russians and Italians on the East Side of New York" who were as attentive to the events in Everett as her present audience. "The only reason there are seventy-four being tried," she said, "is that they were not killed. . . . There is no evidence of the worker guilt, but there is plenty of evidence of the bosses' vengeance." But the day was coming, she assured the crowd "when we will do more than ask for collections, when we will declare the general strike."[88] She appealed for these men "not only for what they are, but for what they represent. They represent our lives and liberty."[89]

This "Bloody Sunday" was in some ways a Peterloo Massacre for the Pacific Northwest, shaping consciousness in a way similar to how the massacre of protesters in Manchester had influenced the English working class.[90] This tragedy so stunned the working people of Seattle—it was a savage assault on all they held dear: free speech, sympathy for the underdog, the very notion of rights— that it became nearly impossible to remain neutral. Opinions hardened, which was not exactly what Everett's authorities had anticipated. Rather, what resulted was the exact opposite: a sea change in working-class opinion and a massive swing to the left.

THE EVERETT PRISONERS WERE HELD incommunicado for more than two months. They were denied reading material, mattresses, and blankets, and were fed vile food. When members of the Cooks and Waiters Union prepared a special Thanksgiving Day meal for them, McRae prohibited it, giving the prisoners

instead a small serving of mush. Nevertheless, they endured, singing and shouting, and protesting by breaking locks and cell doors
and by going on a hunger strike.[91] They composed a letter to the
federal government opposing conscription and war. All seventy-
four signed on.[92]

On March 5, 1917, the trial began—the governor had intervened and moved it to the King County Courthouse in Seattle. It
was to be the greatest labor trial in Northwest history. Certainly,
the Wobblies believed this. The prosecution changed its charges:
originally the case had focused on the murder of lumber manager C. O. Curtis, but he was found to have been shot in the back,
apparently by fellow deputies. So it was changed to focus on the
shooting of Jefferson Beard.[93] Thomas H. Tracy, who at age eighteen had left home due to poverty and worked in various humble
jobs, was charged with murder in the first degree.[94] The prosecution asserted that he had fired the first shot that day and, in so
doing, had "assisted, counselled, aided, abetted and encouraged
some unknown person to kill Jefferson Beard."[95] Sometimes thousands would routinely seek admittance to the courtroom, which
held but one hundred.[96]

In the streets, the fight for justice continued. Seattle's May Day
march, which united the left as never before, was the largest ever.
Setting off from the IWW hall at 10 a.m., "thousands of men and
women fell into a marching line of fours, a committee pinning a
red rose on each marcher."[97] The march was fifteen blocks long. It
wound its way through the city streets and up to Mount Pleasant
Cemetery, there to pay tribute to Everett's dead. There speeches
were delivered in English, Russian, Swedish, Hungarian, and
Italian. The marchers then turned back to arrive at the county
jail, where they sang their revolutionary hymns. As was routine,
they collected money and divided the proceeds, half going to San
Francisco for the Tom Mooney defense.[98]

Anna Louise Strong, then still a member of the Seattle School
Board, covered the trial for the New York *Evening Post*. "I was
not consciously taking sides in any struggle," she would recall; "I

merely sent the news. The news, which still had the power to horrify the average American believer in fair play, was that at every stage the Everett police and private lumber guards took the initiative in beating and shooting workers for speaking in their streets. The lumber guards on the dock had begun the shooting and continued firing as the *Verona* pulled away; yet none of them were arrested. The men on trial for murder were not individually shown to have even possessed a gun; it was enough that someone on their ship, a comrade or an *agent provocateur* had fired."[99]

George Vanderveer was a conservative Seattle lawyer when he was chosen for the defense. Best known for his work as a criminal lawyer, he became known as "the Attorney for the Damned" in the wake of the Everett trial. It was a strange appellation, unless the Wobblies were seen somehow as "damned." He would go on to defend the IWW in the big Chicago trial where one hundred of its leaders were tried for conspiracy. Vanderveer later returned to the Northwest to defend the IWW victims of the Centralia massacre.

In the Everett case, Vanderveer established himself as a meticulous investigator. He spent hours in jail cells with the defendants. He "prowled" the Everett city dock, "taking exact measurements, drawing sketches." He spent days searching for several small boys, locating "nine of them, taking from them evidence, including an assortment of cartridges they had gathered in the aftermath of the shootings—shotgun, revolver, rifle shells. He examined the *Verona*."[100]

The trial, which lasted into May, was in fact a political trial. The prosecution tried the IWW as an organization, not the individual men, such as Tracy, who was the first man charged. In making their case, the prosecutors alleged: "The plot was not hatched in Snohomish County. It was hatched down here in Seattle. The expedition started out from Seattle, not one but many of them. Seattle was the base and it was from here that it started."[101] To debunk this theory, James P. Thompson spelled out at great length the principles and tactics of the IWW. Still, Vanderveer sought evidence. He took the jury, followed by reporters, to the Everett docks. He identified false testimony, contradictions, failing memories, and class prejudice—all of it amounting to a frame-up of Seattle's working class.

In closing the defense Fred Moore, Vanderveer's partner, told the jury it had "the opportunity to settle the biggest labor trial in the history of the Northwest." The conclusion was foregone, since it had become clear during the trial that behind Sheriff McRae stood the Commercial Club and the Weyerhaeuser interests. On the morning of May 5, the courtroom was packed and the corridors jammed solid. The jury foreman, James R. Williams, presented its findings: "We the jury find the defendant, Thomas H. Tracy, not guilty." Judging that there was no point in continuing, the prosecution abandoned the case.[102]

Skid Road erupted in jubilation that night. There were celebrations in Wobbly halls throughout the country and reports of spontaneous singing in hobo jungles. For the fifty thousand workers in the logging camps, the victory showed that anything was possible. The now-released prisoners assembled at Seattle's IWW hall, then traveled together to Mount Pleasant Cemetery. The most fit among them set out for the hills, with the aim of uniting the workers in the lumber industry and preparing for the strike to come.

As catastrophic as Everett was, it enhanced the IWW's reputation. First, they earned sympathy as victims. Then, triumphing in court, they were vindicated. In June 1917, the *Seattle Daily Call* reported that IWW membership had risen to twenty thousand and that it now employed a dozen paid organizers, whereas before there had been just three. Perhaps the *Call* exaggerated the IWW's growth, but it was clear that the Everett Massacre and its aftermath had fueled working-class consciousness.

5. A UNION TOWN

In July 1917, Jimmy Duncan reported the following to Seattle's CLC: "The labor year . . . has been a red-letter year in the history of organized labor. A dozen new unions have been organized, and all of the Seattle unions are flourishing." He singled out the streetcar men (with a membership of 1,600), the "telephone girls" (with nearly 1,100), foundry employees, laundry workers, and cereal and flour mill workers.[1]

The growth of Seattle's unions was real. It was in part the result of declining unemployment in an improving economy. It paralleled an upswing in union membership nationally. Still, Seattle's achievements were extraordinary and its labor movement unique. In these remarkable years, 1916 to 1918, trade union membership in the city had increased 300 percent—from fifteen thousand to sixty thousand. It was a testament to the workers' degree of organization, their politics, and their capacity to organize and fight. Seattle became a "union town," a closed-shop city.

The recovery began in 1914, spurred on by the war in Europe. Nationally it would last into the summer of 1920. Recovery gave millions of workers both the confidence to switch jobs when it was to their advantage and the willingness to strike on a scale that "dwarfed all previously recorded turnover and strike activity."[2] From 1919 to 1922, there were more than ten thousand strikes across the nation involving eight million workers, four million in 1919 alone.[3] In Seattle, thousands would take work in the shipyards where wages were relatively high and "war workers" were exempt from conscription. However, the war also brought inflation, and constantly rising prices, aggravating workers who believed that the cost of living in Seattle was already higher than elsewhere. Wartime restrictions on the right to strike throughout industry added to a deep sense of grievance. One result was "the fusing of economic discontent with visions of a better life,"[4] fueling Socialists and Wobblies, ever more active in both workplaces and communities.[5] This situation alarmed those in power, and not only the employers. Samuel Gompers worried that "the minds of men are not working in the normal manner. The struggles, the sacrifices, the enthusiasm, the highly nervous strain induced by the World War, have brought about a state of almost mental hysteria."[6]

Seattle's achievements had their limits, however. Seattle's longshoremen were as militant as any; indeed, they were the backbone of labor's left and at the forefront of virtually every struggle—from Everett to the General Strike itself. In the aftermath of the General Strike, the Waterfront Employers Association remained cowed, shielding themselves from those irate workers by employing their own force of armed men. However, for the longshoremen, the closed shop remained elusive and the year 1916 brought defeat on the docks, though with contradictory implications.

The waterfront was central to Seattle's economy. It had a near monopoly on the Alaska trade; its canneries shipped fish and inland wheat and fruit came in by rail and went out by ship. Rafts of raw lumber were towed into the port, loaded onto schooners bound for California, Asia, and the South Pacific. The docks were modern. The city's progressives had fought the municipal docks and won. Elected Port Commissioners had developed deepwater piers at East Waterway, Salmon Bay, and Smith Cove; the latter became the largest dock complex on the West Coast, and the East

Waterway pier enabled a ship to be unloaded from both sides onto two docks simultaneously. These piers were also long enough to accommodate the newest vessels plying coastal waters. They were linked directly to railroad lines and featured huge cranes that dominated the waterfront skyline. These cranes—still rare in eastern cities at the time—were mounted on the railroad tracks. They could carry 4.000-board feet of lumber from a rail car to storage or onto a ship's deck, replacing both animal and human power. This meant significant savings for the shippers at the expense of the other coastal shipping centers, such as San Francisco, Tacoma, and Victoria.[7] The Port Commissioners were not only modernizers, but also sought peace with labor. In January 1915, Commissioner Robert Bridges granted union organizers access to the piers, agreeing to work with the union's dispatcher instead of the companies' hiring halls. All this paid off. By 1916, the Port of Seattle ranked first on the coast in shipping, second only to New York nationally. Even if the promise of the Panama Canal had waned by 1914, the waterways there plagued by landslides and strikes, the demands of war seemed boundless.

Nevertheless, for longshoremen, the work on the docks remained crude. The days were long, longer when finishing the job demanded it, because the "ship must sail on time." The work was grinding, backbreaking, and always dangerous. Although the shippers considered the longshoremen to be unskilled, their survival depended both on skill and cooperation, working in gangs on even the most modern piers. Employers might see them as "human machines," but in practice they were far from ordinary. They were required "to push or pull enormous weights, aided only by the most elementary inclines, pulleys, winches, and screws and above all by their own teamwork."[8] Cooperation in turn created a common outlook and a widespread sense of solidarity, despite the classification "longshoremen" embracing a vast array of workers. From skilled riggers to loaders, shovelers, pushers, and general helpers, they were all longshoremen.

This common identity was reinforced by being casual labor

hired according to the practice of the "shape-up." The cruelty of
this system was self=apparent, condemned in vain by industrial
relations specialists almost everywhere. The men gathered each
morning at the gates to the wharf with the hope of being chosen by
the hiring foreman. This gave the employer absolute power to hire
or fire and determine the duration of work, thereby dividing the
longshoremen and empowering the employers. Dave Madison, ILA
Local 38-12's spokesman, explained that, in the system preferred
by employers (and the ILA's national leaders), "the longshoremen
[had] to read the ship's arrival on blackboards and then await the
ship's arrival." This meant that they were "practically forced to frequent rapacious saloons" only to wait there again "to get paid after
the job." Hundreds of men flocked to the piers at all times of day
and night to line up for work. Yet sometimes stevedore bosses hired
only half a dozen.[9] The Seattle longshoremen fought this system.
The employers sometimes used steady gangs, but most often the
shape-up prevailed. It divided workers viciously, institutionalizing
discrimination. Still, the shape-up was also defining: the divisive
experience often had the opposite effect of uniting longshoremen.

In Seattle, as elsewhere, the number of workers on the waterfront almost always exceeded the number of jobs. This was not
just because there were too many full-time longshoremen, but also
because the number of men seeking work swelled seasonally and
when times were hard. The foreman at the gate almost always held
out hope, even if the chance of work was slim. The loggers would
arrive in winter. Harvesters and strikers, together with miners
from as far away as Butte, were known to join these throngs. In
this system, the fear of unemployment became universal. Even the
most skilled veterans—those favored by the waterfront bosses—
experienced long periods without work. So the longshoremen
fought for the closed shop and the orderly, more secure conditions
provided by a union hiring hall.

The West Coast longshoremen were represented by the ILA,
an East Coast–centered union that organized aggressively but
opposed strikes, particularly sympathy strikes. The union had

been founded in the Great Lakes but was strongest in the East and in the Gulf ports. Its president, T. V. O'Connor, was a former tugboat captain from Buffalo, who worked closely with Samuel Gompers and the shippers. Hence, the struggles of longshoremen in these years was, in large part, the fight for a real union.[10]

The first test for the union on the West Coast came in 1912 at Grays Harbor. There longshoremen walked off their jobs in solidarity with striking shingle weavers and IWW mill workers, but with their own wage demands. Seattle and Tacoma dockers secured work for these strikers. Strikebreakers were fined, and the union won its demands. Aberdeen and Hoquiam regained hiring preference, plus wages of fifty cents an hour. In 1913, O'Connor himself negotiated the contract with Canadian and Puget Sound shippers, winning a nine-hour day plus wage increases. The victory, however, had a downside. The ILA recognized the open shop and inserted this contract clause: "Any member of a local who violates any part of this agreement, or agitates a stoppage of work under any circumstances, shall be discharged and will be given no future employment."[11] Thus O'Connor's "triumph" fueled discontent. In 1915, Vancouver shippers went on the offensive, cutting wages, locking longshoremen out, and replacing them with strikebreakers. The West Coast ILA District, believing this was just the beginning, boycotted Vancouver ships. The Seattle dockers, however, recast the boycott. They refused all work unless dispatched from the ILA hall in alphabetical order. This strike, violent from the beginning, lasted into spring, with strikers fighting strikebreakers, armed guards, and police. Federal mediators intervened in March, forcing a settlement with the shippers that no one liked. The strikers would return to the conditions before the Vancouver dispute, there would be no discrimination against union members, and the hiring hall demand would be dropped.[12]

O'Connor settled the Vancouver conflict, only to face trouble in Seattle again in July. This time Smith Cove longshoremen struck, demanding the closed shop and wage increases. The Seattle Washington Employers Union (WEU) refused to settle. Instead, it demanded that the ILA offer "some assurances" of its "ability to handle the Seattle local," insisting that the Seattle and Tacoma locals return to work.[13] The West Coast ILA replied by demanding that the WEU settle with the Seattle strikers or face the possibility of a coast-wide strike. The employers retreated but not much. In a now thriving economy, it promised to hire only union men when available. Pressured by O'Connor, the union gave in, one local at a time, leaving an angry Seattle out alone in September.

The ILA District met in convention in Seattle on May Day, 1916. Delegates demanded better wages, insisting that the employers had prospered while they were victims of inflation. The longshoremen were not alone. In anticipation of the US entry into the war, hundreds, if not thousands, of working people shifted to the higher-paying jobs in Seattle's shipyards, contributing to an already tumultuous labor scene. There were thirty-seven major strikes in Washington State in 1915, fifty-eight in 1916. These included two hundred halibut fishermen who struck on March 12, followed two days later by the strike of five hundred steamboat men. On May 29, 1916, waterfront truckers struck. Meanwhile, the IWW had recovered from earlier losses and rebuilt itself on the waterfront, bringing with it the argument for industrial unions. J. T. Doran, the IWW's popular speaker, savaging the AFL's O'Connor, ridiculed the existence of ten separate, uncoordinated unions on the Seattle waterfront, and the absence of solidarity from the bottom would inevitably lead to disunity and defeat.[14] The ILA District appealed to the marine workers for support and won it from almost all; only the Sailors Union of the Pacific, led by the fierce exclusionist Andrew Fusureth, declined. Indeed, "for the first time in West Coast longshore history, thirty-eight local unions planned to hang the hook together."[15]

The 1916 strike began on June 1 with Sam Sadler leading the strike committee. Twelve hundred Seattle longshoremen struck, demanding $0.55 an hour for regular work, $1.00 an hour for overtime.[16] In the aftermath of the strike, Sadler was elected the local's president. Pickets were identified by green buttons, but there were no strikebreakers. The harbor filled with ships, more arriving by the day, with the wharves full to overflowing. The CLC directed all maritime unions to support the strike. Teamsters joined the picket lines. The waterfront checkers joined the union. All told, three thousand fishermen, steamboat men, truckers, checkers, and longshoremen controlled the waterfront, with pickets along the line from Smith Cove to the grain elevators of West Seattle.

Negotiations for the whole West Coast were held in San Francisco, also embroiled in a harbor-wide dispute. In the meantime, Seattle's employers vowed never to concede the closed shop, alleging that the strike was inspired by the Kaiser. They raised money, hired Pinkertons, bought full-page newspaper ads, appealed to eastern Washington farmworkers to work the Seattle docks, and enlisted strikebreakers. On June 3, there was a brawl on the Milwaukee Road's docks, with fistfights and shots fired. In San Francisco, however, a deal was struck, with the shippers tentatively appearing to have surrendered. Still, the two thousand Seattle and Tacoma strikers rejected the San Francisco recommendations "without one dissenting vote."[17] In any case, the Bay Area strikers returned to work only to learn that San Francisco employers continued to hire non-union workers. The next few days brought the deaths of longshoremen in Oakland and San Francisco. The ILA executive board then ordered the strike to resume. The picket lines were reset, the strikebreakers returned; on Seattle's docks, University of Washington students joined black strikebreakers working behind locked gates.

The WEA denounced the resumption of the strike, again vilifying the demand for a closed shop. "The principle of the closed shop is clearly subversive of individual liberty," they declared. "Under such conditions the labor union becomes an intolerable tyranny and the rest of the people become helpless slaves."[18] Seattle businessmen donated $20,000 to help break the strike. The Employers Association recruited Filipino, other Asians and black strikebreakers, intent on inflaming the conflict.[19] The union on its part prohibited Asian membership. The situation of black workers was more complex, as the ILA had thousands of black members in the South, as well as black officers on its national executive committee.[20] The Japanese Labor Association, committed to achieving a place in the city's labor movement, refused to offer strikebreakers, to its great credit, instead supporting the strikers where it could.[21]

The black population of Seattle grew in the 1910s, though by no means was it the "great migration" that happened elsewhere. Their numbers increased by some 602 to total 2,894 in 1920.[22] Black workers, both men and women, were scattered throughout industry. Of the WEA's 1,500 strikebreakers, three hundred were black, and many went on working in the strike's aftermath. According to historian Quintard Taylor, the strike's defeat caused the ILA to change policy, "sensing the danger to its interests in racially exclusive unionism, [it] quickly incorporated many of the black strikebreakers into its ranks."[23]

There were IWW members in the ILA, "two-card" men, and they participated in the strike as a loyal but radical minority, preaching solidarity. The Wobbly leader J. T. Doran was a popular speaker on the Seattle waterfront, and the IWW used such occasions to openly recruit.[24] The Tacoma ILA invited Wobbly James Thompson to speak, explaining that "the members in Tacoma want to hear the IWW organizer."[25] On Labor Day, a thousand Seattle dockers chartered a steamship and two trains to Tacoma for the annual parade. They marched with the Tacoma strikers, singing IWW songs and leading cheers for One Big Union.[26] In the aftermath of the strike, IWW members in both Tacoma and Portland would take control of locals, even if only temporarily.

The CLC supported the Seattle longshoremen; boilermakers, bakers, salesmen, carpenters, coal miners, Teamsters, garment workers, printers, and waitresses lent support. The waitresses volunteered to walk the picket lines. On behalf of the sailors' union, Furuseth ventured into town. Brazen, typically, he defended the San Francisco leadership, but was chased from the Labor Temple with shouts of "Coward, Quitter." Even so, in a replay of what had happened a month earlier, the San Francisco locals surrendered again in July. Again, too, the Seattle and Tacoma longshoremen unanimously rejected the Bay Area settlement, as did two San Pedro locals and two Portland locals. The Seattle longshoremen held out until October, but by then their strike was lost. At the end, there were 850 scabs working the docks, and the employers had retaken control of the waterfront. For 127 days, the Seattle waterfront had been an outright battleground. "Union longshoremen beat up scabs on docks and ships. There were fistfights, knife fights, dock bombings, pier fires, shooting duels and murders. Spies infiltrated each other's organizations. Gunfire strafed both the Waterfront Employers Union office and the ILA halls. Arrests were frequent."[27] The employers gloated, "No greater victory . . . was ever recorded." The longshoremen had to accept the open shop in place plus the "fink hall," a hiring office whose purpose was to screen out ILA and IWW members. Workers were informed that "all work done on their docks will be strictly on the open-shop principle."[28] In fact, this war was far from over, because defeat radicalized the longshoremen.[29] The ranks of the IWW swelled, and the dock workers' cause became widely known among Seattle's workers. After all, many had been personally involved. The lesson? The strike seems to have again deepened class antagonisms and convinced workers that support for the strikers had been insufficient.

THE YEAR 1917 BROUGHT A FLURRY of labor activity. It began with the steamboat men settling their ten-month strike, with mixed results, but the strikers were rehired and wage gains won. Then the streetcar workers struck. In April, ironworkers struck the Washington Iron Works, "the hell hole of Seattle." They were followed by the laundry workers who struck in June. In July, it was the trainmen's union's turn to strike. The employers imported strikebreakers and housed them in its Georgetown center where they were trained and then armed. The company ran no cars in the first days of the week, then dispatched two cars manned by strikebreakers to test the waters. These were attacked and demolished by strikers when they reached Yesler and Washington Streets, resulting in arrests and some twenty injuries. The trainmen's strike ended in early August when the company agreed to arbitration. The company refused to concede the eight-hour day but allowed that the carmen were entitled to a "living wage," a "comfort wage" (to cover living expenses), five days' sick leave annually, and two days for recreation.[30] That same month, meat packers walked out. Candy and Cracker Workers struck in September, as did Teamsters and twelve thousand shipyard workers in the non-union yards.

DUNCAN'S ASSESSMENT OF THE STATE of Seattle's unions included the situation of large numbers of women workers. The CLC, unlike many of its counterparts, understood the "vital importance of the [AFL] Pacific Coast movement's campaign to organize women workers in all industries."[31] In Seattle, this included domestic workers. In the spring of 1917, the CLC, led by the waitresses' brilliant leader, Alice Lord, set out to organize "household and domestic help." In turn, this drive connected with the growing women's movement and especially the Federation of Women's Trade Unions and Auxiliaries' campaign to unionize all the city's women workers. The Federation would claim that some four thousand women had become CLC members by 1919.

In this context, the workers' movement debated the "woman question," including the issue of whether married women should work outside the home. The debate was contentious, often "acrimonious," with progressives showing themselves to be not always so progressive. Feminists argued for equal access to work. Traditionalists argued for a "moral economy"—that is, work allocated on the basis of need. Central to the concept of a moral economy, of course, was the family. Some women argued that "children needed the special attention that only a mother can provide." To this, others responded, "Not one woman in a thousand gets up early and stands the hardship of a working woman's life for mere nothings." For one woman, changing times meant that a "true mother would rather work than take her children out of school or deny them the advantages the present-day demands. The things that one time were a luxury are nowadays necessities: art, music and education are necessities to the home now."[32] The historian Maurine Greenwald followed this debate as it appeared in the *Union Record*. "It is impossible to tell precisely," she writes, "which viewpoint attracted the most adherents in the Seattle working-class elite. The family wage/moral economy seems to have been especially compelling for male and female trade union leaders, while the female club leaders, many of them housewives, adopted a feminist position." She contended, "Nevertheless, the Seattle controversy demonstrates that feminist ideas were an important part of working-class culture and public discourse that women tailored to their dual commitments to equal rights for women and for workers."[33]

There were also objections from men when women entered previously all-male occupations—another unintended consequence of war. The CLC was divided on the issue but acceded to the women's position only if equal work meant equal pay, that is, avoided wage competition, a race to the bottom. Duncan argued, "No supported married woman has a moral right to answer the call of an unscrupulous employer to enter the competitive field for pin money to the disadvantage of the single girl who must work to live."[34] Frank Turco of the blacksmiths supported the feminists: "I believe in Freedom. Woman should do what she sees fit. As long as the workers believe in a woman staying at home because she is tied up to a certain man . . . we'll have slavery. Man cannot be free as long as woman is not free."[35] Phil Pearl of the Barbers' Union agreed: "I hold that a married woman has as much right to work as anybody." He appreciated that some women disliked housework and wanted to do something else. Wage work enhanced women's lives by helping them develop "independence and originality."[36] On the left, hometown heroes like Sadler spoke out for the full emancipation of women, as did visitors such as Elizabeth Gurley Flynn, Margaret Sanger, and Emma Goldman, all of whom came through Seattle in 1916.[37] Greenwald wrote that this debate—whether married women should hold jobs outside the home and what place women workers should have in

American society—"suggests new social values were emerging in the era of the First World War."[38]

Still, for women there were fights that were neither altogether different in kind nor separate from the other issues of the time. If Everett created angry men, it also produced angry women. "Men and women," wrote one reporter in the aftermath of the massacre, "who are ordinarily law abiding, who in normal times mind their own business, pay their taxes, send their children to church and school, in every way comport themselves as normal citizens, were heard using the most vitriolic language concerning the Commercial Club, loudly sympathizing with the IWWs."[39] He continued, "I heard gray-haired women, mothers and wives, gentle, kindly, I know, in their home circles, openly hoping that the IWWs would come back and 'clean up.'"[40]

One issue upon which there was no disagreement was the right of women to form and join unions. In 1917, 20 percent of the workforce was female, with the largest occupation being trade, followed by domestic service. Women strikers were supported, often celebrated. In June, laundry workers in Seattle launched an organization drive, soon tripling their membership. On June 14, seven hundred female laundry workers struck, joined by two hundred male drivers. It was about time. Alice Lord, testifying years earlier at the US Commission on Industrial Relations, had reported "sad scenes of misery" in the laundries.[41] The strikers were joined by two hundred male drivers. In the face of employers who refused to meet with the union, the women demanded recognition of the organization and a new wage scale. The women, who worked in cramped quarters, breathing steamy air stinking of dirty clothes and cleaning chemicals, demanded better working conditions as well. They lifted and carried heavy bundles of wet clothing, in stifling heat and on damp concrete floors.[42] These workers were widely considered "the hardest worked and poorest paid in the industrial field."[43]

The strike hit Seattle's laundries hard, all seventeen laundries affiliated with the Seattle Laundry Owners' Club. Within a week, the press announced that all the major laundries were crippled or closed. Hotels and clubs experienced shortages of linen. The *Seattle Times* predicted the "family washtub would emerge from oblivion in thousands of Seattle homes." The laundry drivers struck as well, reporting that they were recruiting strikebreakers. "There is honest work for every man [i.e., strikebreaker] in Seattle; other employers are willing to place imported drivers who quit the laundry wagons."[44] Support for the strike was widespread: the CLC endorsed it, the Teamsters pledged financial support, and the Butchers warned members to avoid "unfair establishments." The strikers took their case to the neighborhoods: a fair in Fremont, a parade in Rainier Valley, a march through the city center. Described by the *Seattle Times* as the union's "militant business agent," the strikers' spokeswoman, Joanna Hilts, told the press, "The women were ready and willing to fight for ten years if necessary."[45] On July 7, stung by hostile public opinion, the employers capitulated. granting full union recognition and the closed shop. The laundries agreed to reinstate and meet the pay demands of all employees: laundry workers, engineers, and drivers.

In October, the "telephone girls" struck, that is, the switchboard operators who worked for Pacific Telephone and Telegraph struck for higher wages. The cost of living, as elsewhere, provoked the strikers. They had worked without a wage increase since 1914, while the new wartime economy was opening better, higher-paying work for women. The strikers rejected the claim that they were interlopers in the world of work, "girls" living at home, in anticipation of marriage and homes of their own. "The truth is we have been shamefully underpaid," one member complained to the CLC, "and that we have been forced to fight for everything we ever got from the Seattle Telephone Company."[46]

The Seattle operators had already joined a coast-wide movement to represent women in the western states led by the International Brotherhood of Electrical Workers (IBEW), the union representing the company's male electrical workers. The Seattle operators demanded recognition for their union, and the closed shop, while also asking for wage increases, shift differentials, double time for Sunday and holiday work, straight eight-hour shifts (no split shifts), and paid vacations. Their slogan: "We ask the company for none of its charity; we ask only for justice."[47]

When negotiations in San Francisco broke down, both operators and electrical workers in Washington duly quit work, only to learn that California workers had stayed on the job. The Seattle workers responded by taking charge of the union's Northwest Conference and continuing the strike. The key issues for the men were wages; they joined in the demand for the recognition of the operators' union. Some nine hundred Seattle operators were out. In mid-November, the IBEW in San Francisco reached a settlement, brokered by US Secretary of Labor William B. Wilson, that consisted of wage increases for the men but no recognition for the women. The Seattle-based strike committee rejected the deal, telegraphing Wilson: "We cannot in justice to our cause recede from the paramount issue, full recognition of the operators of the Northwest."[48] They also wired Duncan, then at the national AFL convention in Buffalo, urging him to press for the Federation's endorsement of the strike "as of vital importance to the Pacific Coast movement." Which he did.[49]

In late November, a new settlement was announced from San Francisco. This time additional wage increases for the men (though still less than they had demanded) and recognition of the operators, but no closed shop. The Portland, Tacoma, and Spokane locals voted to accept the offer, but Seattle stayed out, still backed by the CLC. Then, however, the federal government intervened, finding that the strike "hampered the country's effectiveness in war." Secretary Wilson intervened in person. In December the nine hundred operators and 170 electrical workers returned to their jobs. Speaking for the operators, Rhoda Kerr conceded they had not won everything they had wanted, importantly the closed shop. Still, they had won recognition, overcoming long-standing employer resistance and establishing themselves as permanent members of the labor movement.[50] Blanche Johnson, elected business agent after the strike, would go on to become the women's organizer for the CLC. And they would fight again. "Solidarity wins," proclaimed the *Seattle Daily Call*, simultaneously denouncing "the traitorous international officers and the divisions in the ranks fomented by them and the company." Moreover, women workers had gained entry to formerly all-male bastions: the electrical workers, the machinists, the butchers.[51] Seattle's women workers had won widespread respect for organization and militancy. At the same time, according to their historian, Karen Adair, this "experienced nucleus of union women helped build the tradition of cooperation between men and women in the Seattle labor movement."[52]

JAMES DUNCAN'S REPORT WOULD NOT have included that the IWW too was growing. The new Chicago offices, the consolidation of Bill Haywood's leadership, and the explosion of the Agricultural Workers Organization all brought a new enthusiasm to the IWW. In the words of labor historian Melvyn Dubofsky, it "infected" the IWW with a new "enthusiasm." IWW "organizers inundated the mining and lumber regions of northern Minnesota, the forests of the Inland Empire, and the wheat, fruit and hop fields of Washington and Oregon."[53] In 1917, the IWW's national membership was estimated to be 100,000, though that figure might be low. Federal authorities would claim that it had reached 250,000 that year. Fueled by the demands of the European war, the thriving economy promised jobs, and jobs for the IWW meant class struggle. In the Northwest, two of three jobs remained concentrated in the forests and the lumber mills. In Seattle, the war economy meant work on the waterfront, but throughout the city, industry prospered, including in Seattle's booming shipyards. The socialist *Daily Call* estimated there were some 20,000 IWWs in western Washington alone.[54]

The IWW's appetite was unquenchable. Its long-anticipated assault on the timber industry, interrupted by Everett, was now its top priority, yet IWW organizers were simultaneously working in scores of settings. In October 1916, The *Industrial Worker* announced victories in eastern Washington. Supremely confident, a banner headline proclaimed, "Yakima and Wenatchee Licked, Now Let's Get Everett."[55] This referred to October 1916 victories in the apple orchards of Wenatchee and Cashmere. There migrant fruit harvesters found themselves assisted by striking Puget Sound longshoremen working for survival in the harvest.[56] In Yakima, the authorities arrested some sixty strikers and jailed them in an abandoned wooden shack. The prisoners tore down the shack and escaped only to be recaptured by vigilantes who took them to the Northern Pacific Railroad tracks and put them into boxcars to be deported. The railway workers, however, rose to the occasion and refused to move the cars; the strikers were released and then carried on until victory.[57] Not without reprisals, unfortunately. Helen Keller, writing for the *Liberator*, reported, "In Washington State, at Pasco and throughout the Yakima Valley, many 'IWW' members have been arrested without warrants, thrown into 'bull-pens' without access to attorney, denied bail and trial by jury, and some of them shot. Did any of the leading newspapers denounce these acts as unlawful, cruel, undemocratic? No."[58]

In March 1917, lumber workers met in Spokane where they founded Lumber Workers Industrial Union No. 500. They primarily represented former AWO members in eastern Washington, Idaho, and Montana, but delegates from the Great Lakes, Oregon, and western Washington attended as well—the latter returning home to organize the Seattle district of the new union. The membership determined that the first item of business was to strike the Spokane district in the coming summer. Their demands included: "an eight-hour day; a minimum wage of $60 a month and board; springs, mattresses, and bedding to be furnished by the companies; shower baths and drying rooms, and an all-around improvement of conditions in the camp; abolition of the hospital fee; and all men [to] be hired from the Union Hall."[59] In these strikes, the IWW increasingly focused on the workers' most immediate demands. They made no excuse for this, nor should they have. Conditions in the camps were appalling. One non-IWW "lumberjack" reported: "More than 200 of us slept in one big room, with a roaring stove in the middle . . . around which all our wet and stinking clothes were hung. We slept two in a bunk and there were three tiers." The steam "from the clothes was so heavy that our blankets were wet, and you could hardly see across the room. The bunk-house was never cleaned out. In most of the camps the bedding is alive with lice and vermin."[60]

The timber industry was quiet each winter but revived in the spring with the melting snow. The spring of 1917 came with spontaneous strikes throughout the Spokane district. In June, the union met again, this time setting a July 1 deadline for the strike. The workers in the camps, however, would not wait. Wildcat strikes spread quickly from one camp to the next, and the union was forced to call all out immediately. "The men," writes Rowan, "left the woods in the thousands and in a short time practically all the camps in eastern Washington, Idaho and Montana were shut down and the lumber industry of short log country was paralyzed."[61] They established a network of pickets, organized strike camps, and elected delegates to assemble in Spokane as the strike committee.

From their side, the lumbermen too prepared for the strike. The Washington Employers Association first hosted a gathering of management in early 1916, then met again in San Francisco "for the sole purpose of dealing with the labor question."[62] They came together once more in Portland where they were unanimous in pledging commitment to the open shop and founded the Lumberman's Open Shop Association.[63] According to a manager of the Puget Mill, "We are fighting for the open-shop principle, and the right to hire whoever we please."[64] If the employers were at all shaken by the Everett events, it was not apparent in the woods. German agents, they claimed, were behind the strike. They dispatched spies, guards, and gunmen to the camps and recruited strikebreakers, meanwhile pressing their politicians for "Criminal Syndicalism" laws. The first of these was passed in Idaho; by 1918, they were in place virtually everywhere. The timberland press demanded martial law. The government sent troops into the Yakima Valley, arrested hundreds of strikers, held IWW members in "bull pens" without trial, and boarded and searched passenger trains. There were appeals, though these were universally rebuffed. A Pasco judge turned one down, arguing that Washington "was in a state of insurrection."[65]

In the meantime, the loggers of western Washington organized. In July, in Seattle, they sponsored a "convention" attended by delegates from throughout the district. The convention resolved that the strike would be led "on the job"—that is, by the rank-and-file workers. Decision-making would be done in "the real local union," not in district offices. Wherever there are seven or more members, they would "hold business meetings, take in members, collect dues and spread literature" on the job.[66] The convention set July 16 as the strike date. The demands in western Washington were identical to those east of the mountains. The eight-hour day became the chief issue. It gave the strike its identity.

The employers also focused on the eight-hour day demand. They held the ten-hour day sacred, though for no apparent reason, surely not in the summer of 1917, with the boom the war brought. But these lumbermen, Melvyn Dubofsky explains, invoked the old Calvinist ethos: "Work, however miserable, was a blessing, not an exaction; the longer a man toiled, the better he was for it. Rather than see their employees labor fewer hours in the woods and mills and squander their extra hours on books and drink, lumbermen preferred to work their hands longer, and in the process, make them better men."[67]

The strike in western Washington spread as rapidly and thoroughly as that in the east; within days there were tens of thousands on strike, ultimately perhaps as many as 50,000, in the largest such strike ever. The *Industrial Worker* reported thousands of loggers and their wives "signing cards" in what became—in the first weeks, certainly—a sort of rolling festival of mass meetings, picnics, and parades. In Aberdeen at Grays Harbor, a "monster" picnic with food, games, sports, speeches, and singing was organized by the

Finnish IWW. With thousands participating, the strikers chartered boats and offered excursions to the celebrants. One boat visited Aberdeen's "twin," Hoquiam, then turned south singing to onlookers as they passed through industrial shores crowded with mills, to arrive at Westport where waitresses wearing IWW buttons, members of the Domestic Workers Industrial Union, had prepared a banquet.

The strikers paraded through Sedro Woolley, a timber and coal mining town on the Skagit River, to the IWW hall that was packed to overflowing. They learned that all the mills in the Bellingham district were closed. In the spirit of "harmony," the AFL joined them in the struggle for the eight-hour day. The AFL had its own union in the fray—the Brotherhood of Timber Workers. The exchanges between these unions' leaders were harsh and bitter, though it seems that neither the employers nor the rank and file always appreciated their differences. Gompers, as usual, attacked the IWW strikers as "subversives," urging all parties, except the IWW, to negotiate. The employers, not caring which union it was, refused. Robert Bruere, a Bellingham mill owner, put it this way: "In a war—and a strike is a war—anything is fair. We have fought the IWW, we would have fought any attempt of the AFL unions to control the workers in the camps. . . . We have been consistently opposed to collective agreements with either the IWW or the AFL, and we are opposed to the recognition of any labor organization."[68]

On both sides of the mountains, then, the lumbermen stubbornly resisted any hint of compromise. The sheriffs arrested strikers without charge, bull pens became normal sights in the state's small towns and villages. On July 15, Washington's Supreme Court issued an injunction against picketing in the Grays Harbor district. Governor Ernest Lister, who earlier had proposed that a "Patriotic League" be organized in each of the state's counties, ordered in the National Guard to break the strike. This failed, even if hundreds of IWW strikers were arrested and then herded into the bull pens and jails. Three weeks after it began, the strike remained solid. On August 3, the *Oregonian* reported that in Grays Harbor: "Although the strike which is tying up the lumber industry of this section is now nearing the close of the third week, the strikers are firm, and no sign of a possible settlement has appeared. Of Gray's Harbor's 25 mills, only eight are in operation. Of her camps only three are running and all four shipyards are closed down. It is estimated that 5,600 men are idle as a result of the strike."[69] Solidarity strikes broke out in shipyards throughout the state, the result of sympathetic workers boycotting "ten-hour" lumber.[70]

Nevertheless, the strike began to wane in August, with settlements taking place here and there. In Tacoma, five mills agreed to institute the eight-hour day, though the banks backing the employers sabotaged the agreement. At the same time, workers began heading back to the camps, penniless, and often hungry. Then came the inevitable repression, the arrest and imprisonment of the strike's organizer, James Rowan, on August 19, along with twenty others in Spokane. Then the closure of the IWW hall, and the proclamation of martial law. Astonishingly, the city was occupied by National Guardsmen who crossed the boundary from Idaho. Governor Lister, in Olympia, was apparently more concerned with events on his side of the mountains.[71] Cries for federal intervention grew louder, the Northwest's lumbermen loudest, and the "patriots" becoming increasingly hysterical.

In a shameful decision, the government responded. On September 5, federal agents began arresting leaders of the IWW. Historian William Preston Jr., in his prescient account, wrote that "the lumber operators of the Northwest provided the initial impetus in the evolution of federal policy."[72] The months that followed brought vigilantism, military surveillance, police raids, ransacked offices, blacklisting, and mass arrests. This policy would escalate into a savage war on the IWW, and ultimately lead to its effective ruin. The US entry into the European bloodbath had turned dissent into treason. The federal government now attacked the IWW with "gloves off" nationwide, indicting its top leadership. One hundred and sixty-six went on trial the following year in

Chicago, all convicted on an array of conspiracy charges. James P. Thompson, J. A. Macdonald, J. T. Doran, and James Rowan were among the one hundred IWW leaders who would be tried and convicted in Chicago, then sent to the Leavenworth Federal Penitentiary in Kansas.

The federal government then became the leading strikebreaker, organizing a rival organization, the Loyal Legion of Loggers and Lumbermen. This project was the brainchild of US Army Colonel Brice P. Disque, who convinced the Wilson administration to submit the Northwest timber industry to military discipline. In November, with a cohort of one hundred officers, Disque met in Centralia with the leading lumbermen, persuading them to sponsor a new labor organization with the goal of ending the strike—and strikes to come. Individual workers would pledge the following loyalty oath:

> I, the undersigned . . . do hereby solemnly pledge my efforts during the war to the United States of America and will support and defend this country against enemies foreign and domestic. I further swear . . . to faithfully perform my duty toward this company, by directing my best efforts, in every way possible, to the production of logs and lumber for the construction of Army airplanes and ships to be used against our common enemies.[73]

Disque successfully recruited Gompers to the project. Typically, Seattle's metal workers resisted, ordering Duncan to write to Wilson with the demand that Disque be fired.[74] By the war's end, the Loyal Legion would claim one thousand locals and tens of thousands of members.

In mid-September the strike looked as if it were broken. According to Rowan, "The lines of communication [in Spokane] had been disorganized by the jailing and persecution of the men in the strike camps." The Seattle district held a referendum and voted to go back on the job.[75] This the lumbermen hailed as a victory, but it was not.

In fact, the IWW planned to continue the strike "on the job." This meant that a crew would come to work but leave after eight hours, to be followed by the next crew which would do the same. The *Industrial Worker* reported that thirty workers from the Big Lake Camp near Bellingham "worked one day then quit after eight hours. They were fired but this crippled the camp. These fellow workers have gone through three other camps this way."[76] "We are asking for eight hours," a striker explained to Anna Louise Strong. "Well, sometimes we just stay in bed and get up late and have only time for eight hours. And sometimes we go to work on time, but quit at the end of eight hours. Usually we get fired for doing it and then a lot of us quit and the boss has to build the crew again. The new crew acts in the same way."[77] The *Industrial Worker* registered dozens of such examples. Wobblies "malingered, soldiered, walked off the job without warning," leaving the employers with no recourse.[78] The Washington State Council of Defense reported camps operating at only 50 percent capacity, scarcely keeping up with the war demands. It also found workers still joining the IWW. By February 1918, despairing employers began instituting the eight-hour day as the only way to maintain their crews. In March 1918 the employers, pressured by the government, ceded; the result was a sensation. The workers had won the eight-hour day and a long list of improvements in the conditions of the camps. This triumph in the woods—surely one of the IWW's greatest accomplishments—became a source of widespread class pride. It added to the accumulation of radical workers to Seattle, and it deepened consciousness. It also brought repression, foretelling both good and bad to come. Ultimately, the isolation and destruction of the IWW is one of the great tragedies in US working-class history. Its tragic character becomes all the more evident when one reflects on the absence of this movement and these people in the strikes of 1919.

FINALLY, SHIPBUILDING. THE INDUSTRY in Seattle began with the construction of wooden barges, river boats, and the small fleets of schooners, steamers, and cargo craft that plied the Sound, and was enhanced by the Alaskan Gold Rush, then by imperial expansion westward across the Pacific. War in that region meant business, and Seattle's industrialists responded with enthusiasm, as they would again and again in the decades to come. The first result was a steel torpedo boat completed in 1898 and dispatched to the Philippines. Later came the construction of the battleship *Nebraska*. By 1914, there were twenty-six shipyards in operation. The largest was Skinner and Eddy, and by then it was producing for the next war, this one across the Atlantic.

The heavy industry of the shipyards was as "dark and Satanic" as any of William Blake's mills. When the CLC's former president Hulet Wells, was awaiting sentencing for opposing conscription, he sought temporary employment at work at Skinner and Eddy. There he found a "howling bedlam . . . a wilderness of strange machines, whirling belts and belching fires. . . . The human ant heap boiled with all the specialists that fit into the modern shipyard. Everywhere there was deafening noise, boilers rang, planers screamed, long white-hot rods were smashed into bolt machines. Here was the angle-bending floor where black men beat a tattoo with heavy sledges, and here a steam hammer thumped its measured blows."[79] Add to this the wrenching scenes of the injured, the sirens of the ambulances, and the dying or dead being carted off into the chaos of the waterfront roadways.[80]

The yards employed an astonishing array of workers: welders, winchmen, pattern makers, angle smiths, riggers, riveters, crane men, furnace men, press and machine operators, boilermakers, drillers, reamers, blacksmiths, machinists, electricians, molders, carpenters, and painters. The workforce was far from homogenous, with every ethnicity employed, though with young men, most of northern European origin, predominating. A few women and black workers were scattered throughout the yards. Their union status remains unclear. More than a dozen craft unions operated in the sector, all affiliated with the AFL, dividing the workers by job and skill. Nevertheless, the diverse craft unions were united by the

Metal Trades Council, which in turn was affiliated with the CLC. The latter affiliation jibed with the aims of the movement's centralizers and those of the advocates of industrial unionism.

Strikes were commonplace in the shipyards. There were two walkouts in 1915—both at Seattle Construction and Dry Dock—and many took place in 1916. "All through the war," remembered Wells, "the Metal Trades Council, which negotiated as a unit, had been in conflict with the government on shipyard wages."[81] In 1917 and 1918, the city's unions increasingly felt pressure from the federal government and its shipping board. The unions were especially intent on raising the wages of the unskilled and semi-skilled, an immediate necessity in breaking down divisions in the shops. However, wage demands were repeatedly rejected, and by the war's end, the workers felt betrayed by the government. They were bitter, angry with the owners; they feared unemployment and the return of the open shop. The January strike was inevitable.

Seattle's workers daily faced injury and sometimes death. Kate Sadler divided them into "those who have been murdered quickly and those whose lives have been one long agony of toil."[82] They were heavily exploited and lived lives segregated from their exploiters—in space, in quality of life, in expectations and outcomes—and they looked at themselves as a class apart. They lived in poor neighborhoods with poor housing; the poorest still lived in shacks along the tide flats and industrial waterways, some living in houseboats, often little more than rafts with tarps and crude shelters. They lived with poor schools, and poor social facilities, conditions not so different from those that many had left behind.

Still, they called each other "sister" and "brother" and created a culture of their own with scores of newspapers, socialist schools, IWW singing, community dances and picnics, lectures indoors and out, and, of course, their unions and political parties. The idea of "workers' control" was not a utopian goal but a practical one they wanted in the here and now. It was a culture that challenged a system where hunger and cold, prostitution, intemperance, poverty, slavery, crime, premature old age and mortality, panic, and industrial terror pervaded social life: a system that made things out of humans. This culture valued equality, cooperation, and solidarity; its roots were in the utopian settlements and the dream of a workers' cooperative in "God's Country." It was created in struggle. Simultaneously looking backwards and forwards, it envisioned a better world.

6. LEFT, RIGHT, AND CENTER

Eugene Debs, in his own words, was "baptized in Socialism in the roar of conflict," in "practical struggle," "in the gleam of every bayonet and the flash of every rifle the class struggle was revealed."[1] Simultaneously, he embraced industrial unionism. Later he would write, while still a member of the IWW, the pamphlet "Craft Unionism,"[2] in which he confessed to readers: "Speaking for myself, I was made to realize long ago that the old trade union was utterly incompetent to deal successfully with the exploiting corporations in this struggle. I was made to see that in craft unionism the capitalist class have it in their power to keep the workers divided, to use one part of them with which to conquer and crush another part of them."[3]

This was the issue of the day. Even the conservative, craft-dominated AFL had its progressive wing, with a program including amalgamating the crafts, promoting stewards' organizations, a labor party, welfare legislation, and mutual assistance or solidarity. Then there was the example of the coal miners' union, the United Mine Workers (UMWA), long organized on the industrial model. Moreover, the war years brought industrial restructuring, new demands, and deadlines even in old industries, such as shipbuilding where metal workers, "hitherto rather conservative, "became in most countries of the world the characteristic leaders of militant labor organizations."[4]

When he spoke in Seattle in 1915 to the big meeting at the Dreamland Rink, Debs, no longer a member of the IWW, now spokesman for the Socialist Party (SP), repeated this conviction; echoing the IWW's endorsement of industrial unionism, he proclaimed "support for a consolidation of all labor crafts and other organizations of the laboring man and woman into one great industrial union."[5] In Seattle, he was preaching to the choir. There, the consolidation of the crafts into twelve sections—a project identified as "Duncanism" after James Duncan—was already underway. Seattle had 120 separate and independent trade unions organized by jobs—tailors, carpenters, waitresses, barbers, builders, Teamsters. Jurisdiction was assigned accordingly. Plumbers, for example, did not do the work of carpenters. Nevertheless, 90 percent of Seattle's workers, craft workers included, supported amalgamation and industrial unions, unions organized by industry and the closed shop, with union members only to be hired. They were quite willing to fight for these goals. They wanted Seattle to be a union town and saw themselves as organizing a united working-class movement to achieve this.

The IWW was the champion of industrial unionism. But many Socialists were also advocates. Seattle socialists had been influenced by Debs but also by the raw avarice of frontier capitalism. There the "reds" had won a long struggle among factions and were proponents of industrial unionism, while fiercely criticizing the party's national leadership for supporting the craft union-dominated AFL and its leader Samuel Gompers. At one point Debs joined the Western Federation of Miners' president Ed Boyce (alienated by Gompers's refusal to aid embattled strikers in Leadville, Colorado) in a plan to renovate the labor movement through a federation of the miners in the UMW and the WFM. Debs was proposing organizing drives in the new industries and combatting the craft unions. All this made sense to many in

Seattle, even if it was repellent to the Socialist Party's national leaders.

Debs was a man of his times. He was both a product and an agent of a new, widespread mood sweeping through the working-class movements. This mood included the growth of class consciousness, combativeness, solidarity, and a radical spirit reflected in the strikes taking place in these years. Mass involvement and direct action in the strikes led to new solidarities and broke down ethnic isolation. The strikers challenged managerial authority, waging intense, violent battles that sometimes spilled out of the workplace into the working-class neighborhood, even when the issues were pure and simple (wages, hours, working conditions). Workers came to reject the AFL along with its traditions and practices: conservativism, collaboration with employers and the state, insistence on the sanctity of contracts, jurisdiction by craft, and the strict authority of the trade union leaders.

The IWW, too, was the product of these times. And if Debs came to symbolize the mood, the IWW fueled its flames, taking radical, workplace-based socialism into the shops, pressuring others to do the same. The IWW was founded in 1905 in Chicago, "the Continental Congress of the Working Class," according to its best-known member, William "Big Bill" Haywood. Its roots were in the West, however. The IWW championed "job socialism." It insisted it was not a political party. It became known for audacious strikes and fearless confrontations, as well as its revolutionary vision—including One Big Union and the general strike. The latter, its exact meaning and purpose always somewhat vague, might be simply a weapon in the workers' arsenal. Or it might imply the final conflict. Or both.

The IWW originated in the factions of the Socialist Party, but also had roots in the harsh, bloody conflicts in the West, above all in the battles of the hard-rock miners of the Western Federation of Miners. It championed the poorest, the itinerant laborers, and the immigrants. It sought to build a fighting organization, one with its doors open to all, to unskilled workers, blacks, Latinos, women, and workers of all nationalities, reviving the best elements of the legendary Knights of Labor. The IWW shed all interest in political parties, renouncing parliamentary perspectives in favor of direct action at the workplace and industrial democracy. "Parliaments," the Wobblies argued, "are little more than clearing houses for the exchange of vague and sterile platitudes. In so far as they do more than this, they merely further the designs of the big business groups whom they serve as retainers."[6] If the IWW was defiantly revolutionary, it stood with both feet on the ground, focusing on the conditions and demands of real workers. And it fought for them, with ideas—direct, militant action and industrial unions—that were straightforward, even simple.

The term "syndicalism" was taken from *syndicalisme/sindical-ismo*, the French/Spanish words meaning trade union. In its US iteration, syndicalism's adherents, such as those grouped around the IWW, supported One Big Union, focusing on class and class struggle. For them, the working class constituted the force for change, and the economic terrain was its natural battlefield. "Direct action . . . [was] its natural weapon, and self-directed labor associations . . . [were] the natural agencies for uniting, marshaling and applying the collective and ultimately revolutionary power of the workers."[7] The mine, mill, and logging camp became the foci for American syndicalists, as the places where industrial workers came together and where industrial unions seemed most likely to succeed. They rejected the parliamentary road, not only because power sprang from the point of production, but also because many millions of people remained ineligible for the vote: women, blacks, immigrants, migrants, the homeless, those far from home, and those with criminal records.

The IWW believed that its organization would be built through the experience of strikes, strikes that taught workers the reality of the class struggle and strengthened their sense of power. Consequently, the organization felt that the strikes should never be abandoned or signed away with a contract. If the workers settled temporarily with employers, this was in the spirit of truce but never peace. The contract between an employer and a workman, the IWW said, "is no more binding than the title deed to a Negro slave is just." Industrial power, they argued, was the basis of social power. "Whenever the workers are organized in industry," said their spokesman, Vincent St. John, "they will have all the organization they need." They envisioned a future system in which "each worker will have a share in the ownership and a voice in the control of industry, and to which each shall receive the full product of his [labor]."[8]

The IWW fought wherever called upon. Its battles in Lawrence, Paterson, McKees Rocks, and the woodlands in the Deep South are still celebrated and rightly so. Nevertheless, its outlook fit the West, where workers routinely left one job or employer for another. Seniority had little value in that context, making the newly hired less fearful of dismissal. Workers' grievances frequently needed settling at once, encouraging direct action: the slow-down, sit-down, and walkout. The risks in this setting were fewer; these were workers with little or nothing to lose. It was the law of the jungle, but it might be turned to favor the worker—at harvest time or when the ship was meant to sail. By the same token, planning, building strike funds, and time-consuming mediation often seemed extraneous.

The IWW, however, insisted it was not syndicalist—to the contrary, it championed "industrial socialism." It had little time for Georges Sorel, the French theorist who advocated syndicalism, and even less for anarchism or anarcho-syndicalism. In principle, the IWW rejected violence and prioritized organization, though there was always tension given the ferocity of the violence inflicted upon it. Abstract issues were resolved through practice. Were they indeed all leaders? And were the industrial unions to be tightly organized or loosely? Should there be a national office? If so, what would its functions be? The answers to these questions were never entirely clear. And they varied with circumstances. The loggers were scattered across thousands of square miles, isolated in remote camps and mills, this meant that each worker was truly a leader. The longshoremen, by contrast, fought an intense battle to capture the ILA, a battle that in Seattle demanded concerted action over decades.

The IWW's enemies were merciless. AFL chieftains ridiculed the Wobblies as "half-baked and backward," and the right-wingers in the Socialist Party belittled the organization as at best "theoretically underdeveloped." Of course, they also rejected "its calls for solidarity, direct action up to and including ca'canny (the deliberate limiting of output at work), and the irrational strike, reliance on the power of the workers themselves, and the assumption that a final conflict, whether or not in the shape of a General Strike, was sure to follow."[9]

Still, the IWW had its supporters. These included local union officers and individual workers who were the AFL's closed shops, either "captives" there or those who chose to "bore from within"— that is, deliberately seeking employment in AFL shops with the intention of challenging the union there. There were anarchist-syndicalists of various stripes and free-wheeling militants. In the Socialist Party, attitudes toward the IWW were often the dividing line between left and right. The editors of the *International Socialist Review* supported the Wobblies, as did the editors of *The Masses* and its successor, *The Liberator*. *The Messenger*, the voice of the "New Negro," reflected the views of its young editors, Chandler Owen and A. Philip Randolph, who advocated an international workers' movement, allying blacks and whites. They opposed some unions and supported others, first the IWW, which they encouraged blacks to join.[10] Canadian socialists rejected electoral politics in favor of the One Big Union, as did much of Seattle's left.

James Duncan acknowledged his debt to the IWW, calling them "the pacesetters." He was born in Fife, the son of a Scottish shipwright. At seventeen, Duncan began an apprenticeship as a machinist, then took to the sea as a marine engineer. In 1904, at twenty-four, he settled in Seattle, sent home for his fiancée, then married. He was a strict Calvinist, a prohibitionist, and a Sunday School teacher, once reported to have said, "I will make a Sunday School out of Seattle." Katsutoshi Kurokawa, author of *The Labor*

Movement and Japanese Immigrants in Seattle, points to Duncan's inauguration as a "milestone" because of his sympathies toward the Japanese immigrants.[11] Duncan led the progressives in the CLC; it would make no sense to call him a conservative or even a moderate, except in a strictly Seattle context. Clearly, he was not a revolutionary, though he had once been a member of the Socialist Party. Duncan believed in industrial unions, however, and he felt at home in the West. "I found in my travels across the country that in the East the people are more conservative . . . It seems to me that if there is any reform in the labor movement it will come from the West."[12] For Duncan, as for many others, "East" was synonymous with Wall Street, the bankers, and the trusts. He supported the idea of One Big Union, but the "talk of One Big Union in Washington is not very practical here."[13]

Duncan's power in Seattle, as one account of his leadership explained, "did not result from his ability in long-range planning or sophisticated economic analysis, but rather from his force of character, willpower, and willingness to work. For all his toughness and rigid moral views, he was not dictatorial. He would not have dominated Seattle labor without the support of other men with similar views who were themselves well-known and well-placed in the labor movement. With these men, Duncan was *primus inter pares.* He could lead them and the rest of Seattle labor because he knew just how far they could be pushed without rebelling."[14] *Union Record* editor Harry Ault concurred: "We do not have labor leaders here. That is a funny thing. Mr. Duncan is secretary of the Central Labor Council, and we allow him to speak for us officially on most matters. . . . I do not believe that even Mr. Duncan thinks he is a leader. We have not anybody that runs the show here."[15]

For all that, the Seattle labor movement took on the name "Duncanism." He was a centralizer; he believed in strong unions that the CLC would control. For Duncan, trade union solidarity began with close cooperation among all the trades in any industry through trades councils, organizationally linked to the CLC. Also, agreements with management in any given industry had to be set to expire simultaneously, allowing the unions to bargain as a unit. Duncan campaigned for these revisions not just at home, but for the AFL as well. There he proposed the "elimination of the 125 international unions and their replacement by 12 great industrial divisions."[16] Most often he worked with Socialists. The socialist Hulet Wells had preceded him in the Council's leadership, and fellow party member Sam Sadler led the longshoremen.[17] Anna Louise Strong, the *Union Record*'s most prolific writer, was sympathetic to the IWW, if not a member. The Metal Trades Council was Duncanism on the ground.[18] Duncan's home base was the machinists; he was president of the Hope Lodge of Machinists and President of Machinists District Council. He was respected throughout the movement, but it was the Metal Trades Council that gave him power. There discontented craft unionists combined belief in strong organization with a radical outlook, believing workers deserved far better than they then received.[19] Duncan also supported the October Revolution, claiming, "No single event throughout the whole world today can, from the standpoint of workers everywhere, compare in importance with the successful piloting of the Russian Soviet Republic past the treacherous rocks of international capitalist greed and the determination of these plunderers to ruin what they cannot rule."[20]

The Wobblies and their supporters have often been condemned as romantics or perhaps as idealists in the face of the march of history where more cold-blooded theorists might be wanted. Their achievements are condemned as fleeting contrasted to the institutions of the realists. The same has been said about Seattle's socialists. Whatever truth there is to these claims, they seem to misunderstand the Wobblies' project. The IWW was not determinist in any sense, which helps to explain its emphasis on equality, solidarity, education, and action. There was a deep humanism in its socialism as well as a moral horizon. The capitalist system was wrong, they argued, and it followed that Victor Berger's sewer socialism and Samuel Gompers's business unionism was as well; these were not to be reduced to simple practicalities. For the Wobblies, the challenge was not to prop up or accommodate oneself to capitalism but to abolish it. Only the workers could build a movement for emancipation. The legacy of the IWW, then, is less about socialist theory and politics, economic formulas, laws and institutions, and more about the "whys" and "hows" of transforming society. Their impact on others was powerful and remains so.

Consider the stance of Elizabeth Gurley Flynn. In the aftermath of the Lawrence textile strike she wrote this wrenching indictment of the workers' conditions:

> Hunger, want, scarcity of work, drives all workers to accept an ever-lower standard, and women the lowest . . . [still] illusions die hard, and one is "the sanctity of the home." But a visit to Lawrence, Mass. would bring rapid disillusionment. The golden dream of youth, that marriage brings release from irksome toil, is rudely shattered by the capitalist system. Whole families toil for a living wage. The heaviest burden is on the tired frame of the woman. Childbearing and housework remain. Pregnant women stand at the looms until the labor pains commence. A few weeks later, the puny babe is left at a day nursery with amateur "nurses"—with the result that 300 babies out of every thousand die in the first month. The gutter is the babies' playground and amid the deafening clatter of the looms the mother's heart is torn with anxiety about her children. Miscarriage from overstrain is common, and unscrupulous doctors secure exorbitant sums to perform abortions, that the women may keep at work. But to tell these women toilers how to control birth is a state prison offense in the United States; and so, they die, 25,000 yearly from operations.[21]

Haywood in his pamphlet "Industrial Socialism," written in 1911 with Frank Bonn, expressed much the same outlook, in sharp contrast to the utilitarians and determinists. There Haywood described the plight of young workers "born of parents broken and weary from work, and themselves underfed and sent early to the factories . . . They desire rest and leisure, a chance to know their family and friends better, and an occasional vacation in the country. They wish to read, hear good music and go to theaters. Above all they crave better food and more of it and they know that their limbs are stiff because of the lack of enough rest and exercise."[22] Such themes dominated the IWW appeal to the country's ordinary workers; they would fight for better food, but also for a better world.

The IWW fiercely asserted its separation from the mainstream labor movement and mainstream socialists, because on so many points of principle the organizations parted ways. The Socialist Party's motto may have been "Workers of the world, unite," but in truth it had "an extraordinary number of members who were not of the working class. Socialist leadership particularly, as in many of the social democratic parties of Europe, was heavily weighted with lawyers, journalists, and teachers, many of whom had never earned a day's wages with the skill of their hands or the strength of their backs."[23] By contrast, the IWW's Frank Little argued that workers would never achieve their goals if led by lawyers in a "political ballot party," adding, "We can never do it as long as we depend upon going out and sticking a piece of white paper into a capitalist ballot box." Little, a western organizer member of the Executive Committee, identified himself as having "Indian blood." He was a veteran of countless western conflicts and an outspoken opponent of the war. In the summer of 1917, deported from Arizona, he went to Butte, Montana, to help striking Mexican copper miners. On August 1, thugs in the service of the Anaconda Copper Company dragged Little from his bed in the early hours of the morning, then tortured and lynched him.[24]

Seattle's socialists were all too aware of this outrage. The free-speech victory in Spokane put the IWW and Washington State on the radical map.[25] However, the national Socialist leaders (and the right wing of the party) were unmoved. From Milwaukee, a hub of the Socialist Party, the *Herald* called the IWW's founding an "anti-AFL" convention, its supporters destined to "impotently make faces at Gompers from the outside." The Socialist Party's radicals, certainly those in Seattle, were disgusted with Milwaukee's caution, gradualism, its "one-step-at-a-time" policies, and with its general stuffiness.[26] Seattle's Socialist Party was proud to have shared the IWW's pride in Spokane. They too believed in working-class solidarity, understanding it as a foundational principle and seeking to overcome sectarian antagonisms. They also cherished free speech and the right of assembly "as their Holy Bible," wrote O'Connor. Kate Sadler was their charismatic leader, their Elizabeth Gurley Flynn. She was the movement's "flaming embodiment. Her anger at injustice was a beautiful sight . . . her elementary lessons in socialism struck deep. I heard her often and was always amazed at the simplicity of her technique. The workers loved her. Kate was the flame."[27]

Harvey O'Connor grew up in poverty in Tacoma, raised by a single mother. He discovered Debs and socialism in a school debating club project, and then discovered a socialist cigar shop and bookstore on his way home from work after school. The owner's niece, a "red-headed girl" from Kapowsin, a logging camp near Mt. Rainier, recruited him to join the Young People's Socialist League (YPSL). O'Connor went to work in the woods as a youngster, because he "had a mother and sister to support." He joined the IWW in time for the big strike: "I was a Union man and the general strike in the woods was my first labor action. The strike went on sporadically for months. We loggers would advance our demands, and when the camp was obstinate, we'd strike. The boss would fire us. And another crew would come up, and the same thing would happen, over and over, again and again, until the company gave in."[28]

In town, O'Connor's world included Will "Red" O'Hanrahan, a Skid Road radical who ran a newsstand and advertised radical and labor press from the street and soapbox. "Mounting his soapbox," O'Connor remembers, "O'Hanrahan would paraphrase the leading articles and editorials in the *Call,* as he had long done those in the *Industrial Worker* and other papers." O'Connor recalled

O'Hanrahan as one of the best speakers of the time: "His sum-
maries of the *Call's* articles were great advertising [and he was] a
popular educator, [who] often opened his radical soapboxing with
his evening commentary on the day's news in which he dissected,
to the merriment of his audience, the stories in the local dailies,
to their satisfaction, he analyzed the oddities and barbarities of
capitalism." Sometimes hundreds would gather around him for
both education and entertainment. "O'Hanrahan was ecumeni-
cal," O'Connor wrote. "He was for the socialists, the Wobblies, for
any working-class movement. He reflected the Seattle labor movement that had little or no room for animosity among unionists,
Socialists, and Wobblies."[29] Others remembered the same. Anna
Louise Strong registered relief on returning to Seattle from fac-
tion-ridden New York.[30] Milwaukee had its Congressman Victor
Berger, Los Angeles its almost-mayor, Job Harriman, but Seattle's
socialists were working class, united, and "red."

WHEN IN OCTOBER 1917 THE BOLSHEVIKS seized power in
Russia, they inspired reds all around the world. In Seattle, the revolution arrived by boat.[31] On the Friday before Christmas 1917,
under winter skies, the Russian steamer *Shilka,* red flags flying,
sailed into Seattle's Elliott Bay. The *Shilka,* out of Vladivostok, with
a cargo of beans and peas, was commanded by a soviet of Russian
sailors. Seattle's rebels of all kinds—its socialists, Wobblies, dockers, metal workers, waitresses, and shingle weavers—scrambled to
greet the visitors, as did naval officers and city police. There were
arrests, interrogations, and searches, fearing that the Russians
brought "Bolshevik gold" or perhaps munitions. There was
none; the intent of the crew was simply to refuel. Nevertheless,
the visit became cause for an extended stay. The sailors—real-
life Bolsheviks—were feted nonstop. There were testimonials,
speeches, spontaneous songs including the "Marseillaise" and the
"Red Flag," The following Sunday, hundreds of residents jammed
the IWW Hall, greeting a young sailor, Danil Teraninoff, with wild
applause. "Never in Seattle has there been such a demonstration

of revolutionary sentiment as at the moment the Russian fellow worker ascended the platform," reported the *Daily Call*, the voice of Seattle socialism.[32] Thus began the almost incomparable romance of Seattle's working people with the Russian Revolution, for where else, certainly not in the United States, was there such passionate feelings of sympathy and solidarity? Nowhere. In response, the authorities, alarmed when not hysterical, discovered conspiracies virtually everywhere but in the end found none. The fact was simply that thousands of working people welcomed the Revolution. They saw in it what they wanted in their own lives, in the here and now: peace, the workers running the factories, and the peasants taking the land. The Russian Revolution became a factor in Seattle's labor movement, just as it was in the whole wave of workers' rebellions of 1919.

Perhaps more so. The events in Russia became part of the city's self-identification. Indeed, Seattle would be the focus of anti-Bolshevik sentiment. The Bureau of Investigation (soon to be the FBI) described Seattle's radicals in the most extreme terms. They were "the scum of the earth . . . a landless and lawless mob, who, having no property themselves, recognize no rights of property . . . no law and no authority save the policeman's night stick or physical violence."[33] On the other side, Seattle's radicals and their press described the Revolution sympathetically if not glowingly. In the following two years, the *Union Record* reported closely on Russian events, featuring letters from Lenin. The *Union Record* also printed forty thousand copies of Lenin's pamphlet "Soviets at Work," with an introduction by Anna Louise Strong, which was distributed by the unions. There were numerous gestures of solidarity. In December 1918, in response to a resolution from the Electrical Workers, the CLC established a Bureau of Russian Information "to be headed by Strong."[34] The CLC delegates to the AFL's national convention pressed for official recognition of the fledgling workers' state (to no avail). When a train arrived with a load of curious crates marked "Sewing Machines," Seattle's long-shoremen grew suspicious. They "accidentally" dropped a crate to the deck, only to reveal that it was full of Remington rifles, bound for Siberia. It was then revealed that it was the US government that had chartered the ship, the *Delight*, to carry the guns on to Kolchak's "White" Army. The dockers refused to handle the cargo. The IWW longshoremen resolved that they would "rather starve than receive wages for loading ships on a mission of murder."[35]

Seattle's workers saw peasants seizing land, soldiers marching away from the trenches, marching home. They saw people fighting for freedom and welcomed them. Duncan, still the AFL man, steadfastly championed the Russian Revolution, both at home and in the AFL's regional and national assemblies.[36] And when two thousand Seattle longshoremen, overflowing their hall, celebrated the second anniversary of the October Revolution and the sixty-fourth birthday of Eugene Debs on November 7, 1919, they rose in "tremendous cheering," as J. T. Doran, the Wobbly walked to the rostrum and began to speak. Free on bail from the federal penitentiary in Atlanta, Doran delivered "an impassioned speech on the workers' revolution in Russia, 'the most stupendous event since the fall of feudalism.'" This was a high point for the longshoremen of Local 38-12. They had won the battle against the shape-up with jobs now dispatched from a single alphabetized list. There was only one more step to contemplate: "When the longshore cooperative Stevedore Company came into being, the bosses would be driven from the waterfront for all time."[37] Alas, this was not to happen. And Russia's workers would not make the leap into the realm of freedom; instead, they would suffer isolation, invasion, civil war, famine, dictatorship. Seattle's longshoremen, for their part, would have to wait for another generation to take power on the docks—this time in the defeat of the shippers in the 1934 coastal strike and the founding of the International Longshore and Warehouse Union.

The Russian Revolution was one factor in uniting Seattle's left, but events on the ground—the growing collaboration of the IWW, the Socialist Party, and the AFL unions in the CLC—were quite likely even more important. Kate Sadler, the face of Seattle's Socialists, routinely joined Wobblies on the speaking platforms of the day. In July 2017, the IWW held a mass meeting at Seattle's Dreamland Rink in support of the striking lumber workers. Sadler was the featured speaker, along with Doran. The *Industrial Worker* reported that the 3,500-strong meeting began with those assembled singing "Solidarity Forever," followed by Sadler's talk calling for "the establishment of the eight-hour day for the purpose of giving workers of the world a broader and freer life, for the purpose of teaching them that their lives and bodies are sacred; 'One reason we want the eight-hour day now is so that we will have two more hours a day in which to rebuild our strength and intelligence.'"[38]

Collaboration was not limited to the leadership but also took place in the streets, where thousands of loggers, field hands, and harvesters, who were sometimes strikers themselves, fraternized while passing through Seattle. Many stayed on and often found work in the shipyards or the waterfront, where they joined others, workers seeking not just better work but also a place where workers mattered. Importantly, many sought to avoid conscription. Others came because the city was an IWW stronghold, Seattle having a reputation as a workingman's city, a reputation, whether deserved or not, still rooted in the popular imagination. In John Dos Passos's novel, *42nd Parallel*, Mac and Ike, workers sympathetic to the IWW, are fed up with a summer working on the Canadian Pacific Railroad. In a Vancouver flophouse, they talk about escaping to Seattle: "Say Ike, what do you think we ought to do? I think we ought to go down on the boat to Seattle, Wash., like a coupla dude passengers. I want to settle down an' get a printing job, there's good money in that. I'm going to study to beat hell this winter. What do you think, Ike? I want to get out of this limejuicy hole an' get back to God's country."[39] They ended up on Skid Road, hungover, broke. But the idea of exploited workers escaping to Seattle was not all fiction, however. The mayor of Butte, visiting the Seattle shipyards, recognized large numbers of ex-miners from his hometown, which was second to no place as a center of intense class conflict.

The socialists were an important force in the Seattle labor

movement and in the antiwar movement. Seattle socialism cannot be separated from the key individuals involved. Emil Herman was the popular state secretary of the Socialist Party. A shingle weaver, he was unusual because he maintained his membership in the IWW even as he served as a member of the Socialist's Party's National Executive Committee. The son of impoverished farmers from Kamnitz, Herman was born in the Austro-Hungarian Empire, eventually settling in Seattle in 1890. He was arrested in April 1918, charged with violating the Espionage Act, and imprisoned at the McNeil Island Federal Penitentiary.

Hulet Wells was the Chair of the Socialist Party and president of the CLC in 1915 and 1916. The socialist Sam Sadler was a leader of the longshoremen and in 1918 was president of ILA Local 38-12. They both belonged to the National League Against Militarism and both were arrested in 1917 for passing out "NO CONSCRIPTION" handbills. After sentencing, they served two years in federal prisons. Harry Ault, the *Union Record*'s editor, was the son of disenchanted Populists, and his mother had fed the straggling cohorts of Coxey's Army's march on Washington, DC, as it passed through Cincinnati in 1894. They were among those who would resettle in the Northwest. The young Ault grew up in the socialist Equity Colony. At age seventeen, he edited the colony's paper, *Industrial Freedom*. Ault became a figure in the labor movement in 1907 with his coverage of the Idaho trial of radical labor leaders Bill Haywood, George Pettibone, and Charles Moyer, falsely charged with the murder of Governor Frank Steunenberg. "I remember that the first time I got up on a soap box at First and Pike in Seattle," he later wrote to O'Connor, "I began, 'Fellow citizens, the Constitution of the United States . . .' and the cop pulled me off the box and said, 'That's enough kid, come along to jail.'" More than anyone else, Ault was responsible for making the *Union Record* daily and competitive with the mainstream papers, the only union-owned paper in the country.[40]

The Wednesday night meetings of the CLC drew hundreds of delegates and more from its constituent unions. The gallery in the

Labor Temple's auditorium where the Council met "was filled with unionists, radicals, and Wobblies, listening to the dramatic debates and the speeches by visiting luminaries." Strong recalled that "every Wednesday night the Central Labor Council sat till midnight listening to emissaries of suppressed and rebelling peoples. . . . We were stirred by the seizure of factories in Germany, by the mutiny of French troops in Odessa, by the rising of soviets in Hungary and Bavaria."[41] And there, free speech was the order of the day. "The suppression anywhere of ordinary rights of free speech added zest and exhilaration to the scene as people struggled, in guarded and Aesopian terms, to express the ideas that burned within them."[42]

The IWW, the Socialists, and the CLC increasingly found themselves on the same stages, in the same demonstrations, and on the same street corners—collaborating on issues such as Everett, preparedness, May Day, and repression. The IWW remained relentless in condemning craft unions; the Socialists would not retreat on the need for a party; the Duncanites insisted on staying within the mainstream. Yet the IWW was gracious in accepting support from the CLC on Everett, and the CLC and the *Union Record* joined in celebrating the Everett trial victory. Further, it was no secret that Seattle's working people admired the courage and direct action of the loggers and the mill workers, supporting them regardless of their nominal allegiance to Gompers and his acolytes. In 1917 and 1918 there existed a *modus vivendi* on the ground.[43] More, there was a division of labor; the IWW working in the woods and fields, the CLC in the cities and in the shops. On the waterfront, cooperation was complex, but it took the form of a common front against the shippers and the ILA's International.

"I belong to the IWW for a principle and to the AFL for a job": this was the "two-card man." O'Connor suggests there may have been several thousand workers holding both AFL and IWW cards. This allowed the logger to work on the docks, the harvest hand to workers construction, and IWW members to have steady jobs in occupations and workplaces represented by AFL local unions. The national AFL leaders were scandalized; they demanded the expulsion of the two-card men. The CLC, typically, refused. Some of these workers may have been boring from within, in practice "dual unionists." The majority, however, were simply good union workers living with the reality of two working-class movements. The IWWs, the two-card men, and the CLC's rank and file rubbed shoulders, fraternized, and fused into a still provisional but radicalized militant majority in Seattle's labor movement.[44] The IWW's vision certainly pulled the others, but the IWW adapted as well, becoming ever more like the unions it still denounced—with its "on the job" strategy in the woods, its members in the city's AFL shops and local unions, and above all in the shipyard's wild multitude.

Seattle's working class, then, was unparalleled. Of course, there were radicals elsewhere, but they tended to be a fringe. In Seattle, however, there was a radical consensus. Seattle workers welcomed radical ideas as well as radical visitors, and political lines were fluid. Margaret Sanger and Emma Goldman each visited in turn during the summer of 1916. Goldman spoke on "Anarchism and Human Nature" at the Tivoli Theater, Sanger on "The Right of the Child not to Be Born" at the longshoremen's hall.[45] In the aftermath of the Russia Revolutions, Louise Bryant, Albert Rhys Williams, Raymond Robbins, Robert Minor, and Wilfred Humphries came to speak. Strong remembers when Louise Bryant returned from the revolution in Russia to dazzle the smoke-laden air of the close-packed longshoremen's hall: "We heard voices of women's freedom, of the equality of backward [sic] races, of children rationed first when supplies were scant. . . . I spent hours, sometimes days, with each of these lecturers, and wrote whole series of articles from what they told me."

Strong admired "these messengers" yet "not once in those years did it occur to me to leave Seattle. . . . The reason is simple . . . the revolution had begun in Moscow [sic], but not in Moscow alone. It was world revolution that took us in. Its messengers crossed all seas, from India, Ireland, Germany, Hungary. It had begun in Moscow, but it was coming to Seattle; and Seattle was our battle post. We also were part of this new world."[46]

Collaboration in Seattle transcended sectarian divides and carried over into the everyday affairs of the unions, where socialists and IWWs alike were well-respected members and often leaders. The workers tended to look upon the unions as a movement, though a uniquely Seattle movement. Historian Robert Friedheim suggested they were "most conscious of being a member of a Seattle labor organization. This intense localism was unique."[47] The observation is correct to the degree that it is interpreted in class terms, for Seattle was a city divided by class. The CLC's actions demonstrated this class-based unity. It called for amnesty for all political prisoners, including the hundreds of Wobblies imprisoned in the raids of 1917 and demanded that Mayor Ole Hanson stop the practice of jailing people on open charges or for such crimes as selling radical newspapers. Additionally, with the longshoremen, it called for the withdrawal of American troops from Russia. It endorsed the statement in "Program and Principles" affirming that "the cause of labor unrest is the exploitation of producers by parasites, that the earth belongs to the people thereof and therefore cannot belong to any individual, group or corporation, that all wealth is the labor of hand and brain plus natural resources, and that anything of value belongs to its producer."[48] Challenging the AFL's strict hierarchy, the CLC gave skilled workers no permanent place of privilege and represented skilled and unskilled alike. Its Labor Temple was home to all. The unions it represented were sympathetic to municipal ownership of the piers, the waterways, the public markets, and the electric company. They took great pride in what they themselves owned: their Labor Temple, their cooperatives, and their paper, the *Union Record*. The paper linked workplaces and neighborhoods, cooperatives and communities—bringing everything in dialogue with politics and world events. Seattle had its ethnic enclaves, but here space was shared.

Seattle's workers built a culture of their own; the soapbox was its classroom, and the Labor Temple its university.[49] O'Connor remembered: "The first time I heard Debs his subject was industrial unionism, and the very first time I laid eyes on Big Bill Haywood, it was a dramatic soapbox lecture on Samuel Gompers, craft unionism and socialism."[50] The street-corner lecturers included "Red" Doran, Elizabeth Gurley Flynn, Tom Lewis, Tom Hickey, Kate Sadler, and James P. Thompson. The Northwest was a source of radical newspapers of all shades, beginning with the utopian settlements: Home had its *Agitator,* Equity its *Industrial Freedom.* The first of many socialist papers was the Seattle *Socialist,* edited by Herman Titus; the *Herald,* the *World,* and the *Seattle Daily Call* followed. Socialist weeklies came and went in Everett, Tacoma, Bellingham, Aberdeen, and even smaller towns. The *Industrial Worker* was published first in Spokane then moved to Seattle. Bookshops and newsstands carried the *Appeal to Reason* and the *International Socialist Review.* Seattle's intellectuals read *The Masses* (and later *The Liberator*). For O'Connor, the *Liberator* was "the one great magazine in the USA." He recalled how in Raymer's bookstore piles of the magazine reached counter high. A literary agent sold it from union hall to union hall and from mass meeting to mass meeting. More than 3,000 copies came into Seattle each month. The working stiffs liked the magazine; it was theirs. It was for labor, pro-red, for socialism, for the Russian Revolution, and it defended the Wobblies.[51]

"Wherever in the West," wrote John Reed, "there is an IWW local, you will find an intellectual center—a place where men read philosophy, economics, the latest plays, where art and poetry are discussed, and international politics."[52] In Seattle, the *Union Record* held it all together. It began as a weekly in 1900, becoming a daily in 1918. Edited by Ault, published by the CLC, it became the first labor-owned daily newspaper in the country. Ault spearheaded the transformation of the *Union Record.* He was backed by Duncan and Wells. The newspaper supported industrial unionism and frequently but not always backed Socialist Party candidates. Ault composed its mission statement: "The *Union Record* will help you win a greater prosperity. . . . *The Union Record* is the only paper in Seattle that dares be consistent in its fight for the working man. It is opposed to capitalist control of the legislative, judicial and executive branches of government. It gives you all the news the other papers give, and in addition, the news the other papers will not print. It is the one paper that stands between you and industrial slavery."[53]

Ault led the campaign to finance an expanded paper, raising $13,000, and enlisting 20,000 subscribers, overwhelmingly from unions and union members. The 15,000-strong Local 104 of the Boilermakers agreed to pay $1 per person out of its treasury. The editors of the socialist *Daily Call*, then failing, gave over its own subscribers for another 10,000. It took to the streets with the help of the revolt of the newsboys, three hundred of whom formed the country's first newsboys' union. Ault would continue as editor into the twenties, but it was Anna Louis Strong, coming over from the *Call*, who set the format and tone of the paper, writing features, gathering international news, producing a women's page, and contributing a daily poem under her *nom de plume,* Anise. She led the battle to champion the Western Union employees (the telegraph girls) who had been locked out after they formed a union.[54] The women's page for a November 1919 issue, a typical one, included an advice column, "Letters to Ruth Ridgway"; a segment in the series "The Care of Babies"; and a report from the journalist Mary Heaton Vorse, "Women Stay with Steel Strike for Freedom's Sake." In the aftermath of the Seattle strike, the *Union Record*'s circulation rose to more than 120,000, surpassing by far the *Seattle Times,* the *Post-Intelligencer,* and the *Seattle Star.*

The solidarity of Seattle's workers was, by any standard, staggering; in 1919 workers from barbers to boilermakers would cease work. There would be no pickets; there were no strikebreakers. Still, there is a darker side to this story to which attention must be paid. Just seventy-five years before Seattle's great strike, before the ravaging of the forests and the spoiling of the Sound's waters, Seattle was still Indian Country, as it had been for ten thousand years. The Duwamish, a Coast Salish people, lived in a dozen or so villages where Seattle now stands. They lived in a world of plenty, nature's bounty available for all. Exploitation and profit were unheard of, violence as we now know it was rare, and war was rarer still. Washington's Indian Wars were grotesque; even if less obscene than California's, the wars had an outcome that was much the same. The people vanquished, in 1910 they were no longer visibly present. One census recorded possibly just a hundred Duwamish people still in Seattle that year. Nor was Seattle and the Puget Sound country immune to the anti-Chinese movements of the 1880s and 1890s. By 1919, the Chinese in Seattle were few, and the experience of the Japanese, then the city's largest minority, was likewise one of discrimination and exclusion.

The Socialist Party was divided on the "Black Question," not surprising in the reality of Jim Crow America. Debs insisted on absolute equality, and he refused to speak to segregated audiences, though he saw the issue primarily as one of working-class unity, refusing to concede that poor blacks might be worse off than poor whites. William English Walling and Charles Edward Russell, New York intellectuals associated with the Socialist Party, were founders of the National Association for the Advancement of Colored People. Yet Victor Berger, elected to the Milwaukee House of Representatives in 1910, a leader of the Socialist right wing, was an outspoken white supremacist. He insisted that "there can be no doubt that the negroes and mulattos constitute a lower race—and the Caucasian and indeed even the Mongolian have the start on them in civilization by many thousand years." Kate Richards O'Hare, the Socialists' Prairie firebrand, was imprisoned as an opponent of the war. Forever the fighter, she became an advocate of prison reform, but she was also a white supremacist, a supporter of segregation. The IWW, on the other hand, represented black workers in the Louisiana pine country, black longshoremen on Philadelphia's docks, and Asians on the Pacific Coast, and it welcomed without distinction Mexican miners in Arizona's Copper Belt.

Seattle's unions, as elsewhere, excluded blacks, though there were exceptions—the longshoremen and the miners being significant examples. Though the Machinists International's constitution banned black workers from membership, there were in fact blacks working in the shipyards.[55] The union status of these black men and women who worked in the shipyards remains unclear. Overall, the few blacks in Seattle—one percent of the population—found themselves scattered and isolated, unrepresented and exploited, often among the strikebreakers brought in by shippers to break the longshoremen's strikes.

The Japanese, who were the largest minority in Seattle (4 percent of the population), could not be citizens; they were not allowed in unions. Alice Lord, the organizer of the waitresses' union, not a socialist, was a staunch exclusionist, as was her union. However, the historian of the Seattle Japanese, Katsutoshi Kurokawa, has revealed changes at work as well as crosscurrents suggesting that the racial animosities within the working class were neither inherent nor inevitable. In his study of Japanese immigrants in Seattle, he writes, "The IWW's appeal for unity of workers of all countries, and its opposition to racial discrimination was genuine. The Japanese community in Seattle understood this fact." Kurokawa also observed that in the late 1910s a change took place: "Progressive and radical activists who had no racial prejudice increased their influence in the Seattle labor movement." He notes that Duncan and Ault had "little patience with racial prejudice." In Ault's case, bad memories of his youth in the violence of segregation in Kentucky played a role. Anna Louise Strong had been to Japan in 1913.[56] In the *Union Record*, her poetry would register the appalling conditions of women factory workers there. A leading critic of Chinese exclusion, Kate Sadler was an advocate of black workers' rights as well. She spoke at black churches, opposing exclusion and segregation in the workplace and the unions. In Seattle's labor movement, race and racism, if always present, rarely remained uncontested.

The *Union Record* recognized the existence of racial barriers in the West and the need to break them down. The paper sympathized, albeit inconsistently, with the black struggle. Just after Christmas 1918, it reported on the arrest of seventy-five black soldiers in

New York City, "members of the quartermasters corps of the Fifth Infantry," charged with having looted several saloons: "The saloon men had refused to serve the men in uniform, whereupon they helped themselves."[57] On December 28, the paper wrote: "White man's supremacy in the South, following the demobilization of the army, is going to cost more than ever before. Half a million colored soldiers are coming home from camp with a feeling that they have earned the right to better treatment than the white politicians and employers have been accustomed to give them. There is a strong current of racial protest among them."[58]

In the aftermath of the 1919 General Strike, the *Union Record*'s February 27 lead headlines proclaimed, "Council Recognizes Negroes" and "Labor Welcomes Colored Workers," in reference to "the unanimous vote of the CLC on a resolution supporting the equal right of negroes with white men in organized labor."[59] In March, it featured a detailed account of the plight of black women who were domestic and field workers. Its coverage of the bloody nation's northern riots the following summer condemned the employers while endorsing black self-determination. That same year, the *Forge*, the newspaper of the Soldiers and Sailors and Workmen's Council (sponsored by the Metal Trades Council), reported that the ILA delegate, Thompson, a black longshoreman, had placed "a motion before the CLC to adopt and send [a message of support] to the Anti-lynching Congress now in session in Kansas, to the *Union Record* and to the *Messenger Magazine*. The motion carried unanimously."[60]

IN THE WAR YEARS, THE IDEA of a general strike was very much in the air. The IWW evoked it routinely, and more than once the CLC threatened to use it in bargaining with recalcitrant employers. However, it was the Tom Mooney case that brought the issue to the fore. The movement to free Tom Mooney, a union leader accused of putting a bomb in a "Preparedness" San Francisco parade, was perhaps the single most pressing issue for labor's left wing at the time, with the *Union Record* featuring almost daily updates. Mooney was a labor activist born of Irish parents, his father an Indiana coal miner. He started factory work at age fourteen, apprenticed as an iron molder, joining the International Molders Union, where he would remain a member for life. A roamer, he visited Europe where he converted to socialism. Back in the United States, Mooney worked in foundries and fields, eventually making his way to California. He joined the IWW briefly, then left, though remaining a socialist and a militant.

July 22, 1916, was "Preparedness Day." In San Francisco it was meant to be a great celebration by the city's business leaders and militarists. It was also meant as a provocation to the labor movement and to all those who opposed the war. The celebration began with a giant parade, first assembled just off the Embarcadero. There a bomb exploded. The results were grisly; ten people were killed, forty injured. Mooney, then well known to the police, was charged and arrested, as was his wife, Rena, and his friend Warren Billings. There was not a single witness, however, who could offer information incriminating them. "Once Mooney and Billings were arrested," according to the historian Richard Frost, "every lead that did not indicate their guilt was abandoned. Eyewitnesses who told the police of suspicious persons were dismissed if the description did not fit the two prime suspects."[61] Many suspected *agents provocateurs* or the anarchists of the Galleanist anarcho-communist movement. Yet this mattered little; the prosecutors, the press, the "Interests," single-mindedly pursued the Mooneys and Billings. The jury found Billings guilty in September and sentenced him to life imprisonment. Tried in January 1917, Mooney was convicted and sentenced to hang. Rena Mooney was acquitted but held in prison until March 1918, then released on bail.[62] There is little doubt that the three had been framed and that the convictions were intended to discredit both the labor movement and the antiwar movement. The International Workers Defense League (IWDL) organized for their defense carried on for fully two decades. California's governor, William Stephens, spared Mooney's life just two weeks before he was scheduled to hang.

Now sentenced to life imprisonment, he would spend twenty-two years in prison, Billings ten months longer.

In January 1919, the left-wing unions convened a national Congress in Chicago for the purpose of freeing Mooney and Billings. "Shall we call for a general strike May 1st or July 4th?" That was the lead of Crystal Eastman's story on the Chicago Mooney Congress for the *Liberator*, which continued, "These were the main questions fought out in Chicago January 13–17. No one dared to doubt the wisdom of calling a general strike—it was the date over which the "Reds" and the "machine" [the conference leadership] wrangled."[63] Another issue debated was the aim of the proposed general strike: "Shall we strike for the release of all political and class war prisoners, or shall we, as a matter of tactics, strike for the freedom of Mooney alone—with the thought that once feeling our power we can use it for anything we want afterwards?"

Seattle sent a delegation to the Congress that was second only to Chicago's in numbers. It included Duncan but also Frank Turco, a vice president of the Seattle Metal Trades Council, who sympathized with the IWW.[64] An Italian immigrant, Turco came to Seattle from Butte, having been forced to leave Montana. He was a former coal miner and hard rock miner and had lost a leg in a mine accident.[65] Though not invited, there were many Wobblies in attendance. Crystal Eastman reckoned that most of Seattle's delegates may have carried two cards. This meant that resolutions to exclude the IWW and socialist left-wingers were of little consequence, as nearly all carried AFL cards. The "Reds" won the battle to exclude two members of the official, government-sanctioned Italian Labor Commission, then located in Washington, DC. "I am an Italian," cried Turco, "I know! These men don't represent Italian labor. They represent the most imperialist country in the world!"[66]

The Congress, which came after Mooney's sentence was commuted, seemed unlikely to have much life. "I think," wrote Eastman in her article, "everybody felt that when the Governor of California, under threat of a general strike last December, saved Mooney from hanging and condemned him to life imprisonment, he had taken the dramatic force out of the Mooney agitation and it would be impossible to revive it."[67] This turned out not to be the case. Seattle's CLC had led in calling for the Chicago Congress along with the labor councils in Oakland and Chicago. This meant the Congress was more than a mere gathering of the left. The fact that it was delegated expressed this. One hundred fourteen cities and twenty-eight states were represented. Eastman suggested it was "something like a spontaneous expression of the organized workers of this country, the first gathering of its kind."[68]

The Seattle and Butte delegations led the "Reds," but the former was not 100 percent Red. On the question of which date to strike, Jim Lansbury, representing 18,000 Boilermakers, said: "I've had the pleasure of sticking two $1,000 bills through the bars of Tom Mooney's cell from the Boiler Makers of Seattle. We voted 8 to 1 to go on strike on December 9th and that vote holds. I tell you, the Pacific Coast would go out tomorrow. But the East is different. We've got to organize, and it takes time to do it."[69] But Sadler, "an able Socialist spell-binder, one of the 'wild' ones," wanted the strike earlier. "What is holding us back when the case of Mooney has gone around the world? . . . If we were ready for a general strike on December 9th to keep Mooney from hanging, why wait till July 4th to call a strike for his freedom? . . . July 4th is too late. . . . Demobilization will have taken place—the country will be full of unemployed—the employers will have months and months to prepare. . . . And July 4th is the Master's day—it is the day when your Masters set you free to celebrate. . . . Why start a strike on a day like that? Why stop work on the one day in the year when you're allowed to stop work? May 1st is the international day of Labor— July 4th is a national day—Why should we wait? This is the only civilized country in the world where the prison doors are still swinging in for political prisoners now that the war is ended!"[70]

The Seattle delegates and other radicals wanted a follow-up conference, insisting that the general strike be for all political prisoners, including Emma Goldman, Eugene Debs, William Haywood, and Rose Pastor Stokes. The debates were intense; the "machine" won more often than it lost, but its victories were hard-won. The radicals won concessions on Russia and on political prisoners, but these, wrote Eastman, "were nothing to boast about." On the main points, there was no compromise. The worst, however, was when the machine peremptorily adjourned the Congress. "This was the real coup of the organizers, the only thing one cannot forgive them," according to Eastman. "To call 1,182 delegates to a Congress and adjourn them before they wanted to adjourn, before they made any provision for a second Congress, for perpetuating and developing their new representative machinery—that was ruthless, unnecessary, shortsighted."[71] The IWDL would continue to struggle for Mooney's liberation, but its work would be sidelined in the tumultuous months to come, and there would be no general strike.

On the long train ride home, Anna Louise Strong reflected: "I was now rated as a leader of Seattle's workers.... From the day when I walked into the offices of the *Call* to offer my services as writer, I had found both comradeship and freedom so naturally mingled that I never analyzed these blessings till long after they had gone. I planned and carried through my own work and seemed to do always the things I most desired. Yet instinctively when new questions arose, I consulted with others. Our editor Harry Ault, the Secretary of the Central Labor Council, Jimmy Duncan, whom we regularly sent as delegate to meetings of the American Federation of Labor to cast the single vote against Gompers which prevented his election as president from being unanimous. My mind—all our minds—were being made by the same past, the same events, the same comrades, by complaints from the shipyards and letters from the mines. Thus formed, my mind functioned easily with the others, with a sense of both personal liberty and joint achievement."[72]

Duncan always kept some distance from the IWW but considered the organization "a pacesetter" with "radical ideas [that] are being rapidly absorbed by the AFL and what some of us consider radical today will be conservative tomorrow [but saw] no good reason why one has to join the IWW. . . . Good ideas we can absorb. Some of those bad ones that get them into trouble they can keep."[73] Speaking at the national convention of the AFL in Buffalo, he warned: "Controlling the lumber production, they will be able to control ship-building operations to a great extent. Already they have applied so successfully the sabotage known as 'the strike on the job' that a crew of 200 men, who formerly got out 20 cars of logs a day, brought its production as low as three cars, until the employers gave them clean beds and good food and wages higher than they asked for. It is this desperate, silent, elusive, yet terribly effective force which takes the name of IWW but is largely made up of men who consider regular trade unionism 'too slow.' This is the threat to the prestige of trade unionism on the Coast."[74]

IWW commemoration of Everett Massacre,
Mt. Pleasant Cemetery, Seattle, 1917

Woman welder, shipyards, c. 1919

Shipyard sheet metal workers, c. World War I

Women welders on break, c. World War I

Shift change at Skinner and Eddy

Telephone worker

Elizabeth Gurley Flynn in Seattle (between umbrellas lower right)

Food for strikers' cafeteria

Elizabeth Gurley Flynn

James (Jimmy) Duncan,
Seattle Central Labor Council,
February 1920

Shipyard track men

Anna Louise Strong

Kate Sadler drawn by Joseph
Pass, March 1919

Soapbox socialism on Skid Road

Smith Tower and Mt. Rainer

Japanese workers outside bunkhouse

IWW organizers awaiting transport to McNeil Island Federal Penitentiary.
James Thompson is in back row, far left.

Shipyard welder

7. THE WAR AT HOME

There was more than one war in Seattle. The first, ongoing, was with labor. The second, half a world away, came with the August guns. Seattle, like most of the United States, opposed this war. And if there had ever been anything romantic "over there," it had dissipated by the end of 1916. The Great Powers had boasted that military prowess—evidenced by their earlier conquests in Africa and Asia—authenticated their claims of civilization. On learning of victory in Egypt at Tel-el-Kebir in 1882, Gladstone had the bells rung, proclaiming it "a great day for civilization." Then came 1914 with the battle at Ypres and poison gas; Verdun with a million casualties, and the outcome inconclusive. On the Somme, twenty thousand British soldiers died in the first hours, and there would be another million casualties. In the end, the First World War's approximately fifteen million dead shattered the myths of Western superiority.

Millions of Americans resisted joining this war.[1] In Seattle, the unions and the political parties were key in raising opposition to it, which reached very high levels. Seattleites were readers and found in the *Union Record* regular reports from the fronts. The Machinists Union submitted a resolution to the Central

Labor Council asserting that "90 percent of the people of this city and probably of the nation (as far as could be ascertained) were opposed to it and the sentiment was overwhelmingly against conscription and everything resembling militarism."[2] Even the *Seattle Times* and the *Seattle Star*, mainstream papers, were at first skeptical. The socialists savaged the war, with Debs calling it "murder in uniform." Antiwar organizations sprung up. The Women's Peace Party (Crystal Eastman was secretary of its New York branch) presented "a two-mile long peace petition signed by 350,000 children in forty states to Secretary of State Bryan."[3] The American Union Against Militarism (AUAM), chaired in Seattle by Anna Louise Strong, was the most prominent such organization. Following the sinking of the *Lusitania*—the British liner that a German U-boat torpedoed on May 7, 1915—Jane Addams and a group of feminists embarked upon a peace tour of Europe. On returning to New York, speaking to the Women's Peace Party and the Women's Trade Union League, Addams denounced the war: "This is an old man's war." She told how in every nation she visited there were "badly mangled" soldiers who said "they would stop the fighting if they could."[4]

Still, real war rallied supporters, and the antiwar movement would split. In Seattle, in the working class and its organizations, antiwar sentiment remained strong. By contrast, among middle-class progressives the movement stumbled, then succumbed almost altogether. The war fever, begun and orchestrated in the preparedness campaigns, played an important role in this, as did the patriotic frenzy of the war itself, championed and urged on by the war parties, supported by civic organizations, the church, and above all by the press. The majority of workers, however, their unions, and the left-wing parties opposed the war to the end, though the price paid was heavy.

Strong was a "pacifist," progressive, and feminist when she returned to Seattle.[5] She had been elected to the School Board by the city's progressives, including its women's organizations, who insisted the Board needed a woman member, but also by the labor movement. She became a popular member, willing to take on controversial issues, above all the war. She threw herself into antiwar work. "The AUAM, the Emergency Peace Federation, the Anti-Preparedness League," she recalled, "sprang up in the East, New York, Washington, Philadelphia, with varying and perhaps conflicting leadership. . . . We of the Pacific provinces never distinguished between the different leaderships. We all met together—all who opposed war, and of these there was a goodly number—in regular luncheon meetings once a week in a cafeteria, and in occasional Sunday mass meetings, enthusiastically attended. We accepted speakers, campaigns, pamphlets from any national society that chose to send them."[6]

The Socialist Party in the United States, to its credit and unlike its European counterparts, opposed the war from start to finish. The labor movement, however, disgraced itself. Samuel Gompers, with counterparts, supported both the preparedness campaign and the push for an Allied victory, managing to keep the AFL aligned with the Wilson administration throughout the war. There were exceptions: the International Ladies' Garment Workers Union, the International Union of Mine, Mill, and Smelter Workers, the United Mine Workers, the International Typographical Union, the Amalgamated Clothing Workers, and other unions opposed the war. Seattle, too, was an exception. Opposition to the war was near universal, the antiwar movement being increasingly a working-class movement.

In 1914, the CLC, then representing 25,000, unanimously adopted a resolution opposing war. Those against the resolution proposed to run up the United States flag on the Labor Temple; this was met with such a storm of opposition that its proponents withdrew it. Hulet Wells, who would be elected CLC president in 1915, composed the resolution:

> Whereas, the appalling loss of life which will inevitably be the result, the inexpressible suffering from the systematic mangling and crippling of human bodies on a vaster scale than has ever

before been possible, the laying waste of lands and the destruction of homes, the ensuing industrial depression, the agony of bereaved women, and the brutalizing of those who kill their kind—all these hideous results and more will fall with crushing force on the working class alone, while the kings, capitalists and aristocrats remain in safety and

Whereas, no possible outcome of such an international war can benefit to any extent whatever the workers, whose enemies are not the workers of other nations, but the exploiting class of every nation, and

Whereas, the nations now preparing to do wholesale murder are nominally Christian, and a majority of those who do the killing are affiliated with the various churches of the Christian religion,

Therefore, as representatives of the organized working class, we declare the European war to be an international crime and a horror for which there is no parallel in savagery, and we denounce the church, which claims to be founded on the principle of peace and good will, for having failed to interpose its opposition to this orgy of blood;

We further declare that one reason for the suspicious eagerness with which the rulers of all these nations have entered into hostility is because of the universal industrial unrest and the growing spirit of working-class solidarity which, if unchecked, threatens the present ruling class.

To all those workers of Europe who have resisted the war craze we extend our sympathy and respect, and we pledge our efforts against any attempt to draw our own country into a foreign war.[7]

The socialists believed that soldiers, "those who kill their kind," were workers in uniform. In reality, soldiers were often the employers' last line of defense. In 1914, there were still working-class veterans who remembered the great railroad strikes of 1877, broken by federal soldiers. Later soldiers had been dispatched to Coeur d'Alene in the mine strikes of both 1892 and 1899, the

Pullman strike of 1894, the Arizona strikes of 1903, the Goldfield strike of 1907, and the Colorado coal strikes of 1913–14 (which included Ludlow). All workers faced bayonets and bullets. This history included the Washington State ranchers, mine owners, and lumbermen who routinely demanded soldiers. The Washington timber strike of 1917 was in a sense militarized, and in Seattle in 1919 federal soldiers were mobilized but not deployed.

Woodrow Wilson campaigned for reelection in 1916, promising to keep the United States out of the European war. "There is such a thing as a nation too proud to fight," he declared. By winter, however, things were changing. The impasse on the Western Front continued, with stalemate in the trenches where massive troop movements might gain a few miles at best, success sometimes measured in feet. Soldiers crawled through muddy wastelands before waiting machine guns—mincing machines—to reach the "enemy" in the trenches before them. The generals' thirst for more was unquenchable—more men, more guns, more tanks. Nothing short of victory was thinkable.

On the Eastern Front, the line of death was nine hundred miles long; ill-equipped Russian peasants were thrown against the German onslaught to defend Tsar and country. Then the first Russian Revolution, in February, raised the specter of a Russian collapse or withdrawal, with all that that implied. The British and French soon faced a one-front war and the redeployment of Germany's eastern armies. In March, Germany resumed unrestricted submarine warfare, and on April 6, 1917, the United States entered the war. U.S. Socialists now faced firsthand the choice that wrecked the Second International in 1914. What to do? Continue to oppose the war, lie low in hopes of riding out the storm, or, like the Europeans, offer support of some kind?[8] Critical or otherwise? The Socialist Party responded by calling a week-long Emergency Convention in St. Louis. By the time it met, however, the United States was already at war. Kate Sadler led Seattle's delegation; it was all "Red." Among them were Emil Herman, the Everett shingle weaver and Washington State party secretary, and L. E. Katterfeld, the former state secretary and a member of the Party's National Committee. Herman would later serve three years and four months at McNeil Island Penitentiary for opposing the war. On release, he declared, "I am opposed to war. I object to bloodshed. I would not take the life of a human being to save my own. I regard human life as infinitely sacred. I am opposed, therefore to the system that ruthlessly sacrifices human life in the most barbarous manner possible."[9] Katterfeld was charged but never convicted of "criminal conspiracy." He would become a member of the central committee of the Communist Labor Party.

At St. Louis, Sadler was a leading left-wing voice. Nevertheless, she broke with others on the left, voting for a minority resolution presented by Louis Boudin, a New York lawyer who had been the US delegate to the Socialists' 1907 Stuttgart and 1910 Copenhagen conferences. The Boudin resolution was virtually identical with the majority's antiwar position; it concluded: "The working men and women of this country will pay for this war while it lasts in blood and suffering, only to inherit when it is past a world in which their struggle for existence will be harder and the road to their emancipation much more difficult. These reasons lead us to the conclusion that we must oppose this war with all the powers at our command."[10] This position has been called "centrist," but this was not the case at the time, as it implicitly undercut the majority position of Morris Hillquit, Victor Berger and the other right-wingers who contributed to the majority position.

Sadler returned home to learn that her husband, Sam Sadler, the longshoremen's leader, along with Wells and the two brothers Joe and Morris Pass would soon be charged with conspiring "to obstruct, hinder, and delay the government in its prosecution of the war."[11] Their trials in September resulted in a divided jury. Tried again, they were convicted. Joe, a writer, and Morris, an artist, were young New York intellectuals inspired by Eastman's *Masses*. They had returned unsuspecting to the East in 1917, to be arrested for their Seattle "crimes" and imprisoned in the Tombs. Visiting nearly every day, they were counseled by Boudin until they returned to Seattle for trial. Boudin discussed Marxism with them; his final advice, after three weeks, was "to keep in touch with Kate Sadler and follow her counsel."[12] Wells spent two years at McNeil Island and Leavenworth, Sadler two years at McNeil. Their crime? Having helped produce an anti-conscription pamphlet, "No Conscription, No Involuntary Servitude." Anna Louise Strong, who had been involved in producing the pamphlet, of which some twenty thousand copies circulated, insisted that it had been written and distributed before the conscription law was passed. In the trial, she read from its conclusion by Daniel Webster: "Where is it written in the Constitution that you may take the children from the parents . . . and compel them to fight the battles of any war in which the folly or the wickedness of the government may engage?"[13]

Wells explained, "I was present with thirty or forty others when the draft of the leaflet was presented. That, however, was it—except, Miss Strong asked . . . [me] to look after the printing, since . . . [I] had experience in that line. I agreed, took the copy to the shop of George Listman, who was a conservative labor leader, a Roman Catholic, and a Seattle Civil Service Commissioner. He read the copy over carefully, then said, 'Yes, I'll print that. That is what I believe.' It was not until a week after the distribution that the enactment of the conscription law was completed."[14] The dailies demanded blood. The *Seattle Times* headline screamed: "TREASON SEEN IN ATTACK ON CONSCRIPTION SPREAD SECRETLY OVER SEATTLE." The *Seattle Star* printed one word across the entire front page in five-inch-high letters: "SEDITION."[15]

In these years, the city's bankers, lumbermen, shippers, railroad men, and newspaper men (including the millionaire Alden Blethen of the *Seattle Times*) felt themselves surrounded by a radicalized, hostile population, above all by the IWW and its supporters. For this reason, they considered dissent as "treason," anticipating federal laws to come. Treason, for this class, could be opposition to war or insubordination at work. In 1917, the most glaring examples of the latter were the strike in the woods and the new working-class insurgency that emerged in the wake of Everett. They begged the federal government to intervene, and it did, passing the Espionage Act in June and the Sedition Act the following year. The first threatened individuals convicted of obstructing the draft—specifically using the mail for that purpose—with $10,000 fines and twenty years in jail. The second made a federal offense out of using "disloyal, profane, scurrilous, or abusive" language about the Constitution, the government, the American uniform, or the American flag.

Strong's sympathies shifted as the antiwar movement increasingly became socialist and working class. By 1916 she had become a figure in the labor movement. CLC president Wells, with James Duncan, invited her to speak to union members. She was well received, with those in attendance unanimously passing a motion endorsing her views on militarism and the rush to war. That spring her report on the Everett trial to the New York *Evening Post* contributed to associating her with the IWW and labor in general.[16] On the School Board, Strong and another member, Richard Winsor, defied demands to bring the preparedness campaign into the schools. Largely successful, their resistance angered the city's militarists and caught the attention of the Minute Men, a far-right paramilitary organization affiliated with the American Protective League (itself a quasi-military group that worked as the Justice Department's volunteer arm). The Minute Men launched a successful recall campaign against Strong. It was not an easy task for them, however, since she did well in the voting at a time when the pro-war forces were at their strongest. When a friend asked if she had any support at all in the face of the recall vote, she replied, "Oh, yes, I've lots of the biggest organizations in the city. The Boilermakers with 7,000 members is working enthusiastically. The blacksmiths, the longshoremen, the machinists, the electricians and lots of others, the Metal Trades Council, even the conservative building trades. We really have a chance to win." "That's a funny lot of roughnecks," her friend said, "to be backing a girl like you."[17]

The *Seattle Times* was triumphant about the defeat of the city's best-known woman. Blethen himself wrote, "Anna Louis Strong, despite the consolidation on her behalf by every IWW, every Red Socialist, every pacifist, every man and woman who disapproves of the recall principle and the large numbers who came to her aid through the mistaken sympathy for a woman, was ejected from office with creditable neatness and dispatch. . . . The sound of the door locking behind her will be music in the ears of the Seattle boys who have already reached the trenches in France."[18]

The Seattle establishment jumped on the "preparedness" bandwagon. They themselves had long been advocates of punitive patriotism, Blethen having avidly supported the Spanish-American War. On a national level, the pro-war movement's leaders were Senator Henry Cabot Lodge, former president Theodore Roosevelt, and General Leonard Wood, former military governor of Cuba. Calling for a giant military—an army and navy as large as that of any of the great powers—they demanded a harsh response to the sinking of the *Lusitania*. They appropriated the lexicon of patriotism, speaking as "real Americans." Roosevelt attacked the Peace Party, called it "silly and base," "influenced by physical cowardice," and "vague and hysterical."[19]

With thinly veiled pro-British partisanship, Roosevelt and Wood argued that US intervention was inevitable. They promoted citizens' training, held military parades, and pressured (even harassed) the Wilson administration. Veterans of San Juan Hill, Roosevelt and Wood were imperialists with ambitions going far beyond northern France. Wood had been governor of Moro Province in the Philippines, where he oversaw the slaughter of six hundred villagers, many of them women and children. "General Wood was present and looking on," Mark Twain wrote. "His order had been, 'Kill or capture those savages.' Apparently, our little army considered that the 'or' left them authorized to kill or capture according to taste, and that their taste had remained what it has been for eight years, in our army out there—the taste of Christian butchers."[20]

Seattle's CLC responded to preparedness by warning against the propaganda campaign: "Various interests in this community, and more especially the press, are seeking to stampede our citizens on the question of preparedness and are endeavoring to divert our attention from the greater enemies of the workers inside our borders to our lesser enemies in foreign lands." The CLC advised "all trade unionists and truly patriotic citizens to refrain from parading or participation of any kind in demonstrations which can have no other result that to thwart the cool, calm, and deliberate judgement which is so necessary to the proper solution to the question."[21] This stance reflected labor's growing place in the antiwar movement, in a context where pacifist sentiments ran deep, despite waning middle-class participation. In May 1916, for example, three thousand protesters gathered at the Dreamland Rink. Their demands were women's suffrage, federal child legislation, unemployment insurance, higher wages, and legislation to prevent the use of the military during strikes.

Seattle's newspapers cheered on the war party—the *Seattle Times*, the *Post-Intelligencer*, and the *Seattle Star* led what became a ferocious and violent campaign for war that was against the city's "traitors" and "German spies," identified as the labor movement and its supporters. This campaign took its toll, as did the war fever nationally. The Preparedness League's June 1916 rally in Seattle drew tens of thousands, and the April 1917 declaration of war inspired another huge demonstration, this one twenty blocks long. It was led by five hundred Navy Reserves, followed by parties of Elks, Spanish-American War veterans, the Puget Sound section of the American Chemical Company, the Seattle Bar Association, Civil War veterans, the Woodsmen of the World, and the American Red Cross Society. Broadway High School and the University of Washington also sent their noisy contingents. The *Post-Intelligencer* reported: "The Oriental section of the city contributed a spectacular organization to the line of march. Japanese citizens, some 275 strong, marched with lighted paper lanterns over their heads."[22]

The socialists and the labor movement never abandoned the streets, nor did the IWW soapboxers and recruiters. Nevertheless, vigilantes hired "security": thugs, soldiers, and sailors that relent-lessly harassed them and targeted offices, meetings, and newspaper vendors. On July 31, 1917, the Seattle branch of the People's Council of America, a pacifist organization, held a mass outdoor rally to protest the war, the vilification of the press, and the attacks on the radical left. Five thousand men, women, and children gathered in a vacant city lot to hear James Maurer, a member of the Pennsylvania legislature and president of the Pennsylvania Federation of Labor. Fifteen minutes into Maurer's talk, however, a mob of intoxicated soldiers with reinforcements from the University of Washington stormed the platform. They succeeded in interrupting Maurer but failed to end the meeting. The *Daily Call* reported that Kate Sadler, the "great champion of the workers . . . was on her feet and warned them not to break up the meeting" thereby preventing "a disgrace-ful riot." Apparently, Sadler stared down the soldiers and brought an orderly conclusion to the rally.[23]

The antiwar movement persevered. On August 16, the People's Council held an all-day session at the Labor Temple. Speakers included Elizabeth Freeman, the English suffragist; Mrs. Hannah Sheehy Skeffington, widow of the Dublin Easter Rising leader; and Charles Erskine Wood, a Portland lawyer. That evening four thou-sand turned out in an outdoor meeting to hear H. W. Watts of the *Northwest Worker;* H.W. Pohlman, president of the iron mold-ers; George Hanson and W. F. Johnson of the *Seattle Daily Call;* Brice Rodgers, Louise Olivereau, Herbert Mahler, and Sam and Kate Sadler of the IWW; and Harry Ault of the *Union Record.* The *Post-Intelligencer* reported that the IWW was out in full force, but O'Connor explains that it was mostly a Socialist Party rally, though one that included IWW speakers.

That night, police stormed the stage, arresting Kate Sadler whom they claimed had said, "Woodrow Wilson, traitor that you are. . . ." The police attempted to take her to the county jail, but the crowd responded by chasing them down and freeing her, threatened to kill them, then "took the prisoner from them." The police fled before the crowd, and Sadler "returned to the rostrum in triumph."[24] She was rearrested the next week when speaking at a meeting of the People's Conference. Charged with disturbing the peace, she refused bail, preferring to spend the weekend in jail, saying she had committed no crime. The *Daily Call's* editors agreed, writing that her case "shows the determination on the part of the authorities to persecute a woman who has the courage of her convictions. To say things that unbiased people know are true, though they may offend the dollar patriots who are at the bottom of the series of outrages against our constitutional rights."[25]

The Socialist Party nationally would survive the war, though the cost was significant. Vigilantes wrecked its offices, and rank-and-file members together with leaders were arrested and imprisoned. The most isolated Party branches were the first to be destroyed. Overall some 1,500 of the Party's five thousand branches were lost.[26] Then it lost Debs, whom biographer Ray Ginger called the Party's heart and soul, a man who "appeared as a giant bridge . . . who stood with one foot firmly anchored in the present, the other in the future, while the multitude walked across his shoulders."[27] Debs's words at his trial in Cleveland were spellbinding. "Many spectators scarcely heard the sentence," wrote Ginger, "They had been transported into a cleaner, better land by his speech."

Debs spoke for more than two hours in his own defense before hushed spectators and "jurymen leaning forward as if to hear the next sentence before it was spoken."[28] What was his crime? In June 1918, in nearby Canton, Debs had denounced the war and its masters. During the trial, he called no witnesses but defended his right to oppose the unjust war: "The Mexican war was bitterly condemned by Abraham Lincoln, by Charles Sumner, by Daniel Webster and by Henry Clay." Debs also stood up for all those fellow pacifists who had protested the current war—Rose Pastor Stokes, Kate O'Hare, Bill Haywood, and the Wobblies—concluding, "I do not know, I cannot tell, what your verdict may be; nor does it matter much, so far as I am concerned. Gentlemen, I am the smallest part of this trial. I have lived long enough to appreciate my own personal insignificance in relation to a great deal that involves the welfare of the whole people. What you may choose to do with me will be of small consequence, after all, I am not on trial here. There is an infinitely greater issue that is being tried in this court, though you may not be conscious of it. American institutions are on trial here before a court of American citizens. The future will tell."[29] Several of the jurymen cried. Nevertheless, they found Debs guilty. Debs, sixty-three and in poor health, would be found guilty on three counts of sedition and sent to Atlanta to serve ten years in the federal penitentiary.[30] Awaiting sentencing he wrote, "Your Honor, years ago I recognized my kinship with all living things, and I made up my mind that I was not one bit better than the meanest of the earth. I said then, I say now, that while there is a lower class, I'm in it, while there is a criminal element, I am of it, while there is a soul in prison, I am not free."[31]

Following May Day, 1919, Cleveland's trade unionists and Socialists turned out in protest, with thousands converging on the city's public square. Police and vigilantes—and later soldiers, armored trucks and tanks—participated in confrontations that spread throughout the city center and lasted most of the day, leaving two people killed, forty injured, and one hundred arrested. Charles Ruthenberg, the Party secretary, was arrested and charged with "assault with the intent to kill."[32]

The CLC wired Debs expressing its "heartfelt appreciation for your splendid efforts to secure for the American wage slave a life of comfort and beauty."[33] Seattle's socialists would have to endure reactionary expressions of patriotic fury. In January 1918, a mob totally destroyed the *Daily Call's* presses.[34] The solution was to hasten already underway plans to disband the *Call* and shift its 15,000 readers over to the *Union Record*, about to be first published at that time. The *Union Record* became the largest socialist daily in the country, building its readership up to 50,000 by the end of 1918. As much as anything, the new paper held the radical movement together and allowed it to regroup in the storms that would follow the war.

Socialists were usually safe at work, though not always. Wells, convicted but free on appeal—the *Union Record* paid his legal fees—went to work at the huge Skinner and Eddy shipyard.[35] The yards were overflowing with workers, many of whom were new to Seattle and its unions. Since these workers knew "only what they read in the papers," they could easily be turned against Wells. Just after Labor Day, with its rallies and picnics that brought the usual torrent of abuse from the press, Wells learned that there were workers planning to kill him. A friend, who was an electrician, warned him to get out of the yards. Wells recalled thinking, "What might happen if I made no resistance? I might not be badly hurt, but would be jeered and roughly handled, hoisted on a rail and paraded as an object of derision. If I could make any real resistance, I would be badly beaten or killed, and the report would be, 'He said, To hell with the flag.'"[36]

Alone in a long open shed, Wells searched for an escape route, but finding none feared the worst. Time passed, but to his surprise nothing happened, though the threat had not been a hoax. "The truth is that I had a narrow escape. I was saved by my good friends Jimmy Duncan and Charlie Doyle, the latter a member of the painters' union. Hearing of the plot against me, they rushed down to the yard and, as Jimmy told me, 'read the riot act' to the mob, threatening them with expulsion from the labor movement if they carried out their plans." The painters had been turned against Wells indirectly by the *Star*'s "Wipe Out This Libel on Labor" in reference to his court case, and "by a business agent, a young man who was one of my enemies on the Council. He was a German hater and war fanatic who denounced the Council for its lack of patriotism."[37]

With the peace movement in disarray Anna Louise Strong became despondent, though she was far from alone: "Nothing in my whole life, not even my mother's death, so shook the foundations of my soul. The fight was lost, and forever! 'Our America' was dead!" The profiteers, the militarists, the "Interests" had won, steamrolling the peace effort. "I could not delude myself, as some did, that this was a 'war to make the world safe for democracy.' I had seen democracy slain in the very declaration of war—and got it. There had been a deep mistake in the whole basis of my life. Where and how to begin again I had no notion."[38]

So Strong sought escape, turning "like a wounded beast to the hills for shelter. Like the pioneers of old I fled to the simpler wilderness from the problems of human society that I could not face. Week after week on the high slopes of Rainier I was busy with problems of pack-trains, commissary, cooking, hikes. Eight or ten hours a day I led parties on the glaciers. Few newspapers reached me; I did not read them. I shrank from every mention of the war. I drugged myself with forests, cliffs and glaciers. It was the end of youth, the end of belief, the end of 'our America.' I could not face the ruins of my world."[39]

8. WINTER IN SEATTLE

In July 1917, the strike in the woods was then in full force. Half or more of the camps and mills had been closed. The IWW, it seemed, ruled. The lumber barons now responded with an all-out assault on the IWW and on immigrants.[1] The Seattle Chamber of Commerce held a meeting of a hundred logging bosses together with lumber and shingle manufacturers. The lumbermen present were angry and fearful. They faced an enemy that, they believed, "poisoned the wellsprings of patriotism and loyalty . . . [and was] slimy and soul-destroying."[2] In Seattle, they formed the Lumbermen's Protective Association, pledging to fight all-out with the strikers. They vowed, above all, to defeat the movement for the eight-hour day. They did this in the name of immediate profits. They were aware, however, that the prevailing winds were shifting. The war changed everything—and in their favor. "United as never before, the industry, with the US government now in tow, resolved to destroy the IWW, doing this while 'capitalizing on its shrewd feel for the temper of wartime America.'"[3]

The lumbermen proclaimed, "Without respect for neither God, government or men, these traitors have spewed the spawn of hate and sung their hymns of venom all over this fair country. . . . The flag of our fathers and of our common country has been defiled and vilified—all in the name of labor and the sham pretense of the uplift of the workers."[4]

This heightened the pitch of Seattle's other war, the war against labor. There had been ongoing skirmishes, even battles, plenty of them, but now began a fight to the death. President Wilson would offer his blessings to the Protective Association, convinced that the trouble in the West was not about workers' grievances but rather about the spruce, cedar, and fir needed to carry out the war. The key issue was sabotage, obstruction of the war effort, and strikers on German payrolls. Concerning the reports he had received from Seattle, Wilson wrote to Attorney General Thomas W. Gregory: "If true, they state a very grave situation. . . . It is thoroughly worth our while, to consider what, if anything, should and can be done about the influences proceeding from Seattle."[5]

In truth there was some basis for these fears. Labor historian Melvyn Dubofsky describes the strength and ambition of the IWW on the eve of America's entry into the war: "The IWW stood poised to open a new and more successful chapter in its history. It appeared ready to generate a sense of solidarity and a spirit of organization among workers long neglected by the trade unions." These included Minnesota loggers, Western hop and fruit pickers, harvest hands following wheat crops from Texas to Canada, black dockworkers in Philadelphia and Baltimore, white and black American as well as Spanish-speaking seamen sailing the Great Lakes and the seven seas, hard-rock miners in Arizona's company towns and the anti-union bastion of Butte, and riggers and day laborers in the oil fields of Kansas, Oklahoma, and California. "The IWW hoped to accomplish what no other American labor organization had ever done, or even attempted: organize America's disinherited and dispossessed."[6]

The Wilson administration paid high tribute to Seattle in considering it to be a "hotbed of unrest and of possible outbreak" and a "staging ground" for regional and national unrest.[7] By defining IWW members as traitors, the federal government gave a free hand to extrajudicial repression. The Minute Men, veterans of the Spanish-American War, implacable reactionaries, numbered several thousand. They assumed the right to detain and question suspected radicals, as did vigilantes of all sorts. The federal authorities' local officials guided the Minute Men and the lumbermen gave them confidential information about their workers. They were financed by Seattle's largest corporations, while the lumber companies in western Washington sought to extend the campaign statewide, pledging a thousand dollars each month for counter-radical surveillance.[8] By the end of 1917, the Minute Men claimed to have "tracked down the most rabid leaders and agitators among the IWW, and [to] have been instrumental in making several hundred investigations and having caused many arrests."[9] The military joined in. On the one hand, the army counterintelligence division from nearby Camp Lewis was dispatched to protect its troops and the civilian population from alleged German-inspired agitators. On the other, the navy assumed "control" of the city's harbor and docks, granting itself the authority to search and seize members of the IWW and the ILA without cause, as did off-duty soldiers and sailors.

Then there was fighting in the streets. The *Seattle Times* blamed anarchist organizations for reported "fistfights occurring in the city." It called for a "cleanup" of an unspecified element, which likely included both Wobblies and Socialists. IWW? Socialists? Little distinction was made.[10] On June 16, hundreds of soldiers and marines, said to be "on leave," surrounded an IWW assembly on the corner of Occidental and Washington Streets and then followed them to their hall, intending to break in. Military police forced the crowd to move on, but it later regrouped. When shots rang out, this brought the Seattle police who, despite themselves, saved the hall, but seized the opportunity to arrest fifty-one IWW members.[11] The entry of the United States into the European bloodbath turned dissent everywhere into treason. And a long-simmering dispute became a bloody war at home, though rather one-sided, as vigilantes attacked and looted the offices of IWW and Socialists across the country, including in Seattle.

The IWW conventions routinely approved resolutions denouncing war and patriotism. It charged the European working classes with "ignorance" for their failure to oppose the war and the devastation it would bring. Its fire was aimed chiefly at the Social Democratic movements, vilifying them for succumbing to the wave of patriotism that swept Europe. The 1916 convention resolved the same. "We condemn all wars and, for the prevention of such, we proclaim anti-militarist propaganda in time of peace . . . and, in time of war, the General Strike in all industries."[12] Actual war, that is, the entry of the United States into the European war, presented the IWW with a problem: how to oppose the war without jeopardizing opportunities to organize. The IWW's answer was a mix of fatalism, realism, and opportunism. The solution was to play down opposition to the war without abandoning it. *Solidarity*, the IWW's Eastern paper, responded to critics by opposing "meaningless gestures." "In the case of war, we want the One Big Union . . . to come out of the conflict stronger and with more industrial control than previously. Why should we sacrifice working-class interests for the sake of a few noisy and impotent demonstrations? Let us rather get on the job of organizing the working class to take over the industries, war or no war, and stop all future capitalist aggression that leads to war and other forms of barbarism."[13] Antagonists, inside and out, found this wanting. The question was, they asked, what to *do* about war?

The issue became academic. On May 24, 1917, the IWW's Chicago headquarters were ransacked and their records and correspondence seized. A couple of weeks later, in Bisbee, Arizona, heavily armed "deputies" loaded 13,000 striking miners, their families, and neighbors into cattle cars and sent them into the desert without food or water. Later in the summer, Frank Little was lynched in Butte. Finally, on the morning of September 5, US Attorney General Thomas Watt Gregory ordered federal action against the IWW. Coast to coast, federal agents raided IWW offices and homes, seizing tons of material. Not mincing words, Gregory explained, "Our purpose being, as I understand it, very largely to put the IWW out of business."[14] Then the Justice Department organized a Chicago grand jury which proceeded to indict 166 Wobblies, accusing them of "interfering with congressional acts and presidential proclamations, conducting strikes which constituted criminal conspiracy, influencing members to refuse to register or to desert the armed forces, causing insubordination with the armed forces and lastly conspiring to defraud employers."[15]

The Chicago trial of 113 Wobblies, presided over by Judge Kenesaw Mountain Landis, began on April 1, 1918. A peculiar jurist, Landis had once fined Standard Oil (they didn't pay), and he would become Major League Baseball's commissioner in the aftermath of the Black Sox scandal. John Reed, just back from Russia and writing for the *Liberator*, described how Landis "abolished pompous formality. He sits without robes, in an ordinary business suit, and often leaves the bench to come down and perch on the step of the jury box."[16] The government's lead lawyer was Frank Nebeker, who had represented copper-mining corporations in the Rocky Mountain West. Seattle's George Vanderveer represented the defendants. To strengthen its case, the prosecution dismissed all charges against women defendants, and decided not to put either the Bisbee deportees or the Butte strikers on trial for fear of what they might reveal about repression. Vanderveer and his collaborator Cleary responded with what Reed called "one long bloody pageant of industrial wrong: Coeur d'Alene, San Diego, Everett, Yakima Valley, Paterson, Mesabi Range, Bisbee, Tulsa."[17] The trial lasted into August. With the arguments completed, Judge Landis gave instructions to the jury, who deliberated one hour and found all the defendants guilty on each count. The result was that Haywood, Chaplin, Fletcher, Speed, St. John, James Rowan, Red Doran, Thompson, Herbert Mahler, Charles Ashleigh, Harry Lloyd, J. A. MacDonald, and Walter Smith went in chains to the federal penitentiary in Leavenworth. Kansas. Trials in Fresno, Omaha, Wichita, and Sacramento produced similar outcomes.

John Reed described, without exaggeration, what was at stake. "One Big Union—that is their crime. That is why the IWW is on trial. In the end, just such an ideal shall sap and crumble down capitalist society. If there were a way to kill these men, capitalist society would clearly do it; as it killed Frank Little, for example—and before him, Joe Hill. . . . So, the outcry of the jackal press, 'German agents! Treason!'—that the IWW may be lynched on a grand scale."[18]

ANNA LOUISE STRONG WAS STILL in her Mt. Rainier camp in 1917 when a new periodical began to appear. It was the *Seattle Daily Call*, the creation of Thorward G. Mauitzen, who described himself as "a cowboy, hobo, rancher, soapboxer, editor and publisher who wouldn't stay put." Newly arrived to Seattle, Mauritzen had been inspired by the Everett decision, the growth of the IWW, and workers' councils in Russia, to found a newspaper. He had raised a mere $500 by the time the first edition appeared on July 28, 1917.

Strong found the *Call* "four pages, poorly written, badly printed—[but] it said what I wanted to say about the war. It said them in harsh words and poor English—the things that respectable folks had ceased to say." The *Call* jeered at the Wilson slogans, "a war to end war," and "a world safe for democracy," insisting that America went to war to protect her loan to the Allies and to make money for war profiteers. Strong credited the paper with bringing her back to the movement: "The call for the workers of all lands to get together and end the war gave me a reason for coming back from the mountains; it gave me a home again."[19]

She joined Mauritzen, the young Harvey O'Connor, plus the veteran socialist Lena Morrow Lewis on the staff. Lewis had been a national organizer and lecturer for the Socialist Party from 1908 to 1914. She had spoken in auditoriums and halls, but also in lumber camps and mining districts, before audiences in every state except Mississippi. Lewis had been elected as a member of the National Woman's Committee from California and as a delegate to the Socialists' 1910 Copenhagen Conference. She had also written the pamphlet, "The Socialist Party and Woman Suffrage," which had a distribution of 200,000 copies. She came to Seattle from Alaska where she had been an organizer, living alone in a two-room cabin. From the home of a black miner where the socialist local met, she and her co-workers launched a paper, reviving an abandoned weekly. Miners in the region, whose Tanana Valley union had just been smashed, avidly read it. "Arguments raged during the long Alaskan winter nights," O'Connor explains, adding, "The miners turned out in droves for the socialist meetings and Mrs. Lewis became a prized possession in their lives."[20]

Lewis was older and more versed in Marxism than Strong, but it was the latter who became the workhorse of the *Call*, as she would become at the *Union Record*. Writing under the pen name "Gale," she covered the city hall scandals, the Loyal Legion in the woods, and the trials of socialists and union leaders. Strong later recalled: "We worked fourteen to sixteen hours a day . . . editorials, news, features, satirical poems were pounded out by me while I shivered from the cold cement floors of our unheated offices."[21] The trials and prisoners kept coming. Before he left for prison, Wells addressed the Labor Council at the Labor Temple. The delegates cheered him for a full ten minutes when he told a story expressing his solidarity with the Wobblies: "Someone who thought he was a friend of mine recently stated that he would like to see me freed but that he wanted to see the IWWs kept in jail. I don't want my liberty on any such terms as that."[22] Strong testified for Wells as a main witness in the conscription trials, helping to get a hung jury, though Wells and Vanderveer warned her not to.

Louise Olivereau was a stenographer for the Lumber Workers section of the IWW. The child of immigrants, she was born in Wyoming. While earning a degree from Illinois State University, she learned of Francisco Ferrer, the Spanish anarchist, and the Modern School movement, which proposed that children would best thrive in an unstructured, loving environment. Later, she taught in day classes for children and evening and weekend classes for adults. "Olivereau," the journalist Jessie Lloyd O'Connor observed, "was a gentle, warm-hearted young woman who in 1917 had a job typing in a Wobbly local hall." Before that, she had been a cook at resort camps. "She was evidently well-educated: she never failed to write 'shall' when grammar demanded it, even in letters to close friends. She had left her parents somewhere, geographically or spiritually, for she told nothing about them."

Olivereau's response to the war was intense personal pain. She could not bear that the youth of our country should follow Europe into the meatgrinder without a protest. Jessie Lloyd O'Connor: "She had long taken a motherly interest in the high school youngsters who sought out the Wobbly Hall looking for adventure in the great task of improving conditions." On summer evenings, she met with small groups of them, reading poetry and philosophy aloud, and discussing beliefs, economics, and the future of the human race.[23] Quoting the pacifist intellectual Randoph Borne, Olivereau said, "War is the health of the state." She was also a veteran of free speech fights in Sacramento, San Diego, and Fresno. Moving to Seattle in 1915, Olivereau briefly joined the Socialist Party, then left, turning instead to the writings of Emma Goldman and Alexandra Berkman. She may have joined the IWW.

When the draft summonses began to arrive, Olivereau took $40 from her salary—more than $800 in today's money—to purchase writing materials and stamps. She composed a letter to draftees, mimeographed it, and sent it out. On September 5, federal agents raided the Seattle IWW hall. The next day at work, Olivereau discovered her desk had been ransacked. The *Star* reported that there had been no arrests, but that subversive materials had been confiscated.[24] She contacted an agent of the Department of Justice and went to his office to retrieve her property two days later. The agent tried to establish that the IWW was responsible for the letters, but Olivereau insisted that she had acted entirely alone. Accompanying Olivereau to her Wallingford residence, the agent then confiscated more documents. She was then arrested, taken to the Pierce County Jail in Tacoma, and charged with violating the Espionage Act. The nine counts against her included obstructing recruitment and using the mail for attempting to cause disobedience in the military forces, matters urging insurrection or any other offense. Bail was set at $7,500. Strong sat with her during the long trial where the focus was her "philosophical anarchism." They would enter and exit the courtroom "with locked arms," the *Seattle Times* noted.

Olivereau was not a spy, of course; nor was she a German agent. She did believe, however, in direct action and civil disobedience. In court, she chose to defend herself. She would answer as truthfully as she could, even when others complained that she weakened her own case. She insisted on telling the world just exactly what she thought it needed to hear. It's not clear that lawyers could have achieved a better outcome. The jury was comprised of a retired banker, a real estate broker, a wealthy hardware merchant, and a man who had seven sons all serving in the army.[25] The prosecutor closed by saying that Olivereau's anti-draft letters were meant "to sow the seeds of mutiny and disloyalty to law and order . . . the evil fruit of such regards which we know would be similar to those terrible acts now transpiring in Russia." He appealed to the jury to act "for the very life of the nation," claiming that people like the defendant "strike at the very foundation of government and outrage the feelings of true Americans."[26]

Olivereau responded by saying, "Anarchism is the working philosophy of those who desire to bring about a condition in society in which force and violence will have no place. . . . I am convinced that violence breeds violence, hatreds, and fears and revengeful desires which lead to other wars."[27] The *Post-Intelligencer* (*PI*)reported that her voice was "deep, clear and her words are chosen for effect," and the *Seattle Times* stated that she was "one of the most widely known anarchistic leaders in the United States."[28] Olivereau argued that "constitutional freedoms including free speech have always been limited to 'freedom within the law,' which is not freedom at all." She said that "patriotic duty involved placing the good of the country above obedience to its laws," and she went on to give her views on conscientious objection, Wilson's war policy, and organized labor, emphasizing the government's complacency in the face of crimes and offenses against the working class: "The murderers of the Everett victims walk free; so far as I know, no investigation of the Butte affair has been made except one made by Miss Rankin, and it has had no results. The Phelps-Dodge Company may continue to censor telegrams without fear of anything more than a reprimand from the government." She also pointed out that capital had used the situation to cut back labor's rights: "When war was declared, there was the demand by corporations that all labor legislation be set aside . . . in order that women and children might be employed in occupations now closed to them, in order that employees might be worked an unlimited number of hours." Conversely, she explained, "attempts to secure better working conditions or shorter hours have been bitterly opposed. The workers have been told that it was unpatriotic for them to desire more money or more leisure in war time."[29]

Olivereau concluded her hour-long defense saying that she had love for her country, but explained that the autocratic US government was on par with the "militaristic system of Germany we are fighting."[30] Defiantly, she told the jurors: "These things will go on, whether I am in prison or out of it. They will go on, even though every Conscientious Objector, every pacifist, every IWW and every member of any other union who endeavors to secure better conditions for the workers and a freer atmosphere for thought and personal life, be thrown in jail." In a great worldwide movement, she argued that "the individual is of little importance; it is the propagation of the idea which is important. And all those who are thus thrown into prison for the crime of loving humanity and working for its emancipation, we know that they are in good company; to them there will come the spirits and the memory of not only our own Revolutionary forefathers, and the Abolitionists, breakers of the laws of their time, but of all the great host of free-souled thinkers of all ages, from Jesus to Frank Little, Revolutionists from England, France, Russia—there is no lack of good company for those whom we imprison today."[31]

In her autobiography, Strong remembered scolding Olivereau for her conduct as defendant. "She asked me to sit beside her in court," Strong recalled, "so she might have a friendly word to relieve the soul-crushing atmosphere of American justice. . . . I was neither prepared nor unprepared for the eight-column headlines which greeted the fact that the woman school director, already under attack for recall, had befriended an anarchist."[32] The dailies harried Strong, and the women's clubs deserted her.

The court sentenced Olivereau to ten years in the Colorado State Prison in Canon City, the nearest federal prison for women. Noting her intelligence, Judge Jeremiah Neterer said he hoped she would change her mind about organized government. He reminded her that every leaflet she had posted was an offense punishable by five years of imprisonment and on that basis he could have sent her to the penitentiary for ten thousand years.[33] She would spend twenty-eight months at Canon City.

WALKER SMITH KEPT LISTS of the Everett IWWs; Strong's Everett notes include interviews as well. Virtually all listed were native-born, white, most often Northern European in background, and often migrants in Seattle seeking rest, looking for the next job. Still, the idea of the IWW as literally alien took hold. Businessmen and public officials envisioned the deportation of thousands as "undesirable" aliens as a simple, practicable solution. Here too, the gloves were off.

Immigrants were sought out and punished on a large scale. The immigrants found the Immigration Bureau's proceedings—conducted in English and rarely with competent, unbiased translators—to be bewildering. When arrested, immigrants were separated from family and friends, with bail set impossibly high. Swedes and Finns were the most persecuted. Italians were also under attack, it being a time when "anarchist" and "Italian" were all but synonymous. The interrogators worked virtually without rules, not allowing defense counsel and often seeking self-incrimination. Few, if any, interrogators spoke anything but English, none were familiar with the ideas or organizations of the left, except perhaps the IWW, and then only as a demonic caricature. Supporting the IWW could be proved by anything: reading a paper, donating in support of a strike, or placing a pamphlet on the bookshelf. Seattle officials argued that any such action helped spread the IWW's message, which was itself illegal. Not bothering to search for evidence or find out what one actually did, interrogators spent their time subjecting suspects to ideological cross-examinations, trying to find out what one read, what one believed, and who were one's friends.

The radical Seattle lawyer Mark Litchman kept papers containing notes on cases of immigrants he defended in the course of the crisis. Born in New York City, he tramped the world as a youth, settling in Seattle in 1908 where he attended the University of Washington's Law School, passing the bar in 1913. Traveling, Litchman recalled, gave him "both a heart and a viewpoint for the underdog, and my early ideal, which furnished the dynamic urge, was to become a lawyer for the downtrodden." He joined the Socialist Party, routinely representing them in court and took up the defense of the *Union Record* in its sedition case. Litchman was an advocate of the eight-hour day, but in these years, he was especially devoted to the cause of the Red Scare's immigrant victims.

Litchman's papers include many cases. In one cache, the defendants are coal miners from the hills east of Seattle, employed at the Black Diamond Mine on the Cascades' western slope and at Cle Elum on the eastern slope. They were all foreign-born Italian immigrants and poorly educated, if at all. Jailed and unable to pay bail, they were charged with reading *Cronaca sovversiva*, a journal that included writings of the anarchist Luigi Galleani on direct action and armed resistance to the state, thereby violating the Immigration Act of February 1917, Section 19.[34]

Here are examples taken from Litchman's notes:

Giuseppe Bertoletti, 32, was charged with "advocating or teaching anarchy, or the overthrow by force or violence of the Government of the United States or of all forces of law, or the assassination of public officials." Litchman's notes describe him as a coal miner from Cle Elum, a member of the United Mine Workers, employed Northwest Improving Company, five years, married with one child, owned his own home. Name found on the subscription list of the anarchist journal *Cronaca Sovversiva*, In jail three months, $5,000 bail. Denied knowledge of the journal or its point of view. Left school in Italy in third year. "Well, I want to say that since I came to this country, I took out about four to six tons daily, and as a reward was arrested in the mine without having committed any crime, and I think it unjust. Since war broke out in Italy, I worked every day in this country, using my salary to keep up my old mother, and two families, and so I would like to know if I can be released under bond as I would like to go home and work." Denied.

Pietro Belli, 29, charged with "advocating" etc., In good health. "a fact which I cannot truthfully state now—he has been in jail more than five months." Itinerant laborer, followed mine laboring, two years resident in the United States, never arrested. No evidence of ever teaching, "he is not of that stamp." No knowledge of *Cronaca sovversiva*. $5,000 bail.

Ottavic Bonnani (same charge), coal miner, Pacific Coast Coal at Black Diamond, WA, ten years. Lives with his wife and child, born in the United States. Member of the United Mine Workers, owns his house, has never been arrested. Books found in house. Officer believed them anarchistic, some had "red paper covers." Disclaimed ownership of all with the exception 11 volumes of "Natural Medicine." In hearing, it was disclosed that none of books were anarchistic—"the alien breathed a sigh of relief, and the inspectors gave way to laughter with great gusto." Hearing officer: "If you are released, Mr. Bonnani, and you find out that this paper is anarchistic, and it is a crime to read it, you will refuse to read it?" "I don't want to read it. I got in enough trouble. I wish to go home right away, I got enough trouble."

"This is the situation faced by the foreign-born workers," wrote John Reed in the *Liberator*, "most of whom are not protected even by the inefficient labor organizations affiliated in the AFL—or are members of the IWW, which has been practically outlawed (although the government pretends it is not), and whose members are hounded from city to city, arrested and beaten, and even lynched."[35]

Beginning in late 1917, the Bureau of Immigration significantly eased the procedures for arresting members of the IWW. Then came a deportation crusade that was huge in scope and based on the assumption that Wobblies and aliens were in fact the same.[36] The Seattle authorities believed that these deportations would bring an end to the IWW threat in the Northwest. "The deportation of alien IWWs," a committee representing all federal officials in Seattle concluded, "would be the most adaptive and persuasive technique of repression."[37] This way costly, time-consuming jail time and trials might be avoided, as well as the onerous process of charging and convicting every individual defendant. The Bureau of Immigration thus set out to arrest and deport "IWW aliens" who were deemed "undesirable" or "pro-German in their activity."[38] The roundup quickly filled the Bureau's own detention centers, forcing it to scatter prisoners throughout the county jails of western Washington.

"Success came easily," writes William Preston, "because the inspectors used almost any excuse for an arrest. The district office detained aliens 'supposed to be ... prominent and active members of the IWW [and] aliens who looked like IWWs.'"[39] The lumbermen eagerly collaborated with the Seattle office to find and rid themselves of suspected IWWs or anyone else they didn't want. If a mill manager suspected a man to be a picket, he could have him arrested for deportation; merely reporting that he was a troublemaker was often sufficient for immigration officers. "In none of the cases," Preston explained, "was there sufficient evidence under the 1917 act to justify issuing a warrant. Arrest was, rather, a convenient method for the removal and detention of undesirables. Besides, there was always the chance that an alien might incriminate himself during the hearing."[40]

According to Reed, Seattle was the epicenter of the anti-immigrant hysteria and the Red Scare: "Since December,1917, foreigners active in the Labor Movement had been quietly arrested in the West, and after cursory hearings, alone (no lawyers permitted), threatened with physical force while being questioned, scores have been held for deportation under the Immigration laws." "The center of the movement," he wrote, "was the great Northwest, where the IWW had been organizing the timber workers and lumbermen. This was the scene of the Everett Massacre, where deputy sheriffs and private detectives fired upon a steamboat full of labor organizers from Seattle and killed six. The same business men and manufacturers who inspired the Everett Massacre were behind the deportation scheme."[41]

The end of the war made legal defense more feasible for the Wobblies, improving their situation somewhat. Vanderveer returned from Chicago and entered the fray. He demanded writs of habeas corpus, and policy revisions from the Bureau. Writing to Frank Walsh, co-chair of the National War Labor Board, he reported that the inspectors had thwarted his efforts: "With only one exception, every immigration official has denied me access to both defendants and the records and has questioned my authority in a manner that no court has yet attempted in all my practice of law. Not only that, but they have frequently stated that their purpose was, if possible, to prevent the men from securing a hearing in court, notwithstanding that they have been restrained of the liberty and denied their legal rights all the way from seven to seventeen months."[42]

The Seattle deportation campaign was, in the end, a failure, since it resulted in very few deportations. "The northwestern officials had turned out to be extremely incompetent detectives and lawyers, and equally untrustworthy judges." Still, it had done much damage to the IWW in what would become a nationwide campaign against organized labor and radicals. When immigration officers and the administration in Washington, DC, had to choose a course for their own ongoing crusade against leftists

and immigrants, they opted for following Seattle's extreme interpretations of policy and enforcement (instead of Labor Secretary
William Wilson's preference for strict definitions of law and focusing on individual guilt). "The anti-radical hysteria of one city,"
found Preston, "thus projected its purely local campaign onto a
national scale, initiating a chain of events culminating in the alien
communist roundup by A. Mitch Palmer's 1920 raids. If Seattle
had wanted to be rid of its seditious elements—a little neighborhood repression would have served the purpose. [Instead] by the
winter of 1918 . . . an unsettled lumber strike, a vacillating attorney, a neutral city administration, and the annual appearance of
large numbers of migratory workers set the stage for widespread
lawlessness."[43]

The final episode in Seattle's anti-immigrant campaign took
place on the eve of the General Strike in anticipation of an "insurrection." The US Attorney in Seattle telegraphed the Justice
Department: "Intention of strike is revolution led by extreme element openly advocating overthrow of government."[44] He insisted
that the radical aliens then held in Seattle must be removed immediately, no later than February 4, the date set for the General
Strike. The operation went forward. By the time the strike began,
fifty-four prisoners had boarded the "Red Special." "Heavily protected with armed guards," the New York Call wrote, "the phantom
train, traveling on a 'mystery schedule' bearing 54 'very dangerous
persons' across the land of the free, whisked across the continent
from Seattle."[45] Thirty-six supposedly unrepentant and desperate
IWWs were on board, headed toward New York City, there to be
shipped off to Europe. The trip to New York involved one calamity
after another for the authorities. In Butte, "a great crowd of one
thousand stormed the station," hoping to free the prisoners but
found that the train had made a detour and been rerouted north
through Helena.[46] In Chicago, dozens of plainclothesmen had to
patrol the platforms at Union Station. For the rest of the route to
New York the federal government needed to induct every county
sheriff and constable along the way.[47] In New York City, a series of

mass protests, organized by the Socialist Party, received the train. Even the barge passage to Ellis Island, where the prisoners were kept incommunicado, was not easy. A row broke out, and soldiers had to be dispatched. In the end, awash in legal challenges, the government released twelve of the "Red Special" prisoners. Five accepted deportation; the Labor Department secured the release of two more. Those remaining sued for writs of habeas corpus. In the end a total of seven were deported.

9. FIVE DAYS THAT MATTER

On Thursday, February 6, 1919, at 10 a.m., Seattle's workers struck. Here it was, finally, a general strike in the nation's most radical city. It was the first such strike. An estimated 60,000 left their jobs, the number of union members in the city. There was no evidence of strikebreaking. The strikers were "jubilant." "They were impressed—if somewhat awed—by the demonstration of their own power."[1]

Seattle's thirty thousand shipyard workers plus fifteen thousand of their fellows in Tacoma were already on strike. Now, with the call for a general strike, streetcar workers came on board, as did waitresses, painters, Teamsters, miners, barbers—workers from almost all the city's unions. Railroad and postal clerks said they would be jailed for striking since the law prohibited federal employees from doing so. Some struck knowing there could be reprisals—the hotel maids were few in numbers yet voted for the strike. Like other newly organized women's unions, they were especially vulnerable to future retaliation yet remained nearly unanimous in favor of the strike. Myrtle Horworth reported to the strike's Executive Committee that "the union was a small union with about 100 members and that they had voted about 7 to 1 to strike, realizing that many of them would lose their positions when they cast their vote." Members remained on strike, however, notwithstanding the fact that several of the proprietors had tried to bribe some of them into scabbing.[2] The longshoremen risked loss of their recently won closed shop. Musicians initially opposed the idea of the strike but voted six to one in favor once it began.[3] Coal miners pledged statewide support.

The strike's critics have contested the figure of sixty thousand strikers, but the real number may have been higher. This is because there were unknown numbers of participating workers still not organized. "How many individual workers struck without the protection of a union will never be known but there were many," one witness wrote in the *Liberator*. "There came to my notice an elevator boy in an office building who calmly quit, saying that he hoped to get his job back again, but he wasn't going to work during the strike. Two men working for a landscape gardener did the same and lost their jobs. Newsboys arose in school and left at 10."[4] There were even unemployed workers who supported the strike—it was extraordinary. There were families on strike, and still more children who walked out of school. Mrs. Eric Lindquist, wife of a shipyard worker, urged mothers, wives, daughters, sisters to support the strikers, recalling, "History tells of no greater bravery than that of the Spartan mothers. What was the task of those noble women? To hold up the hands of their men fighters; to encourage them on the one hand and on the other make them understand the only way to win their approval was to win in battles."[5] Altogether it is likely that half, if not more, of the city was on strike or supporting it.[6] Power, at least for the moment, was in the hands of Seattle's working class.

The strike, set as it was in the far Northwest, was at once an isolated event and yet connected. The Seattle strike, recorded an alarmed *Nation* magazine, was "extraordinary" in an "extraordinary time." It represented "the most extraordinary phenomenon of the present time . . . the unprecedented revolt of the rank and file. . . . In Russia it has dethroned the Czar. . . . In Korea and India and

Egypt and Ireland it keeps up an unyielding resistance to political tyranny. In England it brought about the railroad strike, against the judgement of the men's own executives. . . . [In the United States] it brought about the New York longshoremen's strike and kept the men out in defiance of union officials, and caused the upheaval in the printing trade, which the international officers, even though the employers worked hand in glove with them, were completely unable to control. The common man . . . losing faith in the old leadership, has experienced a new access of self-confidence, or at least a new recklessness, a readiness to take chance on its own account . . . authority cannot any longer be imposed from above; it comes automatically from below."[7] The Seattle Strike, as much as any single event, set this in motion.

The *Post-Intelligencer*, the *Seattle Times*, and the *Star* vilified the strikers. "A handful of radicals precipitated this absurd and indefensible conflict" claimed, the *PI*. "They . . . put Seattle in the position of staging a revolution against the government of the United States. These radicals must go, and it is the business of employers to see that they do, by co-operating with conservative labor in the reconstruction."[8] Edwin Selvin, editor of the *Business Chronicle*, insisted that "the labor leaders be hanged on the nearest telephone pole." His printers, however, all union members, refused to set this in type. Softening, Selvin demanded that all labor "agitators" on the job be replaced by returning veterans. He called Seattle "the most labor terrorized city in America," declaring that it was "overrun by red-flag agitators in the guise of labor leaders."[9]

Soldiers occupied Seattle's city center. They installed machine guns that commanded the downtown's street corners. Camp Lewis suspended demobilization and resumed training of soldiers. Warships stood by in the bay. Bremerton's sailors were on alert. The governor resisted invoking martial law, although University of Washington president Henry Suzzallo and the city's employers demanded that he do so. Well-to-do businessmen dispatched family members to hotels in Portland and California. The *Star* reported "No Guns Left in Shops Here."[10] The mayor swore in six hundred new police and deputized 2,400 more. University of Washington students volunteered for anti-strike duty.[11] A hardware dealer reported "400 requests for guns and ammunition" though "not one from a laboring man."[12] Despite the printers being on strike, the *Seattle Star* cobbled together an "emergency" edition announcing that "clubs, revolvers, rifles, carbines, automatics, and machine guns were being distributed among the fearful."[13]

The General Strike's principal aim was to support striking shipyard workers. The Metal Trades Council had requested the strike to back up their dispute with the shipbuilders, which had begun with a shipyard strike launched two weeks earlier. Expected, indeed long postponed, the strike was "absolutely clean," according to A. E. Miller, chair of the Metal Trades. "The men walked out *en masse*, none remained in the plants." The thirty thousand strikers in Seattle showed "splendid solidarity and great enthusiasm"; cheering throngs, undaunted by the winter rain, left the yards and swarmed into the city's streets. Tacoma followed suit with fifteen thousand more workers, then Aberdeen. No one came to take their places.

The shipyard strike was about wages, pure and simple. Yet Seattle was on edge, filling up with unemployed, homeless, demobilized young men, and few were unaware of the stories coming from Russia. Just three nights earlier, thousands of Seattle's workers had packed the Hippodrome to announce the formation of a "Soldiers, Sailors and Workers' Council." It was a project of the Metal Trades Union, who feared the use of discharged soldiers as strikebreakers. The meeting went forward despite the authorities, who surrounded the hall with military police. Several thousand workers also gathered in Tacoma, just miles north of Camp Lewis, the nation's largest army base. Bert Swain, a leader of the Engineers' Union, reported encountering large numbers of men, "returned soldiers with only $4 or $5 between them," searching for work.[14] The recently demobilized soldiers were making their way to Seattle, as loggers and harvest hands had done before them, looking for work and some place to stay.

Speaking on behalf of the Metal Workers, John McKelvey defied the owners. The "shipyard millionaires," he reminded those assembled, "have been getting all the credit for the ships we have built. Oh yes, they're the ship builders. If they think they can build ships, let 'em go ahead and build them! They've got the yards. Can they build ships?" The Boilermakers' official Dan McKillop, responding to the shipbuilders' threats to close, also was undaunted by the threat of moving all shipbuilding to the East: "Well, let them try it. If they want a revolution, let 'em start it."[15]

The idea of a General Strike was not new in Seattle. The IWW had routinely threatened to stage one even though the closest it came was the big timber strike, sometimes called "a general strike in the woods." The *Union Record* had covered the great European strikes of the era, with regular reports from the Scottish shipbuilders of the River Clyde, who had struck in 1915. "I was taken by surprise," Wells admitted, "but I saw at once that if the general strike was ever to be given a test, that it could not be undertaken at a more propitious time. Never before had such a generally militant spirit prevailed. After the long steady grind of the war years most workers would be glad to have a short rest. All of them had more savings than ever before." Finally, he advised, "being a strike against the government, it was political in its nature, and nothing but a spectacular demonstration would have any chance of success."[16]

The *Post-Intelligencer* and *Seattle Times* desperately sought ways to divide the workers, insisting that the rank and file did not support the strike, which was merely a project of the radicals. Yet some of the best-known radicals were still en route from the Chicago Mooney Congress (in defense of the imprisoned labor leaders Mooney and Billings) when the strike was called. Seattle's forty-member delegation included Duncan, Turco, Strong, and Kate Sadler. It has also been suggested that the absence of this contingent somehow cleared a path for the other radicals. This makes no sense. There was no group, this or any other, including Duncan's, that would have defied the shipyard workers' request. In fact, it was the shipyard workers who led the strike, and in that sense, they were the radicals, infuriated by the stonewalling and intrigue of their employers and the federal government. The shipyard workers were proud of their wartime achievements: in 1918, Seattle's yards were the most productive in the country, providing ninety-six ships, sixty-one of these steel-hulled freighters. They had done so even as wages had been frozen by wartime regulations. US government policy during the war had allowed for gains for labor, though the Wilson administration limited these by collaborating only with "responsible" trade unionists. The wartime industrial and labor boards insisted on uninterrupted production and no strikes. In exchange, compliant unions enjoyed growth in membership, recognition, bargaining rights, and participation on the labor boards themselves—in the name of peace and productivity on the shop floor. The situation changed at the war's end, when government policy shifted to containing inflation, making wage restraint the central feature of its labor policy. Consumer prices had doubled during the war. In the postwar years, however, the government instructed those labor boards not already disbanded to unbendingly resist concessions to the unions.

Seattle's shipyard workers believed they had already sacrificed. They had worked with standards set nationally, even when believing themselves punished by these standards. It was indisputable that prices were higher on the West Coast, above all in Seattle, than in the East; yet the government pressed for national standards. The workers believed themselves to be held hostage by the national agreements which Eastern-centered international unions had made in violation of their constitutions. Seattle's metal workers complained that the national leadership had traded their right to strike for recognition of the union, which they already had. Authority now rested with the Shipbuilding Labor Adjustment Board (the Macy Board), named after its chair, V. Everit Macy, and formed by agreements between the US Emergency Fleet Corporation and the presidents of the unions involved. It controlled their wages (among other things) with the result that neither the Metal Trades Council nor its twenty-one-member unions had much say. This amounted to running roughshod over the craft unions' constitutions, where theoretically the rank and file had the last word.

When the war ended, the Metal Trades Council demanded general wage readjustments. Its president, James A. Taylor, traveled to Washington to confer with Charles Piez, director of the Emergency Fleet Corporation, and with the Macy Board. Writing in the *Liberator*, Joseph Pass highlighted Taylor's shrewdness: "He will not budge an inch if it is to the detriment of the working class. Theory was foreign to him. From the everyday battles of life, he learned the desires and hopes of his class. He gave Charles M. Schwab and Charles Piez many an unpleasant hour in Washington and Philadelphia. This vigorous labor man of the West stood up and fought these various boards with means that were unknown to labor leaders in the East."[17] When the Board's appeals committee split on the Seattle wage issue, Taylor returned to Seattle confident that he had been given permission to negotiate directly with the shipyards.

The shipyards' owners appeared to agree. Preliminary to negotiations in November, the Metal Trades held a strike vote, and majorities were carried in most unions. On January 16, 1919, negotiations opened on demands for an $8 scale for mechanics, $7 for specialists, $6 for helpers, and $5.50 for laborers. The Council calculated that its wage demands would leave the shipyard owners with ample profits. The owners refused, responding with desultory offers for skilled workers, nothing for laborers. Intrigue followed—misdelivered letters and ultimatums from Piez. Had the employers themselves requested these? Who really was in charge? Piez ordered the shipyard owners not to give in to wage demands; the shipyards would receive no steel if they did so. The Macy Board would set all terms itself and assume total authority in all negotiations. The union demands were rejected. They were up against both employers and the government.

The *Union Record* brought news of the strikers' plight to its fifty thousand subscribers, supporting the strike without qualification. Next to its front-page lead on January 2, "45,000 Men Out in Sound

Cities," it ran an article titled, "Tremendous Profits Made by Seattle Shipbuilding Firms," revealing the businesses' costs, sales, and profits.[18] The day's editorial, "A Great Strike," explained: "The whole question of wages is bound up in the tremendous increase in the cost of living in Seattle."[19] There are some, it argued, "who will, perhaps, refer to the demand of '$1 an hour' as an outrageous demand. It should be remembered, however, that $8 per day in these days of mounting living costs equals but $4 a day when the yardstick of 'purchasing power' is used to measure wages. No REASONABLE man will say that sum is too great a wage for a skilled worker engaged in hazardous labor." The editorial continued: "It should be remembered that the wage applied to but a limited number of workers in the yards. By far the greater number of workers in the yard are $4.16-a-day men. . . . It would hardly be necessary to argue as to the inadequacy of a $4.16 wage scale in Seattle today. No thinking man will contend that it is possible to maintain a family on such a wage —especially when it is remembered that it is almost an impossibility to get in what amounts to full time."[20]

"The idea of a general strike swept the ranks of organized labor like a gale," wrote Harvey O'Connor. Statements of solidarity were rushed in from the shipyards of Anacortes and the Grays Harbor towns, and from metal workers in shops and mills along the shores of the Sound. On January 22, in an assembly of the CLC in the Labor Temple, the metal workers requested that Seattle's workers join them in a general strike. The aim would be not only to win their demands but also to present a show of force in the face of the employers' renewed open-shop campaign. They believed that the fate of the organized labor movement itself was at stake.[21] Representatives of the city's local trade unions and rank-and-file militants packed the Labor Temple. According to O'Connor, "Every reference to the general strike was cheered to the echo; the cautions of the conservatives . . . were hooted down."[22] Or interrupted by shouting, clapping, and singing. The Council proposed a referendum on the strike, which passed unanimously. The enthusiasm that evening brought with it high rhetoric, emotion, even tears. Then came a cornucopia of additional demands; appetites grew, delegates revealing their own grievances and aspirations, hopeful that these too might be addressed. The metal workers, however, insisted that the strike's demands be limited to those of the shipyard workers already out—what they wanted was a "clean-cut demonstration of the economic power of organized labor."[23]

"There are 32,000 workers employed in the shipbuilding industry," declared Hulet Wells, to cheers from those assembled, "and it comes pretty near being the basic industry of the city. The life of it pulses through every industry. It affects the workers in all industries." Why, he asked, should "the weaker industries aid in this strike? The answer is that there is no industry but stands to gain by the success of this strike." Wells then repeated what would become a mantra of the strikers: "The real reason for this strike is to help the poorest paid working men. In spite of all that has been said, the highly paid workers in the shipyards are very few."[24]

The meeting ended in an uproar when delegate Fred Nelson unfurled a banner showing a soldier and a sailor in uniform with a worker in overalls and the slogan "Together We Will Win." This was followed by "a storm of applause which lasted several minutes" abating only when delegate Ben King of the Painters, just returned from the Mooney Congress, recounted "sleeping between soldiers and sailors and they are all with us." The applause "broke out afresh."[25]

This meeting and those that followed only widened the sense of solidarity. According to the reflections of a woman who was there, "The Japanese barbers struck when the American barbers struck and were given seats of honor at the Barbers union meeting that occurred immediately thereafter."[26] "The Japanese and American restaurant workers went out side by side."[27] The Japanese community, formed of Seattle's largest minority, would not be indifferent to the General Strike. The daily *Taihoku Nippo* reported: "Our compatriots are in two unions. One is the Dye Workers Union in which there are 80 associate members. The other is the [Barber's] Union composed of only compatriots, but it acts in agreement with the white union.

. . . The Dye Workers Union executives have already made the decision to go on sympathy strike and in a few days will call a meeting to unanimously pass the resolution."²⁸ The Japanese-language paper continued, "The said unions are the only organization that has joined to [American] union in the United States. This is a test to decide whether the Japanese in America will act in good faith as union men or not, because this is the first time to vote for or against a General Strike. In the days ahead the unions will have an important meaning and will exert a very large influence on our relationships of mutual trust. The sympathy votes of 80 people of the said union, therefore, must be said to be really significant."²⁹

The Japanese Labor Association, led by Katsunari Sasaki, counseled Japanese workers: "The members of this association should stop working during the General Strike. Our friends who do not belong to this Association should also follow the action of unions to which your trades belong." Sasaki then sent the following letter to James Duncan: "Regarding present crisis, we, Japanese Laborers' Assn., hereby declare to join General Strike sympathetically and, however, to make the step with you. We are much appreciate [*sic*] that some local unions of organized labor here in Seattle have had a good feeling toward us while American Federation of Labor is still discriminating us and refusing to become member of organization. Enclosed check of $50 of which we took collection from our members of here office, please place us supporting the General Strike, we are heartily sympathy with."³⁰

The *Union Record* responded to this gesture in its pages: "Even in the midst of strike excitement, let us stop for a moment to recognize the action of the Japanese barbers and restaurant workers who, through their own unions, voted to take part in the general strike. The strike here in Seattle is proving the biggest demonstration of internationalism that has yet occurred in this country. The Japanese deserve the greater credit because they have been denied admission and affiliation with the rest of the labor movement and have joined the strike of their own initiative. We hope that this evidence of labor's solidarity will have an influence on the relations between the two races in the future."[31] In his study of Japanese immigrants and the labor movement, Kurokawa argued that "the action of Japanese unions toward the General Strike helped to change the attitude of organized labor to Japanese workers."[32] The effects were felt as early as the second day of the strike, when two Japanese men recognized new feelings of fraternity among white workers toward them.[33] *Taihoku Nippo* reported: "During the turmoil of the General Strike two Japanese men ventured into the Labor Temple where executives were solemnly evaluating a strategic plan. One man is Tsuchiya, an inspector general who was responsible for peace and order of Jackson Street, and the other was Tsukuno, president of the Restaurant Union, which was in the vanguard of the sympathy strike. As soon as they found the two men, the executives in the Temple gathered to shake hands with them and guide them to a meeting room. Every man there, with one voice, expressed their appreciation for the sympathy of the Japanese and they said they would not forget this favor for as long as the Labor Council exists. When the two men were about to leave after they had heard about the situation, the people there thanked them again for coming and gave them a ride to their house."[34]

Duncan, the "moderate," home from Chicago, with the others, joined the movement, saying. "The gauntlet has been thrown down by representatives of the government who think more of building ships than building men. . . . They feel it was all right for us to talk about democracy as long as they talked about democracy, but when they stopped, it was time for us to stop."[35] The city's elites were stunned, unprepared, then panicked by the sheer pace of these developments, and confounded. They did not understand the strike. Yet as A. E. Miller of the Metal Trades pointed out, the procedure for calling the strike was straightforward: "The question has been asked," said Miller "if the strike was called by the rank and file. The membership took a vote following the decision of the Macy Board. The question submitted was, 'Shall we accept the Macy Award, or shall we go on strike for the original demands?'

Both a majority of the unions and a majority of the membership voted for the strike."[36]

Still, it was not simply a strike, albeit bigger than most. It was a radical strike in radical times. The *Union Record*'s front pages, crowded with international news, were evidence of a world in turmoil. The editors routinely updated readers on the revolution in Russia and the strikes in Britain. It also covered the fighting in Budapest and in Germany, including the bloody street confrontations in Berlin, where the Spartacists were "demanding the end of the ministry. . . . Wives and sweethearts of the mutinous sailors seized rifles and joined in the defense of the royal palace against the loyal guards." It reported that "Liebknecht, Rosa Luxemburg and two Russian envoys, Adolf Joffe and Karl Radek" had proclaimed that the "final fight for the revolution" was in sight.

Piez himself jumped into the fray, with full-page newspaper advertisements. Apparently, he believed that this way he could reach into the rank and file. The ads addressed the workers directly, pleading that they honor their contracts and threatening to halt shipbuilding in the Northwest. This was too much for Upton Sinclair, the California muckraker and socialist, who wired Piez asking if the government had paid for the ads. "If it's your money, all right. If it is mine, I protest with the utmost vigor."[37] Seattle became a test case for the government and the Shipping Board. The nation's ports would continue to be sites of conflict in the postwar years.

Piez made the wrong calculation. The only trade unionists consistently against the strike were the international unions' officers and staff. The strike had been proposed unanimously by the Metal Trades and the city's local unions sanctioned it, so it was wrong to argue that the strike "was out of the hands" of the recognized leaders of all ideological hues, and also that "the rank and file seemed to have gone over to the radicals."[38] Surely, it was the labor movement itself that was radical. It followed then that the Strike Committee of 300 was radical, as was the Executive Committee of 15 (though less so than the Strike Committee). The

latter was composed of all well-known people, at best two or three
self-identified revolutionaries among them. "The fact is that the
strike," wrote Wells, a member of the Executive Committee, "was
conceived and carried out entirely by craft unions of the American
Federation of Labor with the sole object of assisting shipyard
workers to win their strike for an increase in wages. Nevertheless,
the general strike would not have been possible had it not been
for the radicalism of the Seattle labor movement."[39] The proof was
at once apparent in results of the referendum. As the days passed,
sometimes hours, the city's unions signed on. "Favor Having
Great Strike on February 1," the *Union Record*'s lead story read on
January 24: hotel maids, unanimous; laundry workers, 600 strong,
"favorable"; candy makers, "every member to come out"; journey-
man tailors, "no opposition"; "unanimously endorsed by a largely
attended meeting of the building laborers union."[40] Carpenters
would follow, also electrical workers, streetcar workers, printers,
Teamsters, cooks. In each case there were, in miniature, replicas
of the big Labor Temple gatherings with speeches and cheering,
mini festivals celebrating class solidarity. The new women's unions
were near unanimous in support of the strike and in staying out
for the duration. On January 26, the striking Boilermakers packed
the Hippodrome Arena, 6,000 strong. Unanimously, they voted to
support the general strike.

On the morning of the strike, the *Union Record* led with its
now famous editorial, brilliantly written by Anna Louise Strong,
though approved by, she would insist, the leaders of the strikers.
And yet, it, more than anything else, is said to have discredited
the strike, ignited the hysteria of the middle classes, the fear and
anger. It was evidence, the mainstream papers argued (in a claim
that historians have echoed ever since), that proved the strikers'
revolutionary intentions.

UNION RECORD - FEBRUARY 4, 1919

ON THURSDAY AT 10 A.M. There will be many cheering
and there will be some who fear. Both of these emotions are

useful, but not too much of either. We are undertaking the most tremendous move ever made by LABOR in this country, a move which will lead—NO ONE KNOWS WHERE! We do not need hysteria. We need the iron march of labor.

LABOR WILL FEED THE PEOPLE. Twelve great kitchens have been offered, and from them food will be distributed by the provision trades at low cost to all.

LABOR WILL CARE FOR THE BABIES AND THE SICK. The milk-wagons and the laundry drivers are arranging plans for supplying milk to babies, invalids and hospitals, and taking care of the cleaning of linen for hospitals.

LABOR WILL PRESERVE ORDER. The strike committee is arranging for guards, and it is expected that the stopping of the cars will keep people at home. A few hot-headed enthusiasts have complained that strikers only should be fed, and the general public left to endure severe discomfort. Aside from the inhumanitarian character of such suggestions, let us get this straight—

NOT THE WITHDRAWAL OF LABOR POWER, BUT THE POWER OF THE STRIKERS TO MANAGE WILL WIN THIS STRIKE.

What does Mr. Piez of the Shipping Board care about the closing down of Seattle's shipyards, or even of all the industries of the Northwest? Will it not merely strengthen the yards at Hog Island, in which he is more interested? When the shipyard owners of Seattle were on the point of agreeing with the workers, it was Mr. Piez who wired them that, if they so agreed —HE WOULD NOT LET THEM HAVE STEEL. Whether this is camouflage we have no means of knowing. But we do know that the great eastern combinations of capitalists COULD AFFORD to offer privately to Mr. Skinner, Mr. Ames and Mr. Duthrie a few millions apiece in eastern shipyard stock.

RATHER THAN LET THE WORKERS WIN. The closing down of Seattle's industries, as a MERE SHUTDOWN, will not affect these eastern gentlemen much. They could let the whole

Northwest go to pieces, as far as money alone is concerned. BUT, the closing down of the capitalistically controlled industries of Seattle, while the WORKERS ORGANIZE to feed the people, to care for the babies and the sick, to preserve order— THIS will move them, for this looks too much like the taking over of POWER by the workers.

Labor will not only SHUT DOWN the industries, but Labor will REOPEN, under the management of the appropriate trades, such activities as are needed to preserve public health and public peace. If the strike continues, Labor may feel led to avoid public suffering by reopening more and more activities. UNDER ITS OWN MANAGEMENT.

And that is why we say that we are starting on a road that leads—NO ONE KNOWS WHERE![41]

This editorial, written for the *Union Record*'s working-class readers, is remarkably clear and prescient. Certainly, it was not a call to arms, whether this was what the authorities claim to have believed or not. First, Strong plainly stated the strikers' intent: to shut down the city, maintaining services essential for life and security. She acknowledges that the General Strike is a step into the unknown, a "tremendous move" never taken before "by labor in this country." Nevertheless, labor would "feed the people," "take care of the babies," and "preserve order." Strong was correct that the Metal Workers' strike alone might not be enough to win, meaning that "the power of the workers to manage" might be decisive. This was the case because the government and the "eastern gentlemen" might well shut down Seattle's shipyards rather than let the strikers succeed. The labor boards faced challenges on many fronts, and the outcome in Seattle was important for them. It was, as some already suspected, just the first round in what would be a year of unprecedented working-class rebellion. She perhaps was mistaken only in underestimating how tenaciously the authorities would resist. At the same time, she recognized that the road led "No One Knows Where."

The strike, after all, was not a conspiracy, and its roots were deep. It was planned, but its outcome could not have been predicted. Few, for example, expected the utter intransigence of the shipyard owners and the government. The strike was, then, a radical departure for US labor: planned, but open-ended, the future not known. How could it have been anything else? Surely all wanted to see the shipyard workers victorious. And all wanted to see the labor movement strengthened in the process. Beyond this, clarity did indeed fade.

"Truth was," wrote Harvey O'Connor, "a revolutionary spark did exist in Seattle in February 1919. The strike leaders knew that as well as the government."[42] There was indeed a far left of dissenters, of revolutionaries, though it was not clear how many. O'Connor himself wrote the text for "Russia Did It," a flyer showing a brawny worker (drawn by Morris Pass) shoving a fat little capitalist into a coffin. There were twenty thousand copies of this flyer, which was aimed at shipyard workers, arguing that the workers should take over the yards.[43] "Take over the management of the shipyards yourselves," it proposed, "make the shipyards your own, make the jobs your own, decide the working conditions yourselves, decide your wages yourselves."[44] There is no doubt that there were workers who responded favorably to the flyer's argument. The ideas were in the air. For example, the Socialist unionists in the CLC demanded that if the strike were prolonged the strikers should "take over the shipbuilding industry, eliminate the bosses, and operate in the interests of the workers," while Sam Sadler advocated confiscating food supplies and declaring a rent moratorium.[45] Seattle, however, was not Gdansk. The yards remained in the owners' hands, defended by soldiers and armed company guards.

The IWW supported the strike, uncritically but passively, though individual members clearly were in the front ranks. They closed the Skid Road gin mills and kept their members off the streets. Nevertheless, they remained targets of arrests and the raids continued. The issue for revolutionaries in Seattle was not revolution versus reform, but rather how to help the shipyard workers win, how long to stay out, and how much they could fan O'Connor's "revolutionary spark." All this seems straightforward. The dividing lines in the strike chiefly concerned duration and effectiveness, and there is no evidence that in this division the revolutionaries were isolated as the authorities so desperately wanted to believe. The Strike Committee's moderates, led by Duncan and Ault, argued for a fixed end date, the radicals for more time and an open-ended strike. On the Saturday of the strike, the Executive Committee called for an end of the strike only to be overridden by the Strike Committee.

Whatever their motives, the owners, the press, and the mayor responded as if a revolution were on the agenda, using Strong's editorial to terrify the city's middle class. Critics echoed this. The historian Robert Friedheim, writing that the editorial was "an artful document," full of "mays" and "mights," and he suggested that it was a conscious exercise in deception. A careful reading of the editorial (it includes one "may" and no "might") reveals nothing of the sort, however. Indeed, the text is remarkably clear about what the strike would bring. In the following five days and nights, the workers did undertake a "tremendous move" never before "made by labor in this country." Likewise, they would "feed the people," "take care of babies," and "preserve order." Friedheim complained that "Miss Strong never mentioned what the goals of the strikers were," and yet Strong wrote, "the power of the workers to manage will win this strike" and everybody knew "this strike" referred to the shipyard strike.[46]

"We do not need hysteria," Strong had written in the face of hysteria, though not that of the workers. In her *History of the General Strike,* published by the CLC in the aftermath of the strike, she describes the bitterness among businessmen, quoting a prominent public official: "It is only necessary to mix among the businessmen of this city and then among the strikers, and hear their remarks, or even watch their faces, to find out which ones have murder in their hearts!" It was a "commonly noticed fact," she continued, "that women on trains running into Seattle, or in clubs, or in gatherings of other kinds, expressed the view that those strikers ought to be stood up against a wall and shot down." Two weeks after the strike, a prominent businessman remarked to friends, "If that strike had lasted a few days longer, there would have been some people hung." The city's elites clearly expected and even desired to see the streets run with blood.[47]

There seems to have been little of this rancor on the workers' part. It was in many ways a rather quiet strike. The socialist newspaper *Appeal to Reason* even thought Seattle's strikers "too polite." Local historian Kathleen O'Connell called it "a calm sort of strike, the tensions all submerged," pointing out that workers walked out "quietly and amiably" into empty streets.[48] This was true in the sense that there was no storming of the Winter Palace and almost no violence. The New York *Tribune*'s reporter wrote, "The normal police docket fell to about 30."[49] This high level of discipline was the work of the Labor Guards—union officers and veterans who belonged to unions—who carried no weapons and wore only white armbands to identify themselves.[50] The IWW had long insisted that workers' power came with "arms folded," and this image of a pacific but assertive worker gets us closer to the truth, for there was no shortage of activity in the strike, nor was enthusiasm in any way absent.

Joe Pass, writing in the *Call*, exclaimed that only "an immortal" could have "lived through the five days of the strike in Seattle and emerged impartial. . . . Men whose temperature in the past remained around the frigid zone suddenly awakened from their cold atmosphere in passionate ecstasy. . . . Professors from the University of Washington, keen students who are studying the labor movement at close range, lose their pedagogical dignity and cheer loudly and wildly the enthusiastic assembly . . . and a woman next to me shedding tears from the pure joy of living." Pass also learned of a union official "dispatched to the city in an effort to halt the streetcar men from 'breaking' their agreement with the company who, " after 24 hours . . . was so affected by the spirit of the hour that he advised the car men to join their striking fellow workers, and so defeated this original purpose of coming. Miracles were the order of the day."[51]

There was indeed virtually no violence, and that is what the strikers wanted, which is perplexing only if radicalism is associated with violence. Certainly, the employers and the press clamored for blood, and the authorities prepared for a confrontation. The workers whose paths home that first morning took them through downtown streets discovered machine guns in place and sandbag barricades. Those who passed by the armory met munitions wagons clogging the streets on all sides and soldiers everywhere. Armed vigilantes gathered on city street corners.

The *Union Record* stated the union's position: "Sane men there are, some, who believe that in the end all peaceful means to abolish the profit system will fail, and the age-long struggle between the suppressors and the oppressed will close with violence. But no sane man believes that time is now." The *Star*, the *Record* explained, "pretends to believe that the unarmed and defenseless workers mean to capture City Hall and run up the red flag in spite of the fact . . . that the workers know that there are thousands of soldiers in Camp Lewis and Fort Lawton. . . . [No] revolution of violence will be started during this strike be the strike long or short."[52] This was the consensus; the strike was in support of the shipyard workers. It was to be the trade unions' show of strength.

A visitor described the city on the first day of the strike:

I have just returned to my room in the hotel in its sixth story, made accessible by walking up six flights of stairs. The room is exactly as I left it at noon. . . . I fail to discern the soft touch of a painstaking chambermaid upon anything. The bed is as I left it, soiled clothes are where I threw them. . . . Among the many female employees of the hotel, the only union girl among them pulled all the others out with her yesterday at ten. Several large posters in the hotel lobby announce to guests that as a result of the strike all employees had walked out, and they were requested to take the inconveniences cheerfully. I went uptown at noon to get a meal at one of the 21 union eating houses, practically the only ones in the city, maintained by the unions themselves in their entirety, operating under a three-hour shift.

The streets are noiseless with the exception of the clatter of feet along the sidewalks, and here and there a private automobile. Every commercial establishment is closed except for two drug stores. Signs on doors and windows tell the reason. "Unfair to Organized Labor," "Closed for Duration of Strike," and some simply have it "Closed." One Japanese restaurant has on the door a permanent sign "We Never Close," but underneath a temporary one saying, "We Believe in Labor's Cause, So We Have Closed." The two adjoining stores have the sign "So Do We." The Jewish quarter tells a similar story.

On Yesler Way a funeral procession passed. On the windshields of the hearse and the ten hired automobiles following, there is the sign in red letters, 'Exempted by Committee.' Above Yesler Way most of the stores are open for business, but there is no business to do. Restaurants, soft-drink places and candy stores are closed. The sidewalks are not crowded by any means. There are no yelling newsboys and the silk-stocking brigade is notable for its absence.[53]

The Metal Trades Council had appealed to the CLC for the strike which it then called after it had obtained the approval of the local unions and then passed authority to a strike committee. This 300-member committee represented 110 local unions, each sending three representatives. The strike committee in turn elected a 15-member executive committee, which met round the clock, managing the strike. The members of these committees worked without pay, as did all the union's officers, by order of the cxecutive committee.[54] The strike was managed with extraordinarily efficiency. No one starved or lacked heat. No children had to go without milk. No sick or injured were denied hospital care. Strikers and those who could not eat at home had access to union kitchens.[55] The executive committee organized committees and authorized the exemptions.

The committee's "Official Statement," published in the *Union Record* on February 6, combined information and instructions: "All business agents and discharged soldiers and sailors belonging to the unions to meet at 7 o'clock to perfect their plans for policing," the statement requested. Then it announced that the welfare committee would have "charge of the health and sanitation of the city in regard to the garbage situation." The public should cooperate "to the extent of segregating the garbage; that is, do not put ashes, waste paper, or other trash in cans where you place swill or other decaying matter, as our garbage man has instructions to collect nothing but garbage the decomposition of which tends to breed disease." The committee ordered the garbage men to carry signs, "Exempt by Strike Committee." The statement also reported on the arrangements "for the supply of milk for babies and the sick and also for the filling of prescriptions by drug clerks." The committee had voted to "postpone the entire shutdown of telephone dispatching wire . . . [because] the continuance of same is necessary in the dispatching of our committees. It must be understood that this is no exemption and the call to quit work must be effective at a moment's notice from the executive committee." It denied an exemption for the janitors at the County-City Building. In other communiqués, the executive committee requested firefighters to stay on their jobs, and approved additional staff for the Cooperative Market to handle the strike kitchens. Most controversial was whether to exempt City Light, the city's source of electricity, or not; the mayor threatened martial law if the electrical workers shut off the power, as they had proposed. Neither happened.

The committee also advised that labor's own enterprises and buildings would be closed: the mutual laundry company, the Labor Temple, and the cigar company, together with the janitorial services at all these locations. The *Union Record* stopped publishing but resumed when the other dailies—the *Seattle Star*, the

Post-Intelligencer, and the *Seattle Times*—began printing again, all with police guard and with distribution assisted by soldiers.[56]

Though the committee's dictates may appear to be excessively controlling and even authoritarian, the situation on the ground was quite the opposite, with spontaneous creativity ruling. Relying on their own skills and commitment, thousands of volunteers took on the strike's tasks, including running the kitchens (which Duncan called "feeding depots"), organizing milk distribution, and policing the city. The process of distributing milk was elaborate. "The dairies supplied by the milk dealers were only eleven in number," the unions' own *History* explains, "so located that it would have been impossible for the mothers of Seattle to secure milk unless they owned automobiles." The milk wagon drivers therefore "chose 35 locations spaced throughout the city, secured the use of space in stores, and proceeded to set up neighborhood milk stations."[57]

Many restaurants offered free use of their facilities. However, the culinary workers, who were one hundred percent organized, decided for fairness's sake to use large halls lest some restaurants be favored, and others left out. Meals were also served at the longshoremen's hall, the Labor Temple, the city jail, and the old Masonic Lodge. Writing as Anise, Strong reported on the thirty thousand meals served on Sunday morning during the strike at twenty-one locations—24 cents a meal for union members, 35 cents for others. "Somewhere near a thousand men and women a day helped in various capacities in the eating houses. Some for a very short time, some for a long time. The shift of work was supposed to be four hours." She reported one volunteer saying, "I want to hand the Teamsters all the compliments your paper will stand without cracking. We couldn't have done anything without them." Some of the "boys," she reported, "come early in the morning and went to sleep in the chairs in the wee hours of the night. The longshoremen also have done a wonderful lot of efficient work for the eating houses. They did our clean-up work, acted as waiters and in every needed capacity, and gave us all the help we asked them for."[58]

Strong asked if they ever gave away meals. "Lots of them," was the response. "We don't refuse anyone, union or non-union if they can't pay." This may not always have been the case. The executive Committee reported a complaint from the IWW that its members' cards weren't being honored. The committee sent out orders that they be fed with "the same privileges in the eating houses that were possessed by members of regular unions."[59] The Wobblies responded with the promise that if any of their members were found causing trouble, "they would put them out of town and keep them out," as "they intended to show the AFL that they could join in a strike and cause no disorder."[60] The strike may well have been the only occasion, before or since, when no one in Seattle went hungry.

"I've held down this commissary job for five days and never used a cuss-word," a worker running a kitchen told the *Union Record*. "If any man can beat that for good nature, I'd like to see him. I've smiled at all and lied to all quite cheerfully." He had told those waiting that "the grub would start in a minute," though the worker had no idea when food would arrive. "But I always figured that I'd round up something somewhere, and I usually did. But take it from me," he added, "when the Bolsheviki do take over the country and start operating industry, I don't want any of these managing jobs or anything in the government line. I'll stick to my own little job of cooking."[61]

During the strike, Seattle's streets may have been quiet, but not the "feeding stations" the union halls, the co-op markets, or the neighborhoods where workers and their families gathered. On Saturday night, the strikers held a dance, and as late as Monday they organized a massive strike rally in Georgetown. The crowd was so large that the building sank somewhat and had to be evacuated. The meeting reconvened, and with "great enthusiasm . . . it was decided to make the meetings a regular weekly event . . . it was unanimous that the strike should continue until a living wage had been obtained by the shipyard workers. . . . Many of those present expressed the opinion that the scope of the meetings should be enlarged to include the wives and daughters of the workers, and to make them real community gatherings for the discussion of questions in which all are concerned."[62]

In all these places, the strike was the topic. It was analyzed, criticized, extolled, and debated and when the workers' representatives packed the rowdy, emotion-filled strike committee meetings, they came prepared; they were making history and they knew it. The General Strike served notice that Seattle's workers had become a class "for themselves"—class conscious and "there at the creation."

"Consciousness of class arises in the same way in different times and places, but never just the same way," wrote the historian E. P. Thompson in *The Making of the English Working Class*.[63] In Seattle, class consciousness arose in the utopian colonies, in logging camps and mills, in free speech fights, in Everett and on the waterfront, in war and in dissent, in strikes of the telephone girls, waitresses, hotel maids, "lady barbers," and laundry workers, in co-ops and in working-class neighborhoods.

"THE EXHILARATION FROM THE MARVELOUS display of solidarity experienced Thursday and Friday began to give way to apprehension," wrote Harvey O'Connor. "By the third day of the strike they realized that the Seattle labor movement stood all alone." The strike had not spread down the coast to California, nor was there support from around the nation. There was little, O'Connor observed, "to give aid and comfort, even verbally, to the labor movements of Seattle and Tacoma. Seattle, unfortunately, was all too unique in its militancy."[64] And, against them, the response of the authorities was unrelenting, especially the fear-mongers. They frantically forecast a terrible future at hand, Bolshevism, anarchy. Ole Hanson, a real estate agent elected mayor, egged on by the papers, denounced the strike as "un-American" and refused to negotiate. The *Post-Intelligencer* observed, "The big fact that stands out from the temporary confusion of business is that Seattle, given a brief time for readjustment, would be well off, if not better than before, if the whole of its striking population [were] suddenly withdrawn from the city."[65] The *Seattle Star* in a jingoist editorial titled "Under Which Flag!" declared, "There can be no compromise on Americanism."[66] Hanson threatened martial law, if the strike were not ended by 10 am on Saturday. The "Interests" in New York and Washington, D.C., joined the chorus. Even the AFL denounced the strike, with the Teamsters Joint Council ordering the strikers back to work. There were telephone calls and telegrams, a deluge of intimidation, threats, vilification from the international offices. The AFL censored the Central Labor Council and would later take credit for defeating its "strike." Then the international officers arrived in person, threatening to rescind charters, seize union properties, and fire staff. Meanwhile, the shipyards in the East and California carried on as usual. The risk of the owners shutting down the Seattle yards now seemed only too real.

On Saturday, February 8, several unions returned, though this was by no means a stampede. The executive committee took advantage and voted 11 to 2 to end the strike. They chose Duncan, not a delegate, to speak to the strike committee for them. He tried to convince those in attendance that continuing the strike was futile. He failed. The strike committee, infuriated by Hanson's threats and still committed to victory, overwhelmingly voted to strike. The longshoremen and the Metal Trades voted to continue the strike; the divide increasingly became one between the rank and file, on the one hand, and the executive committee, on the other. Then on Monday, with more unions yielding, Duncan returned to the strike committee. He recommended ending the strike on Tuesday at noon. He requested that those unions that had returned to their jobs come back out so that the strikers could return united; as they had left on Thursday they would return on Tuesday. The shipyard strikers remained out one month more.

How is this strike to be assessed? Harvey O'Connor wrote, "For the majority of Seattle unions, there was no sense of defeat as the strike ended. They had demonstrated their solidarity with their brothers in the yards, and the memory of the great days when labor had shown its strength glowed in their minds."[67] This sentiment was widely shared among Seattle's workers. The CLC's minutes are laden with messages of congratulations: The Metal Trades Council in Aberdeen commended Seattle's workers "for the excellent conduct of the successful general strike [and urged] "one big union and a 24-hour strike on May1st to demonstrate our solidarity." From the Astoria Central Labor Council came a communiqué "complimenting Organized Labor for the excellent conduct of the successful general strike." Mine Workers Locals No. 2917, 1044, 1890, and 4309 sent resolutions "condemning the attitude of the 'Star' upon the strike and expressing willingness to lay down tools if conditions warrant." The King County Pomona Grange pledged support by furnishing produce and finances to the strikers, while cash and expressions of solidarity came from local businesses.[68]

The IWW's *Industrial Unionist* wrote in its editorial: "With its splendid solidarity, with its joining of hands of white and yellow wage workers, with the submerging of petty differences, and with the absence of violence, the Seattle Strike has demonstrated the wonderful power of united labor."[69] Its *One Big Union Monthly* wrote that "thousands of IWW men were involved in this general strike . . . a grand manifestation of solidarity."[70] The Socialist *New York Call,* under the head "Seattle Strike Was Forecast of Fall of Capitalist System," explained its view of the strike: "Every wise American, from the capital to the workers in the humblest home, is today trying to sum up the cost, the import and the essence of the 'Seattle Affair,' and the course of democracy in this country may depend upon how well that sum is calculated. For in the five-day so-called sympathetic strike that bound Seattle with its possibilities were fused all the creeds that propose the overthrow of the capitalist system."[71]

Many years later, in a very different climate of opinion," wrote O'Connor, "some of the leaders began apologizing for what could be excused as a momentary aberration by an otherwise solid body of citizenry." Then the history of the strike would be rewritten so that "blame" might be assigned, with of course the radicals and the IWW "singled out." The new interpretations would efface the "fact that the strike was called by some 300 delegates chosen for this purpose from a hundred local unions, almost unanimously, and that none but these regular delegates and their Committee of 15 made the decisions." Above all, the strike would be recast as defeated, "a disaster."

When the strike ended, Seattle's mainstream newspapers expressed smug self-satisfaction. The *Post-Intelligencer* ran a front-page cartoon captioned, "Our Flag Is Still There," and welcomed the "inglorious" defeat of the "fiasco," all the while heaping praise on Hanson. All three papers applauded the arrests that followed, especially that of Walker Smith at the *International Weekly*, which had printed the "Russia Did It" flyer.[72] The press demanded incessantly that labor "clean house." On the other side of the country, the *New York Times* reported, "the Revolution failed," and lauded Hanson as "a champion of Americanism." The Seattle mayor toured the nation, as the self-proclaimed hero who had saved the city from Bolshevism. Not to be outdone, Samuel Gompers joined in, boasting that instead the AFL had saved the day, rescuing the American labor movement from its many foes, foreign and domestic. Gompers claimed: "Born in a spirit of insubordination, disregarding all rules and regulations adopted by trade unions for orderly procedure . . . the strike was from its inception destined to die an early death. . . . It was the advice and counsel and fearless attitude of the trade unions leaders of the American International Trade Unions and not the United States troops, or edicts of a mayor, which ended this brief industrial disturbance of the Northwest."[73] Next, having pronounced the strike dead, the strike's enemies—all the above, holding their breath—sought to have it buried, its history debased, and its memory deleted.[74]

The academic version of this story, which remains widely accepted, is the work of Robert Friedheim. "The first major general strike in the United States ended quietly at noon on February 11, 1919," he wrote, adding without evidence, "Somewhat sheepishly, Seattle's workers returned to their jobs in shops, factories, mills, hotels, warehouses and trolley barns. The strike had been a failure, and they all knew it. In the days ahead, they were to learn that it was worse than a failure—it was a disaster."[75]

The strike committee, to its great credit, commissioned a committee to produce a history of the strike. Anna Louise Strong penned its findings:

> The vast majority [of workers] struck to express their solidarity, according to *The History of the Seattle General Strike*. And they succeeded beyond their expectations. They saw the labor movement come out almost as one man and tie up the industries of the city. They saw the Japanese and the IWW and many individual workers join in the strike, and they responded with a glow of appreciation. They saw garbage wagons and laundry wagons going along the streets marked 'exempt by strike committee.' They saw the attention of the whole continent turned on Mr. Piez and the Seattle shipyards. They learned a great deal more than they expected to learn—more than anyone in Seattle knew before. They learned how a city is taken apart and put together again. They learned what it meant to supply milk to the babies of the city, to feed 30,000 people with a brand-new organization. They came close for the first time in their lives to the problems of management.[76]

The *History* responded to the presses' claims that the strike was "lost" and to their descriptions of Seattle workers "creeping back to work downcast." "In fact, the mood was quite different," it asserted. "Strange to say, except for an occasional note of regret, the workers of Seattle did not go back to work with the feeling that they had been beaten. They went smiling, like men who had gained something worth gaining, like men who had done a big job and done it well. The men went back, feeling that they had won the strike. . . . They went back proud of themselves for the way they had come out; proud of themselves for the way they had kept order under provocation; glad to have gained so much education with so little comparative suffering; glad to have worked shoulder to shoulder with their fellow unionists on a lot of big problems; and a bit relieved, to tell the truth, that no one had been raided, no one shot and that the labor movement of Seattle was still 'going strong.' For they were quite aware that they had held in their hands a weapon which might have exploded in any one of a dozen different directions. They were glad to find themselves able to use it, to examine it and to lay it down without any premature explosions."

The *History* recounted some disorganization in the early hours. Shutting down the *Union Record* had not been popular among the strikers. The *Record*, under the direction of the strike committee, published a *Strike Bulletin* for free distribution, a two-page sheet with no telegraph service news except when directly relevant to the strike. A crowd of perhaps five thousand eager people surrounded the *Union Record*'s offices on the afternoon of its distribution. The Labor Guard could not keep them at bay and the *Strike Bulletin* only stimulated their desire for further reading matter. "On Saturday, the third day of the strike, after the *Star* had disregarded the strike by sending out papers on wagons with armed police, and after the *Post-Intelligencer* had managed to issue a four-page sheet which was given away at its own doors, the General strike committee directed the *Union Record* to start printing again."[77]

The *History* also addressed what it considered to be the "confusion" accompanying the ending of the strike. It emphasized the strikers' "inexperience." But it wasn't that the strikers were inexperienced as organizers and fighters. Rather, there had never been such a strike before, not in the United States, and their aims were not always clear. Some were striking to gain a definite wage increase for their brother workers in the shipyards. Others, a very few, were striking because they thought "The Revolution" was about to arrive. Even if "strikes and upheavals were in the air," it argued, "the vast majority were striking 'just for sympathy,' just as a show of solidarity." Thus, the extent to which the strikers were also "moved, half-consciously, by the various forms of labor's upheaval going on throughout the world, cannot be estimated, consciously perhaps, not very much; but unconsciously and instinctively, a great deal."

The *History* argued that the labor movement could learn from the strikers' errors. "Possibly," it surmised, "one of the reasons they did not gain a definite end was that no end was stated quite definitely and simply enough … perhaps one lesson that other cities may learn from the experience of Seattle is this: 'If you are striking for a definite aim and refusing to come back until you have gained it, make your aim so clear and simple that everyone in the city will know the one man on whom to bring pressure, and what one act to demand of him." In this case, that man would have been Piez, but would he have yielded?[78] Possibly, but it is quite unlikely. In any case, Piez did not give in, and the government remained immovable in the face of the challenges to its rulings and awards, not just in Seattle but elsewhere in the country. The argument to limit the duration of the strike is most cogent. However, this argument is based on hindsight and presupposes that the strike could not be won, which the majority of the strikers, even at the end, did not believe.

The *History* has been accused of portraying the strike leaders as far more conservative than they were to protect them in the face of federal prosecution and the demands that the unions "clean house." Mayor Hanson and the papers had declared that "the whole Seattle labor movement had come under the control of the radicals." This was not true. The question of how to end the strike was real, and it remains unanswered. Certainly, solidarity had begun to fray. But the fact that so many wanted more is critical as well, though what exactly they wanted is not clear. Speculation now accomplishes little. The possibility of prosecution was real indeed, even though the authorities thought better of it. That they dared not arrest the city's trade union leaders is of the greatest significance.

There were no arrests during the strike of strikers or of any connected with the strike. The authorities instead arrested thirty-nine Wobblies on the charge of being "ring-leaders of anarchy." They also raided the Socialist Party headquarters and arrested the Socialist candidate for the City Council. The Equity Printing Plant was a cooperative press owned by various worker organizations. It too was raided, its manager and others arrested, and the plant closed. Those arrested were charged with passing out leaflets during the strike. The pamphlet "Russia Did It" was singled out.

The CLC appointed a committee to investigate the arrests. It reported that "not one of the leaflets on which charges were passed gave any evidence of anarchy or desire for violence but were rather socialistic in their teaching." This meant that the arrests constituted "an invasion of fundamental rights . . . when they are denied to one, they are denied to all." Despite differences, the CLC's committee called for solidarity with the IWW because they faced "in the interests of solidarity, one common enemy."[79] The authorities would come later for the staff of the *Union Record*, including Ault and Strong, though charges against them were ultimately dropped.

The rank and file, argued the *History*, "went back laughing at the suggestion that they 'clean house of the leaders who had tried to make a Bolshevik revolution.' They had chosen the strike themselves, and it had been a great experience."[80] They had not attempted to dislodge the mayor nor other civil authorities. They had, however, themselves held power in the city for five days that mattered.

Others concurred. The Socialists' *New York Call* wrote: "Whatever may be said of the Seattle strike, it certainly is not a case of 'blind striking,' as the *Journal of Commerce* affirms. It has been calculated and prepared and is one of the finest examples of sacrifice and solidarity that workingmen have displayed in many years. It is a sympathetic strike participated in by workers who have no grievance of the own, at least none that they are raising at this time. They have walked out in support of another group of workers, with the view of aiding the latter to secure a speedy victory."[81] Max Eastman, editor of the *Liberator*, visited Seattle during the strike. The strike committee's minutes reveal that he had joined one session, the guest of Strong. What he may have contributed, if anything, is not recorded. He did, however, record his evaluation: "The General Strike in this city of Seattle filled with hope and happiness the hearts of millions of people in all places of the earth. . . . You demonstrated the possibility of that loyal solidarity of the working class which is the sole remaining hope of liberty for mankind."[82]

The Seattle General Strike was a precursor of what was to come that year, a succession of spectacular battles. Some have seen the Winnipeg general strike, for example, as an extension of what happened in Seattle. Indeed, the Canadian strikers, to the alarm of authorities on both sides of the border, feted James Duncan and a delegation from Seattle as a gesture of international solidarity. Then came further strikes in diverse sectors—garments, steel, coal, the Boston Police, and the New York longshoremen. All historic, even in defeat.

Seattle's working people opposed capitalism, exploitation, and war. They imagined the working class in control. They too believed in the inexorable march of history and the final victory for which many would sacrifice themselves. Their goal of workers' control, however, remained elusive. Still, their achievements were real and need retrieving and remembering as they are indeed links in a long chain. Memory is an indispensable element in the struggle and a source of understanding and idealism and strength. History does not die; the history of the Seattle workers is not dead. The Seattle General Strike remains the only true general strike in US history, the only time when workers in this country really ran a city, and those five days are to be celebrated, not forgotten. Today, one hundred years later, these events remain remarkable, and they count—a testament to what a workers' movement can do and offer a vision of another world.

THE OLD WORLD PASSES
BY ANISE (ANNA LOUISE STRONG)

Good-bye,
Nineteen-nineteen!
You have brought to us
Here in Seattle
Many EXCITEMENTS!

The unrest and upheaval!
Of a State LEGISLATURE,
Which always worries the people,
Marked your beginning,
Merging quickly
Into the PEACE and quiet
Of the GENERAL STRIKE,
Which ended again in the tumult
Of Ole's REVOLUTION!
You have seen the Union Record
Steadily emerging
From all DISASTERS
Stronger now than ever.
You have been reasonably good
In all our Local matters,
Nineteen-nineteen!
But in the world's history
You will be known
As the year
Of the GREAT DISILLUSION!
When the people of earth,
Of India and Egypt,
Of Armenia and Syria,
Of China and Persia,
And Ireland,
The peoples of Germany
And all the little Baltic States,
ALL the seeking peoples,
Who saw in their darkness
A GREAT LIGHT,
Bowed down and worshiped
The MAKERS of PEACE —
And found that their GODS
Were Clay!
You have been the year

When the ghosts of those
Who died on Flanders Fields
Giving their lives
For the world's FREEDOM,
For a new understanding
Among nations,
For an END to WAR,
Were CHEATED
By the men for whom they died
You have been the year
When our country's HEROES
To whom we promised
Glory and honor unending
Came home to HUNT for jobs;
And when NEGRO soldier boys
Were LYNCHED
For wanting democracy;
And when the cost of living
FAILED to come down!
You have been the year
When hand-picked representatives
Of Capital and Labor
Consulted together for a week
And NOTHING came of it!
Good-bye, nineteen-nineteen,
Year of disillusions
You have seen the death
Of many false gods,
You have seen the DARKNESS
Before the DAWN
For the False gods must die
That the true gods
May be known![83]

10. SOLDIERS OF DISCONTENT

The workers returned to work "cheerfully," wrote the *Union Record*, "proud" of their strike. Harvey O'Connor remembers the "glow" of the memory of these days. Hulet Wells recalled it all as the workers' "Glorious Vacation." No credible evidence exists to the contrary. The return was not "clean," however, not in the sense that Jimmy Duncan would have preferred. The strike did not end all at once. A few unions went back early, several stayed out longer. So inevitably, emotions were mixed, but if there was disappointment, it was only because so many of the rank and file would have preferred to stay out longer.

Mayor Hanson and the newspapers boasted of having defeated Bolshevism and harped on the need for a "house cleaning." The CLC responded: "We hasten to assure the draft-slacking publisher of the *Star*, all the employers who hate labor, and all those who love to lick their boots, that we know exactly what they mean by 'reds,' we know exactly what they mean by 'bolsheviki,' exactly what they mean by 'cleaning house.'" The CLC emphasized that "organized labor in Seattle was never so proud of itself, that it appreciates the reds more for the enemies they have made, that it has no intention of cleaning house to please its opponents, and that the general strike is permanently in the arsenal of labor's peaceful weapons."[1]

In reality, the employers were relieved, but not because they had defeated the workers. In the course of the strike's five days, there had been no lockouts or significant dismissals. There had been, after all, no strikebreakers, no "replacement" workers needing protection. No mass arrests, thus no search for lawyers, no defense funds to build. There had been no violence—hence no funerals, no wakes, no widows with children to support. The leaders of the strike committee and the Central Labor Council worked to get the strike's handful of victims—casualties were few—back to work. They remained quite capable of achieving this.

The fact was that the employers dared not test the workers, not in the short run. Seattle remained a union city. There was, of course, a sense of things getting back to normal, the exception being the waterfront where the roller-coaster conflict continued. The shippers imposed the open shop, only to have this reversed in August. Now, at last, the ILA achieved job control and a single, alphabetical list. Seattle's workers remained "strike prone," among the most combative in the nation right into 1920–1921. Wages remained relatively high in the city, as did the cost of living, levelling off but remaining above national averages through 1921.

In some respects, Seattle's unions appeared stronger after the strike. The circulation of the *Union Record* grew to 120,000. Readers' loyalty to the paper was legendary. Likewise, the co-op movement continued, together with an array of union initiatives. The movement for industrial unionism was strengthened, and "Duncanism" remained at the core of the CLC's vision. The craft unionists remained loyal to the AFL; Duncan's plan in Seattle was challenged only from the left—the "Federated Unions" and the One Big Union (OBU) movement. With considerable support in western Canada, the OBU differed from the IWW. It proposed working for industrial unions inside the AFL. The CLC joined the short-lived "Triple Alliance," a coalition made up of the AFL unions in Washington State, the independent railway unions, and the Grange. Its name was taken from the then thriving movement in Britain of miners, railway workers, and transport workers. It then supported the Farmer Labor Party (FLP), which morphed out of the Triple Alliance, again in defiance of the AFL, which had its so-called nonpartisan policy. Washington State would nearly top the nation in votes for the national FLP ticket in the presidential race of 1920, second only to Illinois and collecting almost 100,000 votes in state campaigns.

Seattle's black workers fared poorly in these years. Fewer in number than Asians, they were not the prime target for the racist wrath sweeping Seattle and Washington State. Still, Asians pointed to the fact that blacks were citizens, could vote, and escaped the threat of legal exclusion and deportation, but this was cold comfort in the world of work. The chief occupations for black workers were service and domestic work; they were isolated and at the mercy of the employer. On the waterfront some found steady work, but most were held back in reserve by the employers as potential strikebreakers. On the docks, the IWW championed black workers and opened the door for scores of them. In this, the Wobblies met opposition from the Washington Employers Union and the ILA's president, T. V. O'Connor. Nevertheless, in August 1919, three hundred black workers joined the ILA, this time in an agreement that gave the union hiring rights. The shippers called it an "obnoxious" deal.

The future remained uncertain, however. The 1919 "Red Summer" of racist terror, with nationwide pogroms, lynchings, and riots was clearly on the horizon. Yet, in Seattle, improvements continued. The *Union Record*, under the headline "Labor Welcomes Colored Workers," reported: "By practically unanimous vote Wednesday night, the Central Labor Council went on record as unqualifiedly for the equal rights of negroes with white men in organized labor. ... The unanimous sentiment expressed was that if organized labor was to have union organization it should take in all the workers. That negroes were as a race strikebreakers was vigorously denied. They were no worse, however, than white men, delegates declared."[2]

As for Asian workers, the future was equally foreboding. "For several years after the General Strike," according to Kurokawa, "the Japanese community in Seattle maintained a friendly relationship with the white labor movement not only in Seattle but throughout Washington." However, he continued, "the Japanese exclusion movement in the United States reached a peak just after World War 1. In those days, in addition to sporadic acts of violence, the movement to legally restrict the rights of Japanese was strongly promoted in Western states. The influence of this movement reached the Federal Government and the Japanese immigration to the United States was completely prohibited by the Japanese Exclusion Act of 1924. In Seattle those who wished to exclude Japanese formed the Anti-Japanese League and aggressively developed an exclusion movement in cooperation with similar organizations in California and Oregon. The American Legion launched its own anti-Japanese campaign. The *Seattle Star* published many inflammatory articles and became a powerful arm of the anti-Japanese movement."[3]

Nevertheless, the *Union Record* consistently opposed the 1920 Alien Land Act and "declared that the fundamental rights of the Japanese had to be protected."[4] In August, its editor, Harry Ault, was among the fifty who offered opinions in hearings on Japanese immigration held in Seattle and Tacoma. There, he argued against the Japanese exclusion movement "despite the persistent and sometimes antagonistic questioning of the hearings interrogator, John E. Baker, a California representative." Yet his remarks were conditional: while supporting a "suspension of Japanese immigration," on one hand, he insisted that the Japanese who were already in the United States be treated fairly.[5] "A certain proportion of the labor movement," he said, "believes in organizing the Japanese, believes in raising the standard of living of the Japanese to that of the white man, believes in making him economically equal and I believe that a very considerable portion of the labor movement in the Northwest has come to that conclusion. It would not be hard, however, for you to find many witnesses in the ranks of labor and prominent in the ranks of labor who will take a contrary attitude."[6] Ault's statement, wrote Kurokawa, "was warmly welcomed by Seattle's Japanese community."[7]

Seattle, then, continued to defy the AFL at every turn. This included the case of the "lady barbers." Blanche Johnson, an organizer for the CLC, described their conditions: "The woman engaged in barbering is beset with numerous difficulties and temptations, more so, perhaps, than any other line of work." Johnson detailed the high cost and false promises of the barber colleges, the great difficulty in finding openings, piece work, and the constant threat of serious injury. The work was at best irregular. There were hours in the day when the women were idle. Further, the work week was long, with women working Sundays to make up for short wages. These conditions, wrote Johnson, "had a tendency to affect the morals of the women worker. She must let pass, apparently unnoticed, offensive remarks, which she would ordinarily resent, because she realized that her earning capacity, which means her bread and butter, indeed her very existence, is controlled by her customers. She must at all times be courteous and ready to attend to the wants of her patrons."[8] Paradoxically, the women barbers in Seattle had been hurt by "the strength of organized labor [because] patronage of only barber shops which display the union shop card has been one of the objectives, and justly so, of the various unions."[9]

In March 1919, these women kept Seattle's workers on the nation's front pages. They established the Women Barbers' Union in Seattle and applied for a charter from the Journeymen Barbers' Union of America (JBUA). "The determination of these women to win a straight day for themselves was indeed wonderful," Johnson recorded, "and would insure success to any proposition, however many the obstacles to overcome. The support of the local union of men barbers was received almost from the beginning."[10] The problem was that the international union's rules forbade the membership of women, and the barbers' proposed charter was refused by both the JBUA and the national

AFL. In response, the CLC, "realizing the right of all workers to organize for the promotion of better wages and working conditions," recognized the women barbers and "seated their delegates to that body upon the condition that they would at all times demand enforcement of prices and wages in conformity with the Barbers' Union of America in Seattle."[11] The women barbers were not the only women to organize. Others followed, bankrolled by the CLC and other unions. In February, Ida T. Levi, an organizer for the State Federation of Labor, and Blanche Johnson circulated an open letter urging "all women to join the ranks of organized labor. . . . It is up to the women to take the lead and to be ever on the alert to improve our standards of living. If they become reduced you have no one to blame but yourselves. Insist that your effort, the little that you can do, will go down in history as having improved the conditions of all women and children."[12] In May, Seattle's union women formed a branch of the Women's Trade Union League.

On the industrial front, there was by no means retreat. And politics? The Mooney defense continued into the year with supporters debating when to call a general strike. In Seattle the call for a strike was narrowly defeated in referendum, yet tens of thousands of Seattle unionists supported what would have been the second general strike of the year. The CLC proposal from the strike committee for a 24-hour strike on May 1 "to show our solidarity" was tabled. At the same time it heard a report on the activities of the "Russian Bureau" including its arrangements for the meeting with Louise Bryant in March.[13] Reiterating its support for the Soviet Union, the CLC condemned the arrests of Russian immigrants, demanded recognition of the Soviet Union, supported federal aid to the Soviets, and selected a delegate for the Red International of Trade Unions.[14] Other projects of the CLC were a "pact with colored and Oriental labor," support for municipal ownership of utilities, endorsement of equal pay for equal work for women and men, and approval of the dockers' refusal to handle munitions bound for the Soviet Union.

James Duncan represented Seattle at the 1919 AFL Convention in Atlantic City, "a pleasure resort," as John Reed described it in his report for the *Liberator*. There Americanism was praised, the Mooney Defense was attacked, and the Seattle strike was mentioned just once—to ridicule prohibition and the General Strike. Duncan and a handful of others led the fight against "the machine." He proposed, for example, "a referendum throughout the country on recognizing the Soviet Union," but in the end worried that the machine was "too powerful to combat here." Reed noted the preamble of the IWW: "The working class and the employing class have nothing in common." This was wrong, he suggested: "They have the AFL in common."[15]

In March, the shipyard strike ended inconclusively, with the workers going back to conditions as they had left them, including the closed shop. The employers moved immediately and forced the open shop into the yard's weakest links. The US Shipping Board had assured all that it would honor wartime contracts. In the case of Skinner and Eddy, this meant that the company was to complete forty-three additional ships in the immediate postwar years. In April, in stark reversal, the Board cancelled contracts for twenty-five vessels. Then, in 1920, the Board abandoned all its Seattle contracts. The company delivered its last ship in February 1920, one year after the strike. When in the postwar slump an assistant to the company attempted to lease their yards to run on a closed-shop basis, the open-shop forces responded aggressively. They pressured local bankers to deny him the necessary loans and contacted Judge Gary of US Steel to prevent him from securing the needed material. In effect, Seattle was expendable.

The shipyard layoffs were the first blow. By the end of 1919, the 1920 depression was in full force in Seattle. Thousands of shipyard workers joined demobilized soldiers and wandering migrants on Seattle's streets. Then, the real 1920–21 depression hit Seattle. It had begun earlier in Seattle and lasted longer. International in scope, coming in the wake of the war, it consisted of a sharp economic downturn marked by rapid deflation and rising unemployment.

It was fueled by demobilization and the termination of government wartime contracts. It undermined the workers' movements
everywhere. In Seattle 10 percent of the wage-working population
was unemployed. In the working-class neighborhoods, hunger
returned. The Associated Industries, the employers' organization
rooted in the timber wars, was revived and bankrolled with massive corporate contributions. Egged on by the press and the new
right wing, it set out to present Seattle's labor movement with a
united front, knowing well, as Duncan noted, that "winter was
coming." Nevertheless, the shipyard unions notwithstanding,
Seattle's labor movement survived and was not broken. It followed
national patterns, indicating that the depression was more a factor
than the open-shop campaign. The CLC continued to press for
industrial unions, though this ensured a running battle with the
AFL in Washington, DC.

In February, the authorities, in the face of an intact labor movement, had hesitated. But this was not the case for the revolutionary
left, closing the IWW's Second Avenue hall, and arresting thirty-
nine members, even as the "Red Special," bearing Seattle workers,
mostly immigrant coal miners, was making its way to New York
City. The press identified them as inspirers of the General Strike.
They were charged with sedition, even when "utterly unknown" to
the leaders of the CLC, then taken in chains to Ellis Island where
they "joined hundreds of other unfortunates, huddled in squalor
and despair." Escaping only as the result of a campaign by New
York's socialist *Call,* they would be released. "Penniless as they
entered, most managed to work their way back to their homes in
the mining camps."[16]

Then, in April, the entire editorial staff of the *Union Record* was
arrested; their crime was acting to "incite, provoke and encourage
resistance to the United States . . . by presenting and purporting
to advance the interests of laborers as a class and giving [them]
complete control and ownership of all property . . . through the
abolition of all other classes of society described as 'capitalists'
[or] the 'master class' . . . and of using the post office to distribute

indecent and unmailable matters."[17] Bail was $2,000; Anna Louise Strong was set free by the Boilermakers Union. The other editors followed, bailed out only to have charges quietly dropped in January the next year. Others, arrested at random, suffered the same—printers, schoolteachers, people with German names. Mrs. Anna Falkoff, of Russian origin, a former resident of the Home Colony, was "a teacher and anarchist, attracted to the ideas of Francisco Ferrer of Tolstoian cast. Falkoff plodded about barefoot in her garden in the University District and conducted a modern school for children. The inquisitors were certain that this was a hotbed of young revolutionists."

"The Great Red Scare," wrote O'Connor, assessing the outcome, "could have been worse." Savage as it was, it "should have taken its greatest toll in Seattle. That penitentiary sentences were awarded only to Louise Olivereau, Wells, Sam Sadler and the Pass brothers (although scores had been jailed for weeks and even months) was a tribute to the solidarity and power of the radical and labor movements there." Tens of thousands, he wrote, "angry at the war and at the federal and state sedition laws, formed a solid ring around those indicted. Seattle juries, when honestly chosen, would not convict, whether in the Everett Massacre trial, in the criminal anarchy farce, or in any other cases. Only the blue-ribbon juries handpicked in federal courts could be relied on, at the behest of the Department of Justice, to scrap the First Amendment and traditional American freedoms."[18] Olivereau, Wells, and Sadler had been charged in 1917 of seditious conspiracy, the result of their connection with the anti-conscription leaflet. The Pass brothers were charged with failure to register for the draft.

On June 5, 1919, Seattle's left packed into the Labor Temple for a banquet in honor of those soon to be imprisoned. "All Seattle friends of freedom were represented among the guests," wrote the *Union Record*, "and many of them had served jail sentences themselves in free speech fights all over the country." Harry Ault was toastmaster; George Vanderveer, just back from defending the IWW in Chicago, spoke, as did W. D. Lane, a city councilman and acting mayor during Hanson's lecture tours. Strong also attended, contributing this verse as Anise:

> *Hulet Wells the convict*
> *Whose conviction has damned*
> *Judges and Courts forever*
> *And written "PREJUDICE"*
> *Over the gates where once*
> *Was written "JUSTICE."*

Strong stayed on at the *Union Record* in the aftermath of the strike, as well as on behalf of the CLC, writing poems, editorials, whatever she was called upon to do. She also wrote about hiking in the Cascades, arranging picnics for visitors, and leading car caravans into Mount Rainier National Park. She continued to advocate cooperative camps for low-cost outdoor recreation for workers,[19] though here too in the face of opposition from Seattle's "Interests." With the Co-op Campers, she organized "summer expeditions and local walks, promoted conservation ethics, and taught good camping skills. Unlike the Mountaineers, a middle-class, social climbing organization, however, [the Co-ops] did not require members to purchase gear or indulge in high-class get-togethers."[20] The National Park Service objected, favoring the car campers. Ultimately the co-ops were driven from the park, much to the applause of Seattle's business leaders.[21] Strong also helped organize a labor theater group. As late as July 1920 she attended the State Labor Federation's convention in Spokane where she joined Alice Lord and M. Mayo of Centralia as CLC delegates, taking part in what one reporter called "the largest gathering of labor women ever in the State of Washington."[22]

Nevertheless, she was increasingly unhappy. Even summer camp and August on the glaciers seemed less than satisfactory. A brief conversation in the Café Blanc with her old friend Lincoln Steffens set in motion her departure from Seattle. Steffens suggested that greener pastures were to be found in Russia, and

Strong, easily convinced, packed up and fled, first to Poland then Russia, arriving in Moscow in August 1921. It was Seattle's loss. Strong's contribution to the labor movement in these years had been nothing short of extraordinary, peerless in many ways. It included her time on the school board, her coverage of the Everett trial, her life as a journalist for the *Daily Call* and the *Union Record* where her contributions of poetry, news articles, and editorials rivaled those of the editors. Surely few people with her background have made themselves so thoroughly a part of the labor movement: an activist, an educator, a propagandist, a historian.[23] She was rather modest about all this in her autobiography—her role promoting socialism, championing women's freedom, and the movements of black people and Asians. Sadly, she wrote very little about her love of the high wilderness suggested by her reaction to Chicago and yearnings to return home to the Northwest and "wild nature."[24]

IN SEPTEMBER 1919, THE CLC held an open-air rally for Debs, Mooney, and the Seattle prisoners. Three thousand heard the artist and writer Robert Minor report on his European trip in which he had interviewed Lenin and Bela Kun. Another meeting drew six thousand to hear reports from McNeil Island and the torture of Hulet Wells, who was confined there. At this time Woodrow Wilson, back from Europe, was touring the country promoting his peace plan. The labor movement prepared a "silent protest" to receive him. The CLC had a hundred thousand badges printed reading "RELEASE POLITICAL PRISONERS." As the parade came up Second Avenue, block after block of people greeted the president with folded arms, silent and reproachful, their badges fluttering in the breeze. At the great meeting that night, half the audience wore badges and sat on their hands during the president's speech. It was "the Seattle Treatment." The longshoremen, having won in August, still ruled the waterfront in October.

Organized labor continued its resistance, which was all the more remarkable considering the fate of the revolutionary left. The

Associated Industries demonized labor in the eyes of the middle classes. It called the open-shop plan "the American Plan." It made a real and symbolic target out of the IWW, presenting the organization as if it were still robust and still "threatening the American way of life." Anti-red fear-mongers told stories of rabid loggers and sawmill workers confronting the poor embattled lumbermen, suggesting that tens of thousands of Wobblies were still active in the Northwest woods, ready at any moment to descend upon Seattle. They identified Seattle as one of the three key centers, along with New York and Chicago, of radicalism in the country, estimating membership to be as high as 100,000 on the Pacific Coast, with tens of thousands of Wobblies still in shipbuilding. Sadly, all this was far from the truth. Although the IWW still had members in the Northwest, they were scattered and disorganized. The 1919 Wobbly national convention was a disaster, with only forty-six delegates attending. In effect, the Wobblies had not recovered from the campaign being waged against them since the savaging of 1917. By 1919, the IWW had become an organization focused on self-defense, and this drained off its leadership, militancy, and finances in fruitless resistance. At no time were the Wobblies considered innocent until proven guilty. The Justice Department set the tone when it declared: "This is not an instance in which there is any danger of doing injustice to innocent citizens." The government consistently presumed the Wobblies guilty and acted upon that conviction.[25]

Since 1917 the IWW had been reduced to a shadow of its once magnificent self, its contribution as an organization to the Seattle General Strike little more than cheerleading. The Socialist Party, which had thrived in the years of trade union power, collapsed. In the summer of 1919, its leadership, still a cohort of considerable talent, became engaged in a bitter, fatal, factional fight. Seattle's Socialists were in the thick of it; the General Strike had helped to inspire the Party's left wing. Several from Seattle went on to become founders of one of the two Communist parties that were born in that conflict. Neither would restore socialism (now Communism) to its past fortunes. The Socialists were scattered. Kate Sadler, one of Seattle's "wild ones," the Party's representative on the National Committee, attended the founding meeting of the Communist Labor Party, where she reported that "she had often heard working men in the Northwest say that they would never again put their name and address on a poll book to be used in hunting them out by the master class, but still she believed in political action."[26] She continued to work with Seattle's unions; she campaigned for Debs's release. She joined Haywood, out of prison on appeal, in Portland on his 1920 speaking tour, and then resettled on Vashon Island. She withdrew from active political life and died in Tacoma in 1939.[27]

The Red Scare, the Palmer Raids, the American Plan, the employers' counterrevolution, depression, the battle with the AFL leadership, all took their toll. Then came Centralia, a true tragedy. It is often presented as the death knell of the Seattle movement. It was not, though the terror and utter depravity it revealed demands telling.

There were significant numbers of Wobblies scattered here and there in the camps and mill towns of western Washington who stood fast, active with what Harvey O'Connor called an "uncommon courage." The authorities harassed and brutalized them, attempting to hound IWW members out of the hills. For example, in little Raymond on Willapa Bay, Wobblies were rounded up en masse and tried for vagrancy—refusal to work a twelve-hour day—in a courtroom packed with soldiers. In Centralia, a mill town of 7,000 that sat on the main line rails from Portland to Seattle, a small group of individual IWW members, most youngsters, some veterans, held out. As with so many other towns in southwest Washington, Centralia was a backwater, but one with its own reactionary, small-town elite.

A not-so-secret cabal led by the lumbermen and the American Legion planned to use the Armistice Day parade in November as cover to raid the IWW's hall in Centralia and punish the organization's members there. The Wobblies knew this. "It was typical too of their utter decentralization and local autonomy that apparently it did not occur to any of them to get in touch with the western headquarters in Seattle on a matter which was to prove of transcendental importance to the entire IWW movement."[28] The Wobblies made plans to defend the hall. Several would be stationed inside, others, some armed, would assemble across the street on Seminary Hill. "Prudent men," writes O'Connor, would not have done this, "but prudence was not a Wobbly trait. Rather their shining glory stood out in audacity, courage, and stubbornness in defense of their rights, and for that they are remembered in history."[29] Before the day of the parade, they printed a circular appealing to "The Citizens of Centralia":

> We beg of you to read and carefully consider the following: the profiteering class of Centralia have of late been waving the flag of our country in an endeavor to incite the lawless elements of our city to raid our hall and club us out of town. . . . These profiteers are holding numerous meetings to that end, and covertly bidding returned servicemen to do their bidding. . . . These criminal thugs call us a band of outlaws bent on destruction. This they do in an attempt to hide their own dastardly work in burning our hall and destroying our property. They say we are a menace; and we are a menace to all mobocrats and pilfering thieves. Never did the IWW burn public or private halls, kidnap their fellow citizens, destroy their property, club their fellows out of town, bootleg, or act in anyway as lawbreakers. . . . Our only crime is solidarity, loyalty to the working class, and justice to the oppressed.[30]

On a dreary, drizzly November afternoon the march set off from the town center, led by the ultra-patriots of the American Legion, all in fine regalia. The Legionnaires passed the IWW hall, held back, then reversed, returning to the hall where they joined the town's postmaster and a minister, each dangling a noose in his hands. Shouts came from the mob, "Come on boys! Let's get them!" The marchers paused, then dashed toward the hall, rushed the door, pushing their way in. Now, they were met with gunfire, first from inside the hall, then from the hill across the road. Four Legionnaires were killed and several more wounded. In a fury, the Legionnaires swarmed the hall, overcame the IWWs, and dragged them out, all except Wesley Everest, an ex-serviceman. Everest escaped, but was chased by the mob, some firing. They caught him as he attempted to ford the nearby Skookumchuck River. They knocked his teeth out, then dragged him through the streets to jail with a belt around his neck.[31] That night the town lights went out. A group of men forced their way into the jail and dragged Everest out. They threw him into the back of a car, and castrated him there. "For Christ's sake men," Everest appealed, "shoot me, don't let me suffer this way." At the bridge, he was dragged out and hanged, but still was not dead. He was then hanged again until dead. The killers amused themselves by shooting at the swaying body. In the morning, they retrieved the body and displayed it in front of the prisoners to terrorize them.

"A grisly kind of perverted humor," Walker Smith writes, "marked the coroner's report of Everest's death. Everest had broken out of jail, the coroner said, and taken a rope with him to the bridge. There he tied the knot around his neck, jumped off, but failing to kill himself, climbed back up and jumped off a second time; still alive he climbed back up, shot himself in the neck and jumped off the bridge again; woke up at seven in the morning, cut the rope, fell in the river and was drowned."[32]

Centralia was overwhelmed with angry mobs, demanding vengeance.[33] Those imprisoned were tortured. The authorities scoured the surrounding hills looking for anyone who might have escaped. They managed by mistake to shoot and kill one of their own, another posse. Across the state more than a thousand were arrested; the plan was to use the criminal syndicalism statutes to try them all at once.[34] Warrants were issued for T. F. G. Dougherty and Walker Smith to impede any legal defense. Dougherty fled to Canada. Smith went underground where he began yet another personal crusade, this one for the Centralia victims. Among the

"Interests" there was no shame—this was, exactly, what they had been demanding for years. "From one end of the country to the other came cries to exterminate the IWW with or without due process," O'Connor wrote.[35] The *Union Record* bravely defended the Centralia prisoners. In retaliation, on November 13, the Justice Department raided the paper, seizing the plant and arresting Harry Ault, Frank Rust, and George Listman of the Board, all on sedition charges. Barrels of documents were carted off to the Federal Building.[36] The hearing judge ordered the paper and its equipment returned. Seattle was not Centralia.

The trial of the Wobblies was held in the Grays Harbor County town of Montesano, where fifty Legionnaires assembled each morning to occupy the courtroom's benches. George Vanderveer made the defense in vain, with three of his witnesses being arrested for perjury just as they stepped down from the stand. On April 5, 1920, the jury found seven of the nine defendants guilty of second-degree murder; they received maximum sentences of twenty-five and forty-five years.

"The Centralia incident," wrote Dubofsky, "was of little intrinsic importance to the IWW. It affected no strike, involved no important leaders, destroyed no affiliate. And brought about no real change in IWW attitudes or policies." What it did do was reveal the lengths to which public authorities and private citizens would go to destroy the organization. In the days just after Centralia, prominent Washington State lumberman T. Jerome wrote to an associate: "Ordinarily I do not believe in mob law but the action taken by the citizens of Centralia in hanging the leader of the 'Reds' [Everest] was the only right and proper thing. . . . I sincerely trust that . . . the people of the state will take such action as will result in the wiping out of the entire Red gang."[37]

The blow to Washington State's IWW was lethal. But the history of the Seattle labor movement did not die there. Seattle's unionists became less unique, their history more in keeping with nationwide trends. The causes of the retreat of industrial unionism in the United States during the 1920s are not hard to find. The movements of the 1910s were exhausted, the strikes defeated, and the unions broken. Trade union membership declined to a fraction of its earlier levels. Craft unionism predominated. Union leaders, clinging to their posts, could think of nothing better than cooperation with essentially hostile employers. Organizing took the backseat. The employers in turn offered an alternating mixture of welfare capitalism and repression. As the economy recovered, real wages rose modestly for some of those employed. The majority, however, benefited little from the "Roaring Twenties." Industrial unionism would not take hold until the great strikes of 1934 and the sit-downs of 1936.

The business classes in the 1920s believed that there was no place for unions. For them, collective bargaining was not only bad, it was un-American. This was not news to Seattle's workers, who had built a union city in frank opposition to the ruling classes. In effect, Seattle's workers had formed themselves as a class in conflict—in struggles that took place in the forests, on the waterfront, in cafes, and laundries. They forged their class identity in the long, hard fight for industrial unions and the closed shop, and in the fight for workers' power. At an early moment, the utopians—the colonies and the Cooperative Commonwealth—had preached workers' power. Later, the IWW and the Socialists fought for it, with the CLC, one step at a time, implementing it. The 1910s had been a decade of organizing, cooperating, and striking, the most basic weapons of working people in battles that were sometimes won and sometimes lost. Then came the General Strike and Seattle's workers' giant step toward a future that might be theirs. Alas, it was not to be. Still, they insisted that their vision was by no means the "pie in the sky" of the preachers and politicians. A better world was indeed possible. It still is.

ACKNOWLEDGMENTS

It's been more than fifty years now since Harvey O'Connor published his marvelous memoir, *Revolution in Seattle* (1964), the first and still indispensable account of the Seattle General Strike. Today, the story demands retelling, above all on this centenary.

There are additional accounts worth mentioning, if not of the strike itself, then of the place and the times, for this is well-traveled terrain. I would single out those of participants: Walker Smith's *The Everett Massacre* and *Was It Murder?*; James Rowan's *The IWW in the Woods;* and, importantly *The History of the Seattle General Strike*, commissioned by the strike committee, printed by the *Union Record*, and written by Anna Louise Strong in the immediate aftermath of the strike.

Later accounts must also be acknowledged, and I have made extensive use of these: Melvin Dubofsky, *We Shall Be All, A History of the IWW;* David Montgomery, *The Fall of the House of Labor;* William Preston, *Aliens and Dissenters, Federal Suppression of Radicals, 1903–1933;* Anna Louise Strong, *I Change Worlds;* Philip Foner, *History of the Labor Movement in the United States, Postwar Struggles, 1918–1920* and *Labor and the First World War; 1914–1918;* Richard C. Berner, *Seattle 1900–1920: From Boomtown,*

Urban Turbulence, to Restoration; Ronald E. Magden, *A History of Seattle Waterfront Workers*; Norman Clarke, *Mill Town;* and Mathew Klingle, *The Emerald City, An Environmental History of Seattle.* The most-cited academic accounts of the strike are Robert L. Friedheim, *The Seattle General Strike;* and Dana Frank, *Purchasing Power, Consumer Organizing, Gender, and the Seattle Labor Movement, 1919–1929.* These academic works must be read with care, however—Friedheim's because it is so narrowly framed and relies heavily on the reports of paid informants, and both Friedheim and Frank because they are so not in sympathy with the strikers and their movements.

I have had the good fortune to have been assisted by many staff at the University of Washington. First, I must thank Professor James Gregory not just for generous advice but also for his (ongoing) monumental project, "Labor and Civil Rights History Projects," a massive collection of material now available online, which includes documents, letters, flyers, etc., and highly useful introductory essays by university students. Also, I am indebted to the archivists and librarians in the Newspaper and Special Collections and the lead archivist, Conor Casey.

I must thank Professor Rob Rosenthal of Wesleyan University for lending me his path-breaking MA thesis, "After the Deluge, The Seattle General Strike and Its Aftermath" (University of California Santa Barbara, 1980), as well as a copy of his rock opera, *Seattle 1919* (by Rosenthal and The Fuse, 1985). Much gratitude to Professor Joseph White at the University of Pittsburgh for sharing his deep knowledge of this period and for reading sections in draft.

I have also been fortunate to receive the valuable assistance of Sarah Ryan, the dean of Evening and Weekend Studies at Evergreen College, and Trevor Griffey, co-founder of the "Labor and Civil Rights History Projects" and co-editor of *Black Power at Work.* I want to thank Professor Kathy E. Ferguson of the University of Hawaii for sharing her 2017 LAWCHA conference paper, "Creating a City to Resist the State, the Seattle General

Strike of 1919," and Kathleen Kennedy, author of *Disloyal Mothers and Scurrilous Citizens, Women and Subversion During the First World War*, for suggestions concerning women workers in these years.

I am grateful to the History Department and other related programs at the University of Washington for encouraging and supporting students' research on these years and events, and the many fine MA theses which have been the result. Among these, I wish to single out Melvin Gardner De Shazo, "Radical Tendencies in the Seattle Labor Movement As Reflected in the Proceedings of Its Central Body" (MA thesis, University of Washington, 1925); Karen Elizabeth Adair, "Organized Women Workers in Seattle, 1900–1918" (MA thesis, University of Washington, 1990); Robert Bedford Pitts, "Organized Labor and the Negro in Seattle" (MA thesis, University of Washington, 1941); and Mary Joan O'Connell, "The Seattle Union Record, 1918–1928, A Pioneer Labor Daily" (MA thesis, University of Washington, 1964).

My thanks go as well to the staff at the Walter Reuther Library, Wayne State University, for assistance in working with Harvey O'Connor's papers there, and the staff at the Tamiment Library and Robert F. Wagner Labor Archives at New York University, and finally, but not least by any means, the staff at the Doe Library at the University of California, Berkeley.

The staff at Monthly Review Press responded to this project not just professionally, but enthusiastically and comradely. I cannot say enough. I want to especially single out Michael Yates and Martin Paddio, exceptional editors and individuals. Without them, there would be no new history of this great strike.

I have received the encouragement and support of many. I want to recognize first Tariq Ali, Susan Watkins, and Tom Hazeldine at *New Left Review* for bringing one chapter to light, "Company Town? Ghosts of Seattle's Rebel Past" (July–August 2018). Also, I am indebted to Mike Davis, Steve Early, and Joe White for reading drafts and making necessary comments and corrections. The following editors kindly published chapters or excerpts of the manuscript: Shawn Gude who ran "Seattle, 'The Soviet of Washington'" in *Jacobin* (September 2, 2018); Alexandra Bradbury and Samantha Winslow who featured "Seattle, 100 Years Ago, Labor's Spectacular Revolt" in *Labor Notes* (February 2019); David Groves who included "Seattle, 1919: Labor's Most Spectacular Revolt," in Seattle's AFL-CIO paper, *The Stand* (January 29, 2019); Jeffrey St. Clair who published "The Seattle General Strike, a One Hundred Year Legacy" in *Counterpunch* (February 8, 2019); Miles Kampf-Lassin who featured "Everything You Need to Know About the General Strike That Shut Down Seattle One Hundred Years Ago" in *In These Times* (February 6, 2019).

I am indebted to Conor Casey, Andrew Hedden, and Professor Gregory of the *Labor Archives* for inviting me to participate in the conference "Solidarity City: The Seattle General Strike and 100 Years of Worker Power," held at the Seattle Labor Temple, February 9, 2019. Thanks also to the Pacific Northwest Labor History Association for organizing the unforgettable memorial boat cruise, "We Never Forget," from Seattle to Everett in November 2016, and for the invitation to participate in their 2017 conference in Vancouver, "Echoes of the 1917 Russian Revolution: Decades of Radicalism and Red Scares in the Labour Movements of the Pacific Northwest."

Annie Lee generously provided editorial assistance. Judith Condon, Eric Hoddersen, Jeff Johnson, Steve Early, Will Smith, Michael Watts, David Howell, Craig Merrilees, Deanna Marlow Kraiger, Summer Brenner, Sal Rosselli, John Gillis, Marcus Rediker, Iain Boal, and Dan Smith have provided not only support but, most important, friendship.

Finally, I want to thank my childhood friend Jeff Brotman for supporting this project, his brother Mike, and their late mother, Pearl, a second mother for me in years when I needed support and attention. Another old friend, Allen Spalt, generously gave me support and a home away from home while in Seattle.

In the end, my family—Faith above all, the children, Jessie, Samantha, Rosie, and Matthew, all grown and thriving on their own now, and the newcomers, grandson Theodore and grand-daughter Cornelia—made this book happen by being their wonderful selves.

NOTES

Introduction

1. L. P. Hartley, *The Go-Between*, This is the first line in Hartley's novel, first published in 1953.
2. Padraic Burke, "Struggle for Public Ownership: The Early History of the Port of Seattle," *Pacific Northwest Quarterly* 6 (April 1977): 60–71. Seattle's workers called their masters "the interests." The Chamber of Commerce, recalled Anna Louise Strong, "was composed of big business, the 'interests' by which we meant the great timber and power companies." *I Change Worlds*, (Seattle: The Seal Press, 1979), 49.
3. Richard White, *"It's Your Misfortune and None of My Own," A New History of the American West* (Norman: University of Oklahoma Press, 1991), 237.
4. Katsutoshi Kurokawa, *The Labor Movement and Japanese Immigrants in Seattle* (Seattle: University Education Press, 2006), 39.
5. David Montgomery, *The Fall of the House of Labor* (Cambridge: Cambridge University Press, 1987), 7.
6. Herbert Gutman, "Review of Friedman," *American Historical Review* 71/1 (October 1965): 331.
7. E. P. Thompson, "Revolution," quoted in Cal Winslow, ed., *E. P. Thompson and the Making of the New Left*, (New York: Monthly Review Press, 2014),159.
8. E. P. Thompson, *The Making of the English Working Class* (Harmondsworth: Penguin, 1968), 13.
9. Ibid.
10. William Haywood, *The Writings of Big Bill Haywood* (St. Petersburg, FL: Red and Black Publishers, n.d.), 70.

11. *New York Call,* February 14, 1919.
12. The classic collection of union songs, sung by the Almanac Singers.
13. Sam Howe Verhovek, *Jet Age* (New York: Avery Press, 2010), 63.
14. "Thanks to Amazon, Seattle Is Now America's Biggest Company Town," *Seattle Times,* 23 August 2017.
15. Jeffrey St. Clair, "Seattle Diary: It's a Gas, Gas, Gas," *New Left Review* 1/238 (November–December 1999), 81–96.

1. The Union's Inspiration

1. This phrase is from Earl George, interviewed in Rob Rosenthal, "After the Deluge, the Seattle General Strike and Its Aftermath" (MA thesis, University of California, Santa Barbara, 1980).
2. Chrystal Eastman, *The Liberator* 1/13 (March 1919).
3. Ibid.
4. Quoted in Robert Friedheim, *The Seattle General Strike* (Seattle: University of Washington Press, 1964), 29
5. Haywood, *Writings of Big Bill Haywood,* 63.
6. Ibid.
7. Melvyn Dubofsky "Revolutionary Syndicalism in the United States," in *Revolutionary Syndicalism, An International Perspective,* ed. Marcel van der Linden and Wayne Thorpe (Aldershot, UK: Scholar Press, 1990), 209.
8. *Union Record,* November 9, 1918.
9. *Seattle Star,* November 7, 1918.
10. Ibid.
11. Seattle *Union Record,* January 4, 1919.
12. Ibid.
13. Ibid.
14. *Seattle Star,* February 13, 1919
15. *Union Record,* December 26. 1918.
16. *Union Record,* December 27, 1918.
17. *Union Record,* January 17, 1919.
18. Ibid.
19. *The Nation,* February 1, 1919
20. Alexander Trachtenberg, ed., *The American Labor Yearbook, 1919–1920* (New York: The Rand School, 1920), 167–209.
21. Theodore Kornweibel, Jr., *Seeing Red, Federal Campaigns Against Black Militants, 1919–1925* (Bloomington: University of Indiana Press, 1998), 21.
22. See Cal Winslow, "Black Workers on the New York Waterfront, 1890–1929," *Historical Studies in Industrial Relations* 19 (Spring 2005): 1–19.
23. Ibid., 16.

24. James Weldon Johnson, *Black Manhattan* (New York: Perseus Books, 1930), 274.

25. Owen and Randolph followed events in Seattle. Evidence of communication with the Seattle workers' movement can be found in the *Forge,* the paper of Seattle's Soldiers, Sailors and Workers Council. On September 12, 1919, the *Forge* ran a brief message under the heading "Greetings from our Negro Brothers": "The *Messenger* extends greetings to the *Forge* in its splendid endeavor to arouse the apathetic public mind to the release of class war prisoners."

26. Harvey O'Connor, *Revolution in Seattle* (New York: Monthly Review Press, 1963), 98.

27. *The Colville Examiner,* January 17, 1916.

28. *Everett Commonwealth,* June 7, 1917.

29. *Butte Daily Bulletin,* June 28, 1919.

30. O'Connor, *Revolution in Seattle,* 98. Italics in original.

31. Ray Ginger, *The Bending Cross, A Biography of Eugene Victor Debs* (New Brunswick, NJ: Rutgers University Press, 1919), 174.

32. Charles Pierce LeWarne, *Utopias on Puget Sound 1885–1915* (Seattle: University of Washington Press, 1975), 300.

33. Ibid.

34. See Cal Winslow, "The Albion Nation," in *West of Eden,* ed. Iain Boal, Janferie Stone, Michael Watts, and Cal Winslow (Oakland, CA: PM Press 2014), 137–57.

35. Titus was fondly remembered by many of his contemporaries. *Union Record* editor Harry Ault wrote that Titus's group was "in communication with Lenin, Kautsky and Jaures, and maintained the party would be strictly Marxian and that 'opportunists' like Victor Berger and his kind would not be allowed in party councils." Ault to O'Connor, July 10, 1957, O'Connor Papers, Walter Reuther Library, Wayne State University.

2. Two Cities

1. Joseph Pass, "The Seattle Class Rebellion," *Call Magazine,* March 2, 1919, 1.

2. Murray Morgan, *Skid Road, Seattle Her First Hundred Years* (New York: Ballantine Books, 1951), 160.

3. Lincoln Steffens, *The Shame of the Cities* (New York: Sagamore Press, 1957), The classic account of urban corruption in the Gilded Age..

4. Morgan, *Skid Road,* 170.

5. Norman H. Clark, *The Dry Years: Prohibition and Social Change in Washington* (Seattle: University of Washington Press, 1988) 67.

6. Ibid., 67.

7. Ibid., 66. Mark Matthews frequently gets a pass from historians despite his opposing women's suffrage, helping lead the extreme opposition to the General Strike, and being a nativist and racist. In 1921, Mathews welcomed fifty hooded and robed Ku Klux Klansmen into his church where they sat as a body for services; Matthews reported them as "worshipping reverentially." For an account of Matthews's reactionary character, see Doris H. Pieroth, "Bertha White Landes, the Woman Who Was Mayor," in Karen Blair, *Women in Pacific Northwest History* (Seattle: University of Washington Press, 1988), 150.

8. Ibid.

9. Morgan, *Skid Road*, 165.

10. Ibid, 169.

11. Ibid. 170.

12. Matthew Klingle, *Emerald City, An Environmental History of Seattle* (New Haven: Yale University Press, 2007), 139.

13. Frederick Law Olmsted, called "the father of American landscape architecture," designed city parks in the United States, including Central Park in New York City. The plan developed for Seattle by the Olmsted Brothers, a business involving Frederick and his two sons, was not adopted.

14. Richard Berner, *Seattle, 1900–1920* (Seattle: Charles Press, 1991), 188.

15. Anna Louis Strong Papers, University of Washington Library, Special Collections, Box 10, Folder (file) 30.

16. Richard C. Berner, *Seattle 1900–1920: From Boomtown, Urban Turbulence to Restoration* (Seattle: Charles Press 1991), 256.

17. Anna Louis Strong Papers, University of Washington, Box 10, Folder 34.

18. Strong Papers, Box 10, Folder 30.

18. Ibid.

19. Ibid.

20. Ibid.

21. Ibid.

22. Ibid. Strong includes a discussion of women in the IWW in this unpublished manuscript. She wrote that women in the IWW, who were both workers and wives of workers, were respected members, though few in number. She refers to the wives of imprisoned members as "class-war widows . . . a title of honor."

23. David Montgomery, *The Fall of the House of Labor, the Workplace, the State and American Labor Activism* (Cambridge: Cambridge University Press, 1989), 240.

24. Ibid., 371.

25. *Outlook* magazine, considering the "strikes and rumors of strikes [that] have appeared on every hand," concluded that "in the United States

the labor war in Seattle has been the most extensive and the most dangerous of these." *Outlook,* February 19, 1919.

26. *Seattle Municipal News,* August 22, 1914.
27. Berner, *Seattle 1900–1920,* 169.
28. Ibid., 216.
29. Maurine Greenwald, "Working-Class Feminism and the Family Wage Ideal," in Blair, *Women in Pacific Northwest History,* 105.
30. Ibid., 106.
31. Berner, *Seattle 1900–1920,* 169.
32. Ibid., 170.

3. The Timber Beast

1. Michael Williams, *Americans & Their Forests, a Historical Geography* (Cambridge: Cambridge University Press, 1989), 314, 324.
2. James Rowan, *The IWW in the Lumber Industry* (Seattle: The Shorey Bookstore, 1923), 3.
3. Matthew Josephson, *The Robber Barons, The Great American Capitalists, 1861–1901* (New York: Harcourt Brace and World, 1962), 52, 53.
4. Rowan, 5.
5. Walker C. Smith, *The Everett Massacre, a History of the Class Struggle in the Timber Industry* (Portland, OR: Gregorius Publishing, n.d.), 15.
6. Anna Louise Strong, *I Change Worlds, the Remaking of an American* (Seattle: Seal Press, 1979), 47.
7. Smith, *The Everett Massacre,* 18.
8. Williams, *Americans & Their Forests,* 232–33.
9. Robert E. Ficken, *The Forested Land, A History of Lumbering in Western Washington* (Seattle: University of Washington Press, 1987), 125.
10. "The Casual in the Woods," *The Survey* 44 (3 July 1920).
11. Rowan, *IWW in the Lumber Industry,* 7.
12. Smith, *The Everett Massacre,* 13, 23.
13. Norman H. Clark, *Mill Town, a Social History of Everett, Washington, from Its Earliest Beginnings on the Shores of Puget Sound to the Tragic and Infamous Event Known as the Everett Massacre* (Seattle: University of Washington Press), 59.
14. Williams, *Americans & Their Forests,* 329–330.
15. Melvyn Dubofsky, *We Shall Be All, a History of the IWW* (New York: Quadrangle, 1969), 128.
16. Ficken, *The Forested Land,* 132–33.
17. Ibid., 124–25.
18. Ibid., 135.
19. Ibid., 133.
20. Ibid., 135.

21. Rowan, "Why We Struck," *International Socialist Review* 18/2 (August 1917): 2.

22. Final Report of the United States Commission on Industrial Relations (Washington, 1915) V, 4236–4237.

23. Strong, Strong Papers. Box 10, Folder 30.

4. Hold the Fort

1. Smith, *The Everett Massacre*, 23.

2. Clark, *Mill Town*, 77.

3. Ibid., 132.

4. Ibid.

5. Ibid., 131.

6. Smith, *The Everett Massacre*, 22.

7. Ibid. Other important works by Walker Smith are *Sabotage: Its History, Philosophy and Function*, and *Was It Murder? The Truth about Centralia*.

8. Max Eastman, "Class War in Colorado,"*The Masses*, June, 1914.

9. Ibid.

10. Ibid.; Smith, *The Everett Massacre*, 83.

11. Smith, *The Everett Massacre*, 26.

12. Dubofsky, *We Shall Be All*, 336.

13. Ibid.

14. *Sunset Magazine*, February 1917, quoted in Smith, *The Everett Massacre*, 25.

15. Ibid.

16. Smith, *The Everett Massacre*, 25.

17. Clark, *Mill Town*, 91.

18. Smith, *The Everett Massacre*, 27.

19. Ibid., 24.

20. Ibid., 27.

21. Ibid., 28.

22. Strong Papers, Box 32, Folder 28; Smith, *The Everett Massacre*, 30.

23. O'Connor, *Revolution in Seattle*, 34.

24. Dubofsky, *We Shall Be All*, 178.

25. Ibid., 180.

26. Ibid.

27. Ibid., 178.

28. Ibid., 179.

29. Ibid., 181.

30. Elizabeth Gurley Flynn, "Story of My Arrest and Imprisonment," (1909), in Rosalyn Fraad Baxandall, *Words of Fire, the Life and Writings of Elizabeth Gurley Flynn* (New Brunswick, NJ: Rutgers University Press, 1967), 88–91.

31. Dubofsky, *We Shall Be All*, 173.
32. O'Connor, *Revolution in Seattle*, 36.
33. *Industrial Worker*, March 3, 1917.
34. Smith, *The Everett Massacre*, 30.
35. *Industrial Worker*, March 3, 1917.
36. Smith, *The Everett Massacre*, 29.
37. *Industrial Worker*, March 3, 1917.
38. *Industrial Worker*, July 20, 1916.
39. *Industrial Worker*, September 16, 1916.
40. Smith, *The Everett Massacre*, 31.
41. Ibid., 32.
42. Ibid.
43. Ibid.
44. *Industrial Worker*, August 5, 1916.
45. Clark, 181.
46. *Industrial Worker*, March 3, 1917.
47. Robert L. Tyler, *Rebels in the Woods: The IWW in the Pacific Northwest* (Eugene: University of Oregon Press, 1967), 71.
48. *Industrial Worker*, September 23, 1916.
49. Elizabeth Gurley Flynn, *Industrial Worker*, March 3, 1917.
50. Clark, *Mill Town*, 197.
51. Flynn, *Industrial Worker*, March 3, 1917.
52. Clark, *Mill Town*, 200.
53. Ibid., 199
54. Flynn, *Industrial Worker*, March 3, 1917.
55. *Industrial Worker*, November 4, 1916.
56. Ibid.
57. Smith, *The Everett Massacre*, 71, 79
58. Ibid., 81.
59. Ibid., 63.
60. Ibid.
61. O'Connor, *Revolution in Seattle*, 44.
62. Smith, *The Everett Massacre*, 65.
63. Ibid., 65.
64. Clark, *Mill Town*, 203.
65. O'Connor, *Revolution in Seattle*, 45,46.
66. Smith, *The Everett Massacre*, 66.
67. Ibid., 67.
68. Clark, *Mill Town*, 210.
69. Tyler, *Rebels in the Woods*, 76.
70. Clark, *Mill Town*, 210.
71. *Industrial Worker*, December 16, 1916; Smith, *The Everett Massacre*, 72.

72. Seattle *Union Record*, repr. in *Industrial Worker*, December 16, 1916.

73. O'Connor, *Revolution in Seattle*, 48.

74. I *Industrial Worker*, November 18, 1916; Tacoma *Times*, April 18, 1917, repr. in *Hellraisers Journal*, April 18, 2017.

75. Ibid.

76. *Industrial Worker*, November 25, 1916.

77. Ibid.

78. Ibid.

79. Philip S. Foner, *The Industrial Workers of the World, 1905–1917, History of the Labor Movement in the United States*, vol. 4 (New York: International Publishers, 1965), 340.

80. *Industrial Worker*, November 25, 1916.

81. Ibid.

82. *Union Record*, December16, 1916.

83 *The Masses* 9/4, February 1917.

84. *Industrial Worker*, December 30, 1916.

85. *Industrial Worker*, January 27, 1917.

86. Ibid., January 6, 1917.

87. Ibid., March 3, 1917.

88. Ibid.

89. Ibid.

90. A seminal event in working-class history, Peterloo was the name given to the massacre of protesters in Manchester, England, in 1819. E. P. Thompson wrote of it: "The enduring influence of Peterloo lay in the sheer horror of the day's events. In 1819 the action of the loyalists found many defenders of their class. Ten years later it was an event to be remembered, even among the gentry, with guilt. As a massacre and as 'Peter-Loo' it went down to the next generation. And because of the odium attaching to the event, we may say that in the annals of the 'free born' Englishmen the massacre was yet in its way a victory." Thompson, *The Making*, 779.

91. O'Connor, *Revolution in Seattle*, 50–51.

92. *Industrial Worker*, February 24, 1917.

93. O'Connor, *Revolution in Seattle*, 51.

94. Smith, *The Everett Massacre*, 156.

95. O'Connor, *Revolution in Seattle*, 51.

96. Ibid.

97. Smith, *The Everett Massacre*, 161.

98. Ibid., 162.

99. Anna Louise Strong, *I Change Worlds*, 54.

100. Anna Louise Strong, "Trial Reports," University of Washington Special Collections, Box 6, Folder 70.

101. Smith, *The Everett Massacre*, 201.

102. Anna Louis Strong, "Trial Reports," Box 4, File 10.

5. A Union Town

1. *Seattle Daily Call*, September 3, 1917.

2. David Montgomery, *The Fall of the House of Labor* (Cambridge: Cambridge University Press, 1987) 332.

3. Priscilla Murolo and A. B. Chitty, *From the Folks Who Brought You the Weekend, An Illustrated History of Labor in the United States* (New York: New Press, 2018), 137.

4. David Montgomery, *The Fall of the House of Labor*, 332.

5. Ibid.

6. Ibid.

7. Ronald E. Magden, *A History of Seattle Waterfront Workers, 1884–1934* (Seattle: ILWU Local 19, 1991), 73.

8. Montgomery, *The Fall of the House of Labor*, 61. Cfr. Cal Winslow, "On the Waterfront, Black, Italian and Irish Longshoremen in the New York Harbor Strike of 1919," in *Protest and Survival, Essays for E. P. Thompson*, ed. John Rule and Robert Malcolmson (New York: New Press, 1993), 366.

9. Magden, *History of Seattle Waterfront Workers*, 91.

10. "This history of longshoremen," wrote the late E. J. Hobsbawm, "is filled with dramatic events as well as tragic defeats." Longshoremen were "powerful workers," everywhere "taken seriously by employers," often feared. This certainly was true in Seattle. Ironically, in 1916 the union itself was neither powerful, nor feared. "National Unions on the Waterside," in *Labouring Men* (New York: Anchor Books, 1967), 241.

11. Magden, *History of Seattle Waterfront Workers*, 77.

12. Ibid., 79.

13. Ibid., 80.

14. *Industrial Worker*, May 20, 1916.

15. Magden, *History of Seattle Waterfront Workers*, 83–84.

16. *Industrial Worker*, June 3, 1916.

17. Ibid., June 22, 1916.

18. Magden, *History of Seattle Waterfront Workers*, 89.

19. Berner, 215–16.

20. Cal Winslow, "Black Workers on the New York Waterfront, 1890–1920," *Historical Studies in Industrial Relations* 19 (Spring 2005): 1–29.

21. Berner, *Seattle, 1900-1920*, 215.

22. Quintard Taylor, *The Forging of a Black Community, Seattle's Central District from 1870 Through the Civil Rights Era* (Seattle: University of Washington Press, 1994), 52.

23. Ibid., 53.
24. *Industrial Worker*, November 4, 1916.
25. Ibid., August 26, 1916.
26. Ibid., September 9, 1916.
27. Magden, *History of Seattle Waterfront Workers*, 91.
28. Ibid., 99.
29. Berner, *Seattle, 1900–1920*, 217.
30. Ibid., 240.
31. *Union Record*, July 24, 1917.
32. Maureen Weiner Greenwald, "Working-Class Feminism and the Family Wage Ideal," in Blair, *Women in Pacific Northwest History*, 116, 117.
33. Ibid., 117.
34. Ibid., 122.
35. Ibid., 120.
36. Ibid., 121.
37. Sanger's visit is recorded in the *Industrial Worker*, June 17, 1916. Goldman's appears in the *Industrial Worker*, August 19, 1916. Greenwald summarized part of the debate: "The feminist respondents in the Seattle *Union Record* attempted to reconcile their ideology with class loyalty by insisting on a modification in the practice of mutual obligation. They directly challenged the fairness and appropriateness of the family wage ideal, which held that an adequate wage was one that allowed a husband to provide for his wife and children. Irate at the implication that women's work would be considered superfluous at best, feminists sought to prove that married women's employment would actually enhance working class life." The more traditional view "conditionally approved or disapproved of married women's employment [and] argued that some members of the working-class community had greater needs than others. If the American economic system could not provide work for everyone, then those with greater economic needs, as determined by their ability to meet essential expenses, deserved to work more than others did." Greenwald, "Working-Class Feminism and the Family Wage Ideal," 123, 124.
38. Ibid., 125.
39. *Industrial Worker*, February 19, 1917.
40. Ibid.
41. Alice Lord, *Final Report, US Commission on Industrial Relations* (Washington, DC: 2015), Vol v.p. 4236.
42. Karen Elizabeth Adair, "Organized Women Workers in Seattle" (MA thesis, University of Washington, 1990), 88, 89.
43. *Seattle Times*, November 1, 1917.

44. Ibid.
45. *Seattle Times*, July 15, 1917.
46. Ibid., November 1, 1917.
47. *Union Record*, June 23, 1917.
48. Adair, 91.
49. Ibid.
50. Ibid.
51. Seattle *Daily Call*, September 3, 1917.
52. Adair, 223.
53. Dubofsky, *We Shall Be All*, 319.
54. Seattle *Daily Call*, September 3, 1917.
55. *Industrial Worker*, October 14, 1916.
56. Ibid., 57.
57. *Liberator* 1/1, March 1918, 13.
58. *Liberator* 1/1, March 1918, 13.
59. Rowan, *The I.W.W. in the Lumber Industry*, 30.
60. *International Socialist Review* 18/3 (September 1917): 147.
61. Rowan, *The I.W.W. in the Lumber Industry*, 32.
62. Dubofsky, *We Shall Be All*, 337.
63. Ibid.
64. Rowan, *The I.W.W. in the Lumber Industry*, 39.
65. *Industrial Worker*, July 29, 1917.
66. Ibid.
67. Dubofsky, *We Shall Be All*, 363.
68. Philip S. Foner, *Labor and the First World War, 1914–1918, History of the Labor Movement in the United States*, vol. 7 (New York: International Publishers, 1987), 255.
69. Ibid.
70. Rowan, *The I.W.W in the Lumber Industry*, 44.
71. Foner, *Labor and the First World War*, 257.
72. William Preston, Jr., *Aliens and Dissenters, Federal Suppression of Radicals, 1903–1933* (Urbana and Chicago: University of Illinois Press, 1994), 123.
73. Quoted in Cloice R. Howd, *Industrial Relations in the West Coast Lumber Industry*, Bulletin No. 349 (Washington, DC: Bureau of Labor Statistics, US Department of Labor, 1924), 78.
74. Berner, *Seattle, 1900–1920*, 240.
75. Rowan, *The I.W.W. in the Lumber Industry* 49
76. *Industrial Worker*, October 3, 1917.
77. Strong Papers, Box 10, Folder 30.
78. Dubofsky, *We Shall Be All*, 365.
79. Hulet Wells, "I Wanted to Work," Wells Papers, University of Washington Special Collections, n.d., Box 1, Folder 5, 182.

80. Ibid.
81. Ibid.
82. Kate Sadler, *International Socialist Review* 15 (July 1914).

6. Left, Right, and Center

1.   Ray Ginger, *The Bending Cross, A Biography of Eugene Victor Debs* (New Brunswick, NJ) Rutgers University Press, 1949), 192.
2.   Eugene V. Debs, *Craft Unionism*, Industrial Workers of the World., n.d, in Marvin Sanford Papers, University of Washington Special Collections, Box 11.11.
3.   Ibid.
4.   E. J. Hobsbawm, quoted in *Revolutionary Syndicalism, an International Perspective* (Aldershot, UK: Scholar Press, 1990), ed. Marcel van der Linden and Wayne Thorpe, 10.
5.   *Seattle Daily Call*, Sanford Papers, Box 11.
6.   Paul. S Brissenden, *The IWW, A Study of American Syndicalism* (New York: Russell and Russell, 1957), 232.
7.   Van der Linden and Thorpe, *Revolutionary Syndicalism*, 2.
8.   Quoted in Melvyn Dubofsky, "Revolutionary Syndicalism in the United States," in Van der Linden and Thorpe, *Revolutionary Syndicalism*, 209.
9.   Ibid., 113.
10. Winslow, "Black Workers," 17.
11. Kurokawa, *The Labor Movement and Japanese Immigrants in Seattle*, 39.
12. Friedheim, 28.
13. Ibid.
14. Ibid., 50.
15. Kurokawa, *The Labor Movement and Japanese Immigrants in Seattle*, 36.
16. Seattle *Union Record*, March 20 and 24, 1919. See also Rosenthal, *After the Deluge*, 101.
17. O'Connor, *Revolution in Seattle*, 111.
18. Robert Friedman, *The Seattle General Strike*, 48.
19. Ibid., 47.
20. Philip S. Foner, *The Bolshevik Revolution, Its Impact on American Radicals, Liberals, and Labor* (New York: International Publishers, 1967) 218–219.
21. Flynn, "The IWW Call to Women" (1915), quoted in Baxandall, *Words of Fire*, 106.
22. William D. Haywood and Frank Bohn, "Industrial Socialism" (Chicago: Charles H. Kerr, 1911) 9, 10.
23. David A. Shannon, *The Socialist Party of America, a History* (New York: Macmillan, 1955).

24. Marcel van der Linden and Wayne Thorpe, "The Rise and Fall of Revolutionary Syndicalism," in *Revolutionary Syndicalism*, 3.

25. Shannon, *The Socialist Party of America*, 23.

26. Ibid., 21.

27. O'Connor, *Revolution in Seattle*, 243.

28. Jessie Lloyd O'Connor, Harvey O'Connor, and Susan M. Bowler, *Harvey and Jessie, A Couple of Radicals* (Philadelphia: Temple University Press, 1988), 15–24.

29. Ibid., 28.

30. O'Connor, *Revolution in Seattle*, 103.

31. Charles P. LaWarne, "The Bolsheviks Land in Seattle, the *Shilka* Incident of 1917," *Arizona and the West* 20/2 (1978), 107–22.

32. *Daily Call*, December 24, 1917.

33. Preston, *Aliens and Dissenters*, 165.

34. "Minutes of the Central Labor Council of King County," March 11, 1918, University of Washington Special Collections.

35. *Industrial Worker*, July 16, 1919; Magden, *History of Seattle Waterfront Workers*, 136, 137; Philip Foner, *The Bolshevik Revolution, Its Impact on American Radicals, Liberals, and Labor: A Documentary Study* (New York, International Publishers, 1967), 192.

36. O'Connor, *Revolution in Seattle*, 244.

37. *Industrial Worker*, November 6, 1919.

38. Ibid., July 28, 1917.

39. John Dos Passos, *The 42nd Parallel* (New York: Signet, 1969), 89.

40. Harry Ault to Harvey O'Connor, October 5, 1959, Walter Reuther Library, Wayne State University, Harvey O'Connor Papers.

41. Strong, *I Change Worlds*, 68, 29.

42. O'Connor, *Revolution*, 90.

43. O'Connor, *Revolution*, 129.

44. Kathy Ferguson suspects that there were two-card women, possibly two-card workers of color, though she has found no evidence. I suspect so as well. Kathy E. Ferguson, "Creating City to Resist the State: The Seattle General Strike of 1919," unpublished ms. in author's possession.

45. *Industrial Worker*, August 19, 1916.

46. Strong, *I Change Worlds*, 68–69. *Industrial Worker*. August 19, 1916.

47. Friedman, *The Seattle General Strike*, 27.

48. Melvyn Gardner De Shazo, "Radical Tendencies in the Seattle Labor Movement as Reflected in the Proceedings of Its Central Body" (MA thesis, University of Washington, 1925), 39–40.

49. Ibid.

50. O'Connor, *Revolution in Seattle*, 243.

51. Ibid.

52. John Reed, "The IWW on Trial," *Liberator* 1/7, September 1918.

53. Mary Joan O'Connell, "The Seattle Union Record, 1918–1928: A Pioneer Union Daily" (MA thesis, University of Washington, 1964), 27.

54. *Union Record,* November 9, 1919; Strong, *I Change Worlds,* 69,

55. There were perhaps two thousand black workers, many of these imported as strikebreakers in the longshoremen's strike. In the aftermath they were welcomed into both the ILA (in 1918) and the CLC unions. Black workers tended to support the strike, whereas black opinion was divided on the issue: the *Searchlight* supported the strike, but the Republican *Crayton's Weekly* opposed it. Taylor, *The Forging of a Black Community,* 5; *Union Record,* February 27, 1919. Fourteenth Census, 1920, 1091.

56. Tracy Strong and Helene Keyssar, *Right in Her Soul* (New York: Random House, 1983), 112-113.

57. *Union Record,* December 28, 1918.

58. Ibid.

59. Ibid., February 27, 1919. *Union Record.* Robert Bedford Pitts suggests that there were no blacks on the waterfront prior to 1916, though hundreds worked as strikebreakers that year, recruited mostly from New Orleans and St. Louis. Many stayed on after the strike. During the wartime boom, according to Pitts, "Negroes took an active part in formulating the policies of the union, mainly through the cooperation of members of the IWW. Negroes were elected to many important committees." Robert Bedford Pitts, "Organized Labor and the Negro in Seattle," (MA thesis, University of Washington, 1941), 42. Earl George, who worked on the waterfront after demobilization, went on to become the ILWU's first black local union president.

60. *Forge,* October 10, 1919.

61. Richard H. Frost, *The Mooney Case* (Stanford, CA: Stanford University Press, 1968), 114.

62. Ibid., 195, 242.

63. Crystal Eastman, *Liberator* 3/19, March 1919.

64. Friedheim, 42.

65. O'Connor, *Revolution in Seattle,* 211.

66. Crystal Eastman, *Liberator* 3/19, 19.

67. Ibid.

68. Ibid.

69. Ibid.

70. Ibid.

71. Ibid.

72. Strong, *I Change Worlds,* 73.

73. Friedheim, *The Seattle General Strike,* 48.

74. O'Connor, *Revolution in Seattle,* 78.

7. The War at Home

1. Michael Kazin, *War Against Wars, The American Fight for Peace, 1914–1918* (New York: Simon and Schuster, 2017), 68.
2. O'Connor, *Revolution in Seattle*, 117.
3. Kazin, *War Against Wars*, 45.
4. Ibid., 67.
5. Strong, *I Change Worlds*, 49. The term "pacifist" was used indiscriminately to describe virtually all opponents of the war
6. Ibid., 56.
7. O'Connor, *Revolution in Seattle*, 87.
8. Shannon, The *Socialist Party of the America*, 81–83.
9. Quoted in Stephen M. Kohn, *American Political Prisoners: Prosecutions Under the Espionage and Sedition Acts* (Westport, CT: Praeger, 1994), 106.
10. *The Class Struggle* 1/2 (Summer 1917).
11. O'Connor, *Revolution in Seattle*, 116.
12. Ibid.
13. Ibid., 86.
14. Hulet Wells, "I Wanted to Work," 190, 191.
15. Ibid.
16. Strong, *I Change Worlds*, 54.
17. Ibid., 64.
18. Ibid., xi.
19. Kazin, *War Against Wars*, 47.
20. "Comments on the Moro Massacre," March 12, 1906. https://www.historyisaweapon.com/defcon1/clemensmoromassacre.html (September 24, 2017).
21. *Union Record*, June 2, 1916.
22. *Seattle Post-Intelligencer*, April 8, 1917.
23. *Seattle Daily Call,* September 5, 1917.
24. Ibid.
25. Ibid.
26. James Weinstein, *The Decline of Socialism in America: 1912–1925* (New Brunswick, NJ: Rutgers University Press, 1984), 161.
27. Ginger, *The Bending Cross*, 376.
28. Ibid., 271.
29. Ibid.
30. Ibid.
31. Max Eastman, "The Trial of Eugene Debs," *Liberator* 1/9.
32. *New Solidarity*, May 10, 1919.
33. O'Connor, *Revolution in Seattle*, 151.
34. *Seattle Daily Call*, January 7, 1918.

35. Wells, "I Wanted to Work," 212.
36. Ibid.
37. Ibid.
38. Strong, *I Change Worlds*, 57.
39. Ibid.

8. Winter in Seattle

1. Preston, *Aliens and Dissenters*, 123.
2. Ficken, *The Forested Land*, 138.
3. Ibid.
4. Ibid.
5. Preston, *Aliens and Dissenters*, 153.
6. Dubofsky, *We Shall Be All*, 346–46.
7. Preston, 155.
8. Ibid., 166.
9. Ibid., 156.
10. *Seattle Times*, June 15, 1917.
11. *Industrial Worker*, July 23, 1917.
12. Melvyn Dubofsky, *'Big Bill' Haywood* (Manchester, UK: Manchester University Press, 1987), 96.
13. Ibid., 97.
14. Ibid., 110.
15. Ibid., 110–11.
16. John Reed, *Liberator* 1/7, 21–22.
17. Ibid.
18. Ibid.
19. Strong, *I Change Worlds*, 58, 59.
20. O'Connor, *Revolution*, 106–7.
21. Strong, *I Change Worlds*, 59.
22. O'Connor, *Revolution*, 118.
23. Jessie Lloyd O'Connor, quoted in O'Connor, *Revolution*, 248.
24. Clippings, Strong Papers, Box 10, 5.
25. Sarah Ellen Sharbach, "Louise Olivereau and the Seattle Radical Community, 1917–1923" (MA thesis, University of Washington, 1986), 10.
26. Ibid.
27. Ibid., 11.
28. *Seattle Post-Intelligencer*, December 1, 1917; *Seattle Times*, November 28, 1917.
29. Strong, "Miss Olivereau Confesses Guilt," Strong Papers, Box 21 (Seattle war cases), Folder 14.
30. Ibid.

31. Ibid.
32. Strong, *I Change Worlds*, 64.
33. Starbach, 11.
34. Mark M. Litchman, Court Deportation Papers, University of Washington Special Collections, Box 3/20.
35. John Reed, "The Tide Flows East," *Liberator* 2/9, 1919, 28, 29. "The famous 'American Committee' of Seattle, consisting of the Reverend M. A. Mathews, Pastor of the First Presbyterian Church; Judge Thomas Burke, attorney; J. D. Lowman, Vice President of the Union National Bank; O. D. Colvin, General Manager of the Pacific Car Foundry; J. W. Spangler, Vice President of the Seattle National. Bank; A. E. Haines, General Manager of the Pacific Steamship Co.; W. C. Dawson, General Manager W. C. Dawson Co.; and William Calvert, Jr., President of the San Juan Fishing and Packing Co. issued a secret invitation to the lumber companies to give 'moral and financial support' to a network of detectives to be placed in the camps and mills, with the purpose of securing evidence which would lead to the 'immediate expulsion of all alien agitators and publishers' from the country. A further printed June 1919 statement by the same 'Committee' showed that it was endorsed by thirteen lumber companies. The credentials of one of the Department of Justice agents who arrested the aliens show that he was at the same time a member of the 'Minutemen,' a private secret service of employers authorized during the war by the Department of Justice, and of a private detective agency of Chicago, and also membership secretary of the Seattle Chamber of Commerce and Commercial Club. Another such agent was on the payroll of the Government and a large lumber company at the same time."
36. Preston, *Aliens and Dissenters*, 163.
37. Ibid.
38. Ibid., 164.
39. Ibid., 165–66.
40. Ibid., 166.
41.   Reed, "The Tide Flows East," 29.
42. Preston, *Aliens and Dissenters*, 196.
43. Ibid., 180.
44. Ibid., 198.
45. *New York Call*, January 11, 1919.
46. Ibid.
47. Preston, *Aliens and Dissenters*, 199.

9. Five Days that Matter

1.   Friedman, *The Seattle General Strike*, 124. Ibid.

2. "Minutes of Meetings of General Strike Committee and Its Executive Committee at Seattle, Washington, February 2–16, 1919," University of Washington Box 15, Folder 19, 10.

3. *The History of the Seattle General Strike* (Seattle: History Committee of the General Strike Committee: Seattle Union Record Publishing, 1919), 12.

4. "When Is a Revolution Not a Revolution, Reflections on the Seattle General Strike by a Woman Who Was There," *Liberator*, April 1919, 24.

5. *Union Record*, Day 1, February 6, 1919.

6. Strikers and strike supporters included unorganized workers, retired workers, and family members.

7. Quoted in Howard Zinn, *A People's History of the United States*, Teaching Edition (New York: New Press, 1997), 278.

8. *Seattle Post-Intelligencer*, January 30, 1919.

9. Friedheim, *The Seattle General Strike*, 86.

10. *Seattle Star*, January 31, 1919.

11. O'Connor, *Revolution in Seattle*, 137.

12. *Union Record*, February 10, 1919.

13. O'Connor, *Revolution in Seattle*, 138.

14. *Union Record*, January 4, 1919.

15. Ibid.; O'Connor, *Revolution in Seattle*, 128.

16. Quoted in Rosenthal, *After the Deluge*, 118.

17. Joseph Pass, "The Seattle Class Rebellion," *Call Magazine*, March 2, 1919.

18. *Union Record*, January 21, 1919.

19. Ibid.

20. Ibid.

21. O'Connor, *Revolution in Seattle*, 128–29.

22. Ibid., 129.

23. Ibid.

24. *Union Record*, January 23, 1919.

25. Ibid.

26. "When Is a Revolution Not a Revolution, Reflections on the Seattle General Strike by a Woman Who Was There," *Liberator*, April 1919, 24.

27. Ibid.

28. Kurokawa, *The Labor Movement and Japanese Immigrants*, 45.

29. Ibid., 46.

30. Ibid., 48. The sentiments of black workers, Seattle's next largest minority, were mixed. There were black workers who participated with their unions in the strike, though it is not clear just how many. Metal Trades Council members commented on the problems of racialized union policy: "A motion was made by Turco that the Metal Trades send

a night letter to Washington DC to urge the authorities to investigate the race riots in the eastern cities. One of the delegates said that they could investigate the cause of the race riots in Seattle just as well as in the eastern cities. All of the organizations that refuse to take in negroes as members are cause of the race riots." Minutes of the General Strike Committee, February 10, 1919. 63.

31. *Union Record*, February 8, 1919.

32. Kurokawa, *The Labor Movement and Japanese Immigrants*, 50:
"On the General Strike Committee, on the motion by Phipps of Painters, amended by King of Painters, a member of the Japanese organization was admitted to the meeting and given a seat with rest of the delegates. Resolution presented as follows, signed by Brothers Fred Nelson of Boilermakers, John P. Rankin of Janitors, F. B. Clifford of Shipyard Laborers, J. B. Stats of the Laundry Workers, John. A. Nelson of Carpenters and John F. Kenney of the Office Employees.

"Whereas, one result of the general strike has been a clear-cut demonstration of the solidarity of labor, including the Japanese and some colored workers, who stood by their white brothers and sisters on strike; and Whereas, the best interest of all the workers demand that we should recognize the truth of the statement made by our martyred President Lincoln. "The strongest bond of human sympathy, outside of the family relationship, should be one uniting the workers of all countries, tongues and kindred": and, Whereas, a race problem exists in the West which demands a solution as speedily as possible; therefore be it Resolved, that we arrange for a conference of Japanese, white and colored workers and farmers to enter into a pact based on the following principles: The Japanese and colored workers and farmers will assist and join with the white workers and farmers in maintaining and improving our American standard of living, adopt the American language and customs and as speedily as possible become assimilated into this nation, and in order to maintain such advantages as the workers of this country have gained, we all join in restricting Oriental or other immigration and assist in every way possible to educate and organize our brothers and sisters in Japan, China and elsewhere, so that the workers of all countries may cooperate for the good of all." —Minutes of the General Strike Committee," 12–13.

33. Kurokawa, *The Labor Movement and the Japanese Immigrants*, 50,51.

34. Ibid.

35. *Union Record*, February 4, 1919.
36. Ibid.
37. Friedheim, *The Seattle General Strike*, 93.
38. Ibid., 88.
39. Quoted in Trachtenberg, *American Labor Yearbook, 1919* (New York: The Rand School, 1929), 170.
40. *Union Record*, January 24, 1919.
41. Ibid., February 6, 1919. The uncertainty and open-endedness of the text recalls descriptions of Rosa Luxemburg's work: "To the immense irritation of her opponents and detractors, she elevated uncertainty to a principle, a revolutionary creed. It is, as I see it, the thread that runs through her unwavering belief in democracy and freedom, as well as in socialism," "Rosa Luxemburg," *London Review of Books*, June 16, 2011.
42. O'Connor, *Revolution in Seattle*, 145.
43. O'Connor, O'Connor, and Bowler, *Harvey and Jessie*, 42.
44. Ibid.
45. O'Connor, *Revolution, in Seattle*, 134.
46. Friedheim, *The Seattle General Strike*, 111.
47. "The History of the Seattle General Strike," 47.
48. O'Connell, *Seattle Union Record*, 76.
49. O'Connor, *Revolution in Seattle*, 138.
50. Friedheim, *The Seattle General Strike*, 125.
51. Joseph Pass, "The Seattle Class Rebellion," *Call Magazine*, March 2, 1918.
52. O'Connor, *Revolution in Seattle*, 135.
53. Foner, *Postwar Struggles*, 72.
54. "Minutes of Meetings of General Strike Committee," Box 15, Folder 19, 4.
55. Friedheim, *The Seattle General Strike*, 126.
56. *Union Record*, February 6, 1919.
57. *The History of the Seattle General Strike*, 41–42.
58. *Union Record*, February 10, 1919.
59. "Minutes of Meetings of General Strike Committee," Box 15, Folder 19, 6.
60. "Reflections on the Seattle General Strike by a Woman Who Was There," *Liberator*, April 1919, 24.
61. *Union Record*, February 10, 1919.
62. Ibid.
63. E. P. Thompson, *The Making of the English Working Class*, 10.
64. O'Connor, *Revolution in Seattle*, 145.
65. Ibid., 140.
66. *Seattle Star*, February 4 and February 6, 1919.

67. O'Connor, *Revolution in Seattle*, 141.
68. See Rosenthal, "After the Deluge," 168.
69. *Industrial Unionist*, clipping, O'Connor Papers, n.d.
70. *One Big Union Monthly* 1/4, March 1919: 39.
71. *New York Call*, February 14, 1919.
72. Ibid., 143.
73. Foner, *Postwar Struggles*, 76.
74. Ibid, 60. In the mid-1930s, writing from Moscow, Anna Louise Strong reconsidered the outcome of the strike and by doing so added considerable weight to the pessimists' arguments, with claims such as: "We were red in the ranks and yellow as leaders," and "We lacked all intention of real battle." It is difficult not to suspect that this change of line reflected her change in scenery. Strong, *I Change Worlds*, 82.
75. Friedheim, *The Seattle General Strike*, 146. If so, few among the shipyard owners were celebrating. C. W. Wiley, writing from Tacoma to William H. Todd, president of Todd Shipyards, headquartered in New York City, complained: "The situation in Seattle is not so encouraging, there being a much larger number of men and it will take the conservatives longer to gain control, although I understand there are several of the higher officials of the International Unions in town today and they have served notice on the unions here giving them twenty-four hours, which expire at noon tomorrow, to clean house and get rid of the radical leaders, and it may well be this will help us clean up the situation." Robert L. Freidheim Collection, University of Washington Special Collections, February 11, 1919, Box 1, Folder 1.
76. *History*, 62, 63.
77. Ibid., 55, 56.
78. Ibid., 60, 61.
79. Quoted in Rosenthal, "After the Deluge," 137.
80. *The History of the Seattle General Strike*, 59.
81. *New York Call*, February 10, 1919.
82. *Union Record*, February 11, 1919. The editors of *The Liberator*, in a note following the article "When Is a Revolution Not a Revolution," added, "It is impossible to keep up with Cooperation in Seattle. Just as we go to press word comes of a Cooperative Bank opened March 1st in which the workers of Seattle deposited $1,000,000 on the first day." *Liberator*, April 1919, 25.
83. "Anise," Anna Louise Strong, *Ragged Verse* (Seattle: Pigott-Washington Printing, 1937), 62. This collection was presented to Strong during her visit to Seattle in 1937, speaking on behalf of Spanish democracy. The poems were gathered from the collection of her father, Dr. Sydney Strong.

10. Soldiers of Discontent

1. *Union Record*, March 6, 1919.
2. Ibid., February 27, 1919.
3. Kurokawa, *The Labor Movement and the Japanese Immigrants*, 65.
4. Ibid., 67.
5. Ibid.
6. Ibid.
7. Ibid.
8. *New York Call*, March 10, 1919.
9. Ibid.
10. Ibid.
11. Ibid. In 1923, Gompers was still demanding that the charter of the women barbers be revoked.
12. *Union Record*, February 27, 1919.
13. "Minutes, Central Labor Council of King County," UW Special Collections, February 26, 1919.
14. DeShazo, *Radical Tendencies*, 90, 91.
15. John Reed, "The Convention of the Dead," *Liberator* 2/8, August 1919.
16. Preston, *Aliens and Dissenters*, 206, 207; *New York Call*, February 14, 1919.
17. Tracy B. Strong and Helene Keyssar, *Right in Her Soul*, 79.
18. O'Connor, *Revolution in Seattle*, 156.
19. Matthew Klingle, *Emerald City, An Environmental History of Seattle* (New Haven: Yale University Press, 2007), 166–67.
20. Ibid., 168.
21. Ibid., 167.
22. *Everett Labor Journal*, July 9, 1920.
23. Strong, *I Change Worlds*, 64.
24. Strong credits Steffens with convincing her to leave Seattle. If true, this means he gave her bad advice twice. The Soviet Union in the 1920s was surely no place for someone seeking solace. He then, in 1934, advised her to toe the Party line, saving her life, who knows, but hardly enhancing her reputation as a credible writer, let alone a plausible advocate of socialism. *I Change Worlds* reflects this. Interesting in many ways, its reflections on the strike stand out in utter contradiction to what Strong wrote at the time, giving credence to the strikers' conservative critics. The strike was "lost," she writes; the strikers didn't "have the guns." It had been "sabotaged" by its leaders, and so on. And connected to this her suggestion that the Seattle comrades were insufficiently Marxist; surely this is Moscow Marxism, mid-1930s iterations. Strong, *I Change Worlds*, 82–96.
25. Preston, *Aliens and Dissenters*, 142.

26. *Liberator* 2/10, October 1919.
27. O'Connor, *Revolution in Seattle*, 170.
28. Ibid.
29. Ibid., 174.
30. Ibid., 175.
31. Walker Smith, *Was It Murder? The Truth about Centralia* (Centralia: Centralia Publicity Committee), *Union Record*, November 13, 1919. 37.
32. Smith, *Was it Murder?*, 39.
33. *Union Record*, November 13, 110.
34. Smith, *Was It Murder?*, 41.
35. O'Connor, *Revolution in Seattle*, 179; Dubofsky, *We Shall Be All*, 455–56.
36. *Union Record*, November 13, 1919.
37. Ibid.

INDEX